Pl...
THE ...

Sankar (Mani Sankar Mukherji), one of Bengal's most widely read novelists in recent times, is the author of *Chowringhee*, *Seemabaddha (Company Limited)*, *Jana Aranya (The Middleman)* and *Kato Ajanare (The Great Unknown)*. He also has several non-fiction bestsellers, including a biography of Swami Vivekananda, *Achena Ajana Vivekananda*, to his credit. Two of his novels *(Seemabaddha and Jana Aranya)* were made into films by Satyajit Ray.

He lives and works in Kolkata.

THE
MONK
AS
MAN

The Unknown Life of
Swami Vivekananda

SANKAR

PENGUIN BOOKS

PENGUIN BOOKS

USA | Canada | UK | Ireland | Australia
New Zealand | India | South Africa | China

Penguin Books is part of the Penguin Random House group of companies
whose addresses can be found at global.penguinrandomhouse.com

Published by Penguin Random House India Pvt. Ltd
7th Floor, Infinity Tower C, DLF Cyber City,
Gurgaon 122 002, Haryana, India

Penguin
Random House
India

First published in Bengali as *Achena Ajana Vivekananda* by Sahityam 2003
First published in English by Penguin Books India 2011

20 19 18 17 16 15 14

ISBN 9780143101192

For sale in the Indian Subcontinent only

Typeset in Perpetua by R. Ajith Kumar, New Delhi
Printed at Repro India Ltd, Navi Mumbai

www.penguinbooksindia.com

To
My friend, philosopher and guide
Dr Rama Prasad Goenka

Contents

Contents

Foreword

I wish to offer my heartfelt thanks to my respected headmaster, Sudhanshushekhar Bhattacharyya, who first introduced me to the literature on Vivekananda when I was only eleven. His advice was: Read the original and you will never lose your way.

I am also extremely fortunate to have received great affection and encouragement from my friend and senior at school, Prof. Shankari Prasad Basu. His monumental work, *Vivekananda o Samakalin Bharatbarsha*, took shape before my eyes and has remained a perennial source of inspiration for me.

I began my own journey on Vivekananda with a few articles in Bengali and soon realized that a lot needs to be explored even a century after his demise. The response of readers to *Achena Ajana Vivekananda* has been overwhelming and this has given me the courage to translate the book into English.

My grateful thanks goes to my two friends at the Shri Chinmoy Centre, New York, for their assistance with the English translation, and who feel 'it is not necessary to put [their] names'.

Acknowledgements

First, I am indebted to *The Complete Works of Swami Vivekananda* in both Bengali and English. In the Bengali version some of the letters are still incomplete. The English edition compensates for this lack, largely because of the research carried out by Dr Beni Shankar Sharma and Marie Louise Burke. The latter's six-volume book, *Vivekananda in the West: New Discoveries*, is a wonderful resource.

Swami Vivekananda's brother, Mahendranath Dutta, is a veritable goldmine of information. He has written nearly ninety books and his writings inspire respect. Another invaluable author is Swamiji's youngest brother, Dr Bhupendranath Datta. I have read all but one of his published works and I would highly recommend them to readers.

Other books that I have consulted include Swami Saradananda's *Sri Sri Ramakrishna Lilaprasanga*; the writings of Sister Nivedita; Romain Rolland's biography of Swami Vivekananda, *Life of Vivekananda*; Swami Gambhirananda's *Yuganayak Vivekananda*; Pramathanath Basu's *The Life of Swami Vivekananda*; the collected writings of Brahmachari Akshay Chaitanya; and *A Comprehensive Biography of Vivekananda* by Sailendra Nath Dhar.

There are also many precious memoirs written by monks and devotees in English and Bengali. Many are yet to be translated across the two languages and so readers who are not fluent in both are unfortunately at a disadvantage.

I have been greatly helped by the slim volume in Bengali on legal matters written under the pseudonym Chitragupta. Again, I would not have dared to write if I had not had access to the patiently researched books by Swami Prabhananda. The old issues of *Brahmabadin* and *Prabuddha Bharata* are storehouses of information. The issues of

Udbodhan must also be mentioned, along with issues of the relatively recent magazine *Nibodhata* published by Sri Sarada Math.

I am exceedingly grateful to Pravrajika Prabubdhaprana, the recent biographer of Mrs Ole Bull and Miss Josephine MacLeod. I would like to pay my deep respects to this nun, though I am not acquainted with her. I also offer my pranams to those who have written biographies of Shankaracharya and Sri Chaitanya in Bengali. And am grateful to another outstanding researcher, collector and translator, Swami Chetanananda, who is the head of the St Louis Vedanta Centre in the United States.

I have browsed through approximately two hundred books on Swami Vivekananda, gleaning what information I could in the belief that I could not begin to know this 'great soul' fully unless I could put his ideas and deeds into proper perspective.

Along the way, I have derived much benefit from the advice I received from the following distinguished list. Many of them guided me unerringly to materials that I required. They are: respected Swamis Ramananda, Vishokananda and Sarbagananda of the Ramakrishna Mission; Swamis Bodhasarananda and Satyamayananda of the Advaita Ashrama; Gopa Basu Mullick from the library at the Ramakrishna Mission Institute of Culture, Golpark; Dr Subrata Sen; Dr Tapas Basu; the Late Sunilbihari Ghosh; Harsha Datta; Dilip Dey; Subir Mitra; Badal Basu; Rakesh Das; Bankim Konar; the quiet researcher Shibshankar Ghosh; Bishwarup Mukhopadhyay and many others. To all of them, my heartfelt gratitude.

I am also grateful to Dr Manas Roy, lecturer at Visva-Bharati University; Jayanta Ghoshal, the New Delhi correspondent of *Ananda Bazar Patrika*; Subha Datta, the editor of *Sukhi Grihakon*; and Soumya Bandopadhyay. Were it not for their constant encouragement, it would have been difficult to bring this book to completion.

A thousand thanks to the original publisher of this book, Sri Nirmal

Kumar Saha, and his son, Pradip Saha, a Vivekananda devotee. My thanks also to Sukhen Saha for his enthusiastic contribution to this project.

I am indebted to Shiladitya Sinha Roy, a loyal reader of mine who also happens to be my first publisher. He heads New Age Publishers and has assisted me considerably in editing this book.

Lastly, the photographs. The Advaita Ashrama has, for some time now, been digitally processing photographs of Sri Ramakrishna and Swami Vivekananda. They perform this work with great love, patience and sincerity. I am especially grateful to them. My sincere thanks also to two stalwarts, the photo-journalists Mona Choudhury and Ashok Majumdar, for all their help.

CHAPTER ONE

A Monk and His Mother

The old lady surveyed the young would-be monks around her. 'My son became a monk at twenty-four,' she said, her eyes glistening with pride. She had given birth to him in that very house at Gourmohan Mukherjee Street in north Calcutta. Her son, the legendary Swami Vivekananda ... Her son, who had died almost nine years ago ...

From time immemorial, in this ancient land of spirituality and renunciation, those in search of liberation have relinquished the bonds of *samsara*, earthbound life, to embrace the life of the ascetic. Yet one wonders, is it possible to sever family ties completely? Is it possible for a child to forget the mother who gave him birth and nursed him?

The experienced will know that monks in India perform their *atmashraddha* (own funeral rites) precisely in order to annihilate forever the implications of such questions. But a monk is a human after all. The opposing pulls of the desire for liberation and the obligation towards one's mother is an issue which no one, not even the greatest monks, has been able to resolve with satisfaction. Swami Vivekananda, a modern prophet, himself explicates: '*Sannyasa*, in essence, means to love death. Not self annihilation—but rather knowing that death is inevitable, offering oneself, in mind and body, completely, to the good of others.'

Vivekananda's neighbour and contemporary, the great Indian poet and Nobel laureate, Rabindranath Tagore, declared: 'Salvation through renunciation is not my path!' Instead, he sought 'liberation among innumerable ties'.

Perhaps Vivekananda was a traveller on a different path. A renunciate at the age of twenty-four, he proclaimed the eternal message of liberation. On such a path, one is expected to give up all human ties. But we know that Vivekananda chose not to do so. To the very end, he remained deeply attached to his family.

Some may feel that for this reason he remained caught in a vortex of conflicting interests. 'What kind of a man is this who, even though he asserts he is an ascetic, does not break his ties with the past?' they may ask. 'Is he a misguided itinerant, is he a charlatan, or is he instead just an ordinary human being?'

The object of our enquiry is Swami Vivekananda, the great soul, a man who victoriously attained the pinnacle of manhood. It is with a profound sense of awe that I study this human being who did not shun the most difficult questions about existence, and achieved the impossible task of accepting within his consciousness the opposing forces of love and detachment.

In Benaras, according to Swami Gambhirananda, Premadadas Mitra once saw Vivekananda weeping openly upon receiving the news of the demise of a loved one. Premadadas rebuked Vivekananda, saying, 'It is unbecoming of a monk to indulge in human grief.' His remark evoked an emotional reply from Vivekananda, who said, 'What do you mean? By becoming a monk, have I become devoid of feeling? A true sannyasi's heart is more tender and affectionate than that of an ordinary man. We are, after all, human.' And then came the fiery declaration, 'I do not accept that form of sannyas which expects me to have a heart of stone!' I do not know of anyone who in the past thousand years has so fearlessly expressed what it means to be truly human.

As ordinary beings, however, we are bound to be sceptical. We are unwilling to accept a philosophy without proof. So Vivekananda too had to present an example to validate his point. His vindication comes from the eighth-century saint Adi Shankaracharya who also renounced the world at a young age. The parallel extends further. Shankaracharya lived a very short life—of only thirty-two summers. Vivekananda passed away at thirty-nine. And they both had an immense love for their mothers.

Jagatguru Shankara loved his mother intensely. I will later recount what great ordeals he had to undergo because of this. Then again, there was Sri Chaitanya. The life of Chaitanya (1486–1533) follows a similar pattern of renunciation combined with love.

Today, we can only marvel at the indomitable courage which prompted Swami Vivekananda to publicly announce, 'One who does not worship his mother can never truly rise.' To some, Vivekananda's utterance may seem clichéd, especially in this land which has had a long history of mother worship. However, in our present day and age, devotion for the mother is no longer a reality. And that is why we must pay our respect to this great renunciate who, even after a hundred years continues to inspire us through his own love and devotion for his mother.

It is, in fact, this bold statement of Vivekananda's that provided the inspiration for this book, *The Monk as Man: The Unknown Life of Swami Vivekananda*. My inquiry, then, begins with the question: How is it that someone who had accepted monkhood and performed his own funeral rites, symbolizing his complete renunciation of all material attachments, is unwilling to give up his loving relationship with his mother?

The life of the ascetic is almost impossible for those who remain attached to the world. But Vivekananda said, 'In India, the mother is the centre of the family and our highest ideal. To us, she is representative of God, as God Himself is the Mother of the Universe.' This effort to reconcile asceticism and attachment proved to be a difficult and arduous journey. It is beyond the comprehension of us ordinary mortals. But great figures like Swamiji have achieved the impossible. That is why we have enthroned them in our hearts and worship them with utmost devotion.

Nobody is born a monk. Vivekananda at twenty-four and Shankaracharya at eight left their homes to begin their new lives. During their childhood, they had both been brought up with great love and care by their families. So it would not be illogical to say that monks are families' gifts to society.

Without going back to Swami Vivekananda's childhood and youth when he was known as Bilu, Bireshwar or Narendranath, we will not be able to fully appreciate his deep and abiding love for his mother, as well as for his brothers and sisters. Nor will we be able to understand the agony that he experienced when he felt he was unable to fulfil his filial duties, or the grief and anxiety that plagued his conscience. He remained constantly preoccupied with this thought throughout his life.

❦

Narendranath Dutta (Swami Vivekananda) was born into a wealthy Bengali family. It would not be wrong to say that he was born with a silver spoon in his mouth. As a young child, he was known as Biley, though his mother called him Bilu. There is an incident when Bhubaneshwari Dasi, Vivekananda's mother, visited Belur Math, and called out from the ground floor at the top of her voice, 'Bilu-u-u!' Hearing his name, the famous monk came running down the stairs and got engrossed in deep conversation with his mother.

This is the same mother who became so agitated by her son's restlessness during his childhood that she once remarked, 'I prayed to Lord Shiva for a son like him, and instead he has sent me one of his demons!' But, don't mothers all over the world say such things? Swami Vivekananda's Western disciples were very keen to learn more about his mother, and their writings reveal some valuable insights. Bhubaneshwari Dasi told one such disciple, for example, that not one but two maidservants were needed to look after her mischievous child.

Although he remained eternally 'Bilu' to his mother, at some point Biley or Bireshwar transformed into Narendranath and the more endearing 'Naren'. Sister Nivedita once mentioned to a Western disciple that Swamiji's original name was Bireshwar, an epithet of Lord Shiva, and this name stuck for quite some time, though few people knew of it afterwards. Still another pet name was used by one of his father's uncles, Gopal Chandra Dutta. He was fond of referring to the boy as *'bente shala'*, meaning 'that dwarf'—a clear indication of the physical stature of the members of the Dutta clan, though Swami Vivekananda stood at five feet nine inches!

Vivekananda was not Bhubaneshwari's eldest son, although he did accept all the responsibilities that customarily fall on the eldest. Even after he left home, he did not selfishly ignore these responsibilities and become blind to his duties. There have been many across the centuries who have taken up the life of a renunciate. What makes Vivekananda truly great is the manner in which he resolved this eternal dilemma between responsibility towards one's family life and strict adherence to the life of a monk.

Few know that Vivekananda had nine brothers and sisters. The large family of Rabindranath Tagore, comprising fifteen children in all—nine sons and six daughters—is comparable to this. Rabindranath was the fourteenth. Bhubaneshwari Dasi's eldest child was a boy but since he died during infancy, little is known about him. Later, however, Bhubaneshwari was heard to praise his singular beauty, saying, 'He looked like his grandfather.' An unnamed writer, acquainted with members of the family, tells us that this boy died when he was only eight months old. Unfortunately, it has not been possible to gather more evidence than this.

Bhubaneshwari's second child was a daughter. She also died in her infancy and history has not preserved her name. According to the same writer, she was two-and-a-half years old when she died. The third child, a daughter named Haramani, lived to the age of twenty-two. About her, too, we know very little. The fourth child, however, a daughter by the name of Swarnamayee (also called Swarnabala by the family) lived to the ripe old age of seventy-two. At one time, she even lived in Vivekananda's home. We learn from her youngest brother, Bhupendranath, that after Swamiji's death every year, on the occasion of his birthday, his sister Swarnamayee would offer ten rupees to Belur Math. This practice had been initiated by Bhubaneshwari Dasi. Either Swami Brahmananda or Swami Premananda would personally go and collect the money.

Bhubaneshwari's fifth child was also a daughter. She died at the age of six. Narendranath (12 January 1863—4 July 1902) was her sixth child and he lived for only thirty-nine years. The seventh, a daughter named Kiranbala, died at eighteen or nineteen; the eighth, another daughter, was called Jogendrabala. The ninth and tenth children were sons—Mahendranath (1869–1956) and Bhupendranath (1880–1961). They lived to be eighty-seven and eighty-one respectively. There is a difference of opinion about the date of Mahendranath's birth. According to the municipal corporation records, he was born on 1 August 1869. However, the registry cites 7 August 1869.

We possess scant data regarding the families of Bhubaneshwari's daughters and, for the facts that we do have, we are indebted to Swami Vishokananda (Partha Maharaj) who quietly undertook the difficult task of recovering and restoring Swami Vivekananda's ancestral home at 3, Gourmohan Mukherjee Street on behalf of the Ramakrishna Math and Mission. From various sources we have learnt that there were many families living there when it was reclaimed by the math. These families had to be relocated to new apartments. (Since none of Bhubaneshwari's sons ever married, the families were related to Vivekananda's sisters.)

From certain sources, we have also come to know that Jogendrabala took her own life in her in-laws' place in Simla in north Calcutta when she was around twenty-two years of age. This occurred during Vivekananda's itinerant years. The responsibility of raising her two young daughters fell on Bhubaneshwari Dasi, who did not have any financial support. We also learn that when her son-in-law remarried, Bhubaneshwari went so far as to invite him and his new wife to visit her house. She lavished them with love and care. Even though incidents such as these were not uncommon in Bengali families in those days, the situation must have been extremely painful for Bhubaneshwari. In India, it is a sad truth that mothers are expected to perform their familial duties no matter what the cost, and bear their sufferings in silence.

Even with all the details we have about Vivekananda, we do not know the particulars of his sisters' marriages. We do not know if they took place during the lifetime of Bishwanath Dutta, Vivekananda's father, or if Vivekananda himself had any role to play in arranging these marriages. Vivekananda was twenty-one at the time of his father's death, Mahendranath was fifteen and their youngest brother, Bhupendranath, was a mere toddler of three. All that we know is that the two elder sisters studied English at Bethune College, while the two younger ones went to missionary schools.

Biographies of Swami Vivekananda fail to shed light on Kiranbala and Jogendrabala. Even Mahendranath, who has provided a wealth of details regarding the family in nearly ninety books, has little to offer on this subject. In Swamiji's own letters, however, there are occasional references to his sisters and cousins. On 15 February 1900, for instance, he wrote to Mrs Sara Bull: 'From my sister's letter, I have learnt that her adopted daughter has passed away. Suffering seems to be the lot of Indians! So be it. I have lost all feelings of pain or pleasure!'

I believe it is necessary to furnish some more information about the members of Swami Vivekananda's family in order to fully appreciate his anxiety regarding them and also to understand why he felt he had not been able to fulfil his duties as the eldest son. What strikes us is the grief and hardship that Bhubaneshwari Dasi bore silently until her death—as both a widow and a mother trying to manage in severely straightened circumstances with ten children.

Note the letter that Swamiji wrote at the time of his death: 'I am an incompetent son. I have not been able to do anything for my mother and I have left them all abandoned.' In a voice that throbs with pain, he seems to beg his mother's forgiveness because he could not alleviate her suffering; he merely allowed the family to fend for itself during a period of great adversity.

CB

Those who have seen the Simla Dutta family home at Gourmohan Mukherjee Street will realize that the Duttas of Dariatona were pretty well established in Calcutta. They were Kashyapas from south Rahr (a region south-west of the Ganga). The Duttas had acquired considerable wealth through being successful legal practitioners. This explains why Swami Vivekananda read law at the university and then joined an attorney's office. Bhupendranath Dutta reveals in this connection that Vivekananda however was irritated when he learnt that his younger brother Mahendranath had gone to England to study law.

The Dutta family of lawyers and attorneys suffered extreme reversals of fortune. Ultimately, they lost everything in litigations. This was a frequent occurrence in Calcutta at the time. The annals of the high court are replete with accounts of wealthy people often losing every rupee they had in family-related property litigations.

A series of lawsuits, contested among his own family members, embittered Swami Vivekananda's short life. One cannot help but wonder regretfully that perhaps he might have lived longer had he not been burdened with the agony of these trials. Later in the book, I will present the troubling facts on the issue.

Let us first describe the Dutta family. They hailed from the Dutta-Dariatona village in the subdivision of Kalna in the district of Burdwan. Swami Vivekananda's forefather, Ramnidhi Dutta (of Kashyapa lineage), moved with his son, Ramjiban, and his grandson, Ramsunder, to Garh-Gobindapur (now Calcutta).

Dewan Ramsunder had five sons: Rammohan, Radhamohan, Madanmohan, Gourmohan and Kristomohan. The eldest, Rammohan, was Vivekananda's great-grandfather. Rammohan Dutta was proficient in Persian law and established himself as the 'Farsi lawyer' of the Supreme Court. He was wealthy and led the life of an aristocrat. By judiciously investing his money, he was able to acquire a great deal of property. He had two garden houses in Salkia and large tracts of land in Kidderpore. Rammohan contracted cholera, however, and died at the young age of thirty-six. Cholera epidemics were common during the summer months in those days, and in the unhygienic conditions of north Calcutta, almost every family lost a member to the dreaded disease every year.

Rammohan Dutta was survived by five sons and a widowed daughter. His eldest son, Durgaprasad (Swami Vivekananda's grandfather), worked in a law firm. Bhupendranath writes of the episode that changed the course of his grandfather's life: When his wife, Shyamasundari, was insulted by Rammohan's widowed daughter who lived in the same house, Durgaprasad decided to leave the family residence. Later he became an itinerant monk and wandered about in north India. But occasionally he would return to Calcutta. He would come riding on a horse and stay at Simla Street in the home of his *bhiksha-putra*, the Brahmin boy at whose sacred thread ceremony he had been the alms-giver. Once, in an attempt to force him to return to the family, his relatives locked him up in a room. Three days later, when they opened the door, he was found foaming at the mouth and so they released him. The ascetic Durgaprasad fled, never to return.

Shyamasundari passed away when her son Bishwanath was only twelve, leaving him to be brought up almost as an orphan under his paternal uncle, Kaliprasad, and his wife. After graduation, Bishwanath tried several times to set up his own business. Unsuccessful, he joined the law practice of attorney-at-law Charles F. Peter as an articled clerk on 11 April 1859. On 29 January 1861, he was transferred to the firm of Henry George Temple as an articled clerk. He worked there till 10 October 1864.

On 14 March 1866, he applied to be enrolled as an attorney-at-law or 'proctor' in the court of Chief Justice Sir Barnes Peacock. Along with his application, he submitted two letters of reference dated 7 January 1865. One was signed by Girish Chandra Bannerjee and the other by Digambar Mitter. The application was passed by Justice Walter Morgan (who later became Chief Justice of the North-Western Frontier Province) on the same day. Bishwanath and his partner Ashutosh Dhar started their firm, Messrs Dhar & Dutta.

Bhupendranath also mentions in passing that his father was fond of literature and wrote an entire novel entitled *Sulochana*. Recently rediscovered and republished after remaining in oblivion for more than a century, this happens to be one of the earliest Bengali novels, written even before Bankimchandra's *Anandamath*. Owing to financial difficulties, however, Bishwanath had sold the rights to his grandfather's cousin, Gopal Chandra Dutta, who was a high official with the postal department, and the book was published under this gentleman's name therefore.

A strikingly similar fate awaited Swami Vivekananda who also penned a few books—on music, conversing in English and a few Bengali translations—before he left home to become a monk. Like his

The Monk as Man

father he withheld his name, sometimes even using that of the publisher. Fortunately, Vivekananda did earn some money from these works.

ೞ

Swami Vivekananda's mother was an extraordinary woman. As an only child, she was the apple of her parents' eye. Bhubaneshwari Dasi was extremely beautiful; she could sing well and she had a phenomenal memory. She needed to hear a poem only once in order to be able to recite it from memory. There is no doubt that her sons Vivekananda and Mahendranath inherited this skill from her. There is a word in Sanskrit which describes individuals who possess such a memory: *ekasyantagrahi*.

Even until his last days on earth, when he was suffering from diabetes and other serious ailments, Vivekananda retained his exceptional memory and amazed everyone with his talent. His younger brother Mahendranath followed suit. There is evidence of his astounding memory in the many books that he wrote. In actual fact, Mahendranath preferred to dictate his books rather than pen them by hand. Until the very end of his long life, he could vividly recall events that happened when he was only three years old. It is largely due to Mahendranath's memory that we know so much about Vivekananda's early life. In comparison, his younger brother Bhupendranath made fewer references to his family in his writings. Bhupendranath was born on 4 September 1880 and was, therefore, only twenty-one at the time of Vivekananda's death.

Mahendranath was born on 14 August 1869. From 1896 to 1902, he lived incommunicado, initially in London and then in many far-flung locations, travelling throughout Europe and Asia. During this period, he did not write a single letter to his mother and, understandably, his prolonged absence was a source of tremendous anxiety for her. Finally, upon receiving a telegram from Swami Saradananda that his eldest brother, Swami Vivekananda, was no more, he returned to Calcutta from Kashmir.

Like her husband, Bhubaneshwari Dasi had literary inclinations. We know that she was a poet and loved books. She used to read several hours every day of her life, until she passed away in 1911. She had learnt English from a private tutor and so was able to lay the foundations of Vivekananda's astonishing English language skills. It is also recorded that she slowly conversed with Sister Nivedita in excellent English.

As learned and beautiful as Bhubaneshwari was, it seems her married life was one of endless grief. The untimely deaths of three infant children, the loss of her husband, the tragic deaths of three daughters in the prime of their lives, the fear of extinction of her family line, crushing poverty, long and bitter legal battles with members of her extended family and, ultimately, the sudden death of her world-renowned son—all these misfortunes made Bhubaneshwari a tragic heroine. How could Swami Vivekananda not have worried about such a mother?

Vivekananda is famed as an all-renouncing sannyasi, yet he never ignored his mother's plight. And because of that he emerges as a symbol of compassion.

Bhubaneshwari Dasi kept a close eye on her daughters' education. There was no shortage of home tutors then, and Jogendrabala was taught English by the highly respected Kamini Shil, the principal of Bethune College, the first ladies' college in Bengal. Her second private tutor was an Englishwoman, Mrs McDonald. Four years before her father's death, Jogendrabala was awarded a special prize at a public event for her fluency in English. Tragically however, shortly after her father's demise, she took her own life at her in-laws' home. Swami Vivekananda's other sisters attended Rambagan Mission School.

As an only child, Bhubaneshwari was doted on by her mother, Raghumani Dasi, another woman of remarkable character. Raghumani

Dasi lived to the age of ninety and was a helpless witness to the tide of events: her daughter's miseries in her husband's ancestral home, her widowhood at a tender age and subsequent ousting from the family house, Bhubaneshwari's financial crises and even the untimely death of her beloved grandson, Bilu.

Born in 1825, Raghumani Dasi was the daughter of Gopal Chandra Ghosh. The Ghosh family lived on Beadon Street and were devout Vaishnavas. Even though Raghumani's daughter, Bhubaneshwari, had married into a large joint family, in her darkest hour she had no one to turn to except her mother. Raghumani stood unflinchingly by her daughter's side through all her trials. Together they braved one sorrow after another. The eldest son became an ascetic; the middle son travelled on his own whim and did not keep touch with the family; the youngest joined the struggle for India's independence, went to jail, was released and then left the country incognito to avoid being arrested again. Through all these travails, Raghumani Dasi offered her daughter tremendous strength and support.

This devoted Vaishnavi lived to see her daughter succumb to meningitis on 25 July 1911 and after helping her cross over the ocean of death, within a span of two days she herself bade farewell to the earthly plane, on 27 July. At the time of her death, she was living in Nimtala Ganga Yatri Nibas, a shelter for the dying. The only person she could call her own was her grandson, Mahendranath, and it is his signature we find on the register at the cremation ground. Some discrepancy about the dates arises from Bhupendranath's account of these events, but I present here the one on the corporation records.

Prior to living at the shelter, Raghumani Dasi resided at Ramtanu Basu Lane. This was the house in which her mother, Raimani Dasi, came to live with her after the death of Raimani's husband. Even though Vivekananda did not have a maternal uncle, this was his mother's home and, on a number of occasions, Bhubaneshwari and her children had to seek protection under its roof. Again, it was this house that Bhubaneshwari's eldest son visited regularly and was witness to many heart-warming incidents in Vivekananda's life.

ભ

It would be appropriate at this point to look at some of the members of Bishwanath Dutta's family. As mentioned before, Bishwanath's lack of success in business led him to practise law. He also engaged in buying properties at auctions and trading, operating under his wife's name. Thus he earned a handsome income.

Bishwanath's father, Durgaprasad, had a younger brother named Kaliprasad. Kaliprasad was Vivekananda's paternal grand-uncle. He had two sons, Kedarnath and Taraknath. Taraknath became a well-known advocate in the Calcutta high court. He developed a close acquaintance with Rabindranath Tagore's father, Maharshi Debendranath Tagore, as he used to handle litigations on behalf of the Tagore family involving their zamindary estate. Taraknath had six daughters and we come to know that some members of the Tagore family, including Rabindranath, attended the wedding of one of the daughters in the house at Gourmohan Mukherjee Street. Special seating arrangements were made for these honoured guests, although it must be said that Rabindranath was not so famous then.

Taraknath's widow, Gyanadasundari, is the one who remained at the centre of the long-drawn-out legal crisis which devastated Bishwanath's family, though in trying to cover the legal expenses of the lawsuits she, too, lost everything and was forced to seek Swami Vivekananda's help in her old age. Such is the irony of fate that the very person whose capricious nature had caused so much hardship and suffering to Bhubaneshwari and her family had to seek aid from Bhubaneshwari's renunciate son. There are also accounts of how this same aunt broke down in tears when she first saw Vivekananda's dead body at his funeral services at Belur Math.

There are varying reports of Bishwanath's financial condition during his legal battles with his relatives. Some allege that he was already heavily in debt and that it was to escape his creditors that he left Calcutta in 1877 and went to Raipur to carry on his legal practice. Narendranath was fourteen years old then. After a few months, Bishwanath brought his wife and children with him and Narendranath left the Metropolitan School in Calcutta where he was studying. In his memoirs, Mahendranath gives a marvellous account of the family's journey to Raipur. He also describes an incident on the way when his brother Naren tried to force Mahendranath, who was a vegetarian under the influence of his Vaishnava grandmother, to eat meat.

Bishwanath subsequently moved from Raipur to a few places in north India to practise law, and it does not appear that he lacked work. Narendranath studied in Raipur for a year and a half. In 1879, he sat for the entrance examination in Calcutta and was successful. The following year, on 27 January 1880, he paid the ten-rupee admission fee to Presidency College. A photograph of the receipt has been reproduced in Bhupendranath's memoirs.

Doctors and lawyers generally earn a great deal and lose immense sums through reckless expenditure. Whether Bishwanath's earnings were considerable or meagre during this period would not have mattered but for the charges brought against him by Taraknath's widow after her husband's death. She claimed that Bhubaneshwari's property had been, in fact, purchased using Taraknath's money but using Bhubaneshwari's name. According to her, Bishwanath did not earn enough to buy such a vast property. And that in his absence Bishwanath's wife and children had been provided for in Calcutta with Taraknath's money.

In disputes regarding family property, such accusations and counter-accusations are common and usually not cause for concern. However, in this particular case, the renunciate Vivekananda had to go to great lengths and fight tooth and nail to settle the case in his mother's favour.

From various references in Mahendranath's memoirs regarding the general lifestyle of the family, we can infer that they were, indeed, affluent. Take, for instance, the description of the meals the brothers had. In those days, butchers' shops did not sell the head of a goat. So Narendranath and Mahendranath made a bargain with one particular butcher that he supply them with ten to twelve goats' heads for a price of two to four annas. They then prepared meat curry with the goats' heads and added two-and-a-half seer (around two kilos) of green peas. 'In the afternoon,' Mahendranath writes, 'after coming back from school, Swamiji and I used to eat the curry, along with sixteen rotis.'

Another interesting story from Mahendranath runs like this: 'Bar-da [elder brother] once bought a kettle for five annas from an Anglo-Indian auction house. The cover was sooty. But, O my God, as I started to polish it, I soon realized that the inside was made of pure silver.'

These stories do not suggest that the family was impoverished. On the contrary, they indicate a certain easy affluence. Remember, we are talking about the years 1880–84, when an educated Bengali middle-class worker earned a salary of around fifteen rupees a month. During this same period, Bhubaneshwari's domestic expenses were a thousand rupees per month!

Let us come back to Bhubaneshwari Dasi. Swami Vivekananda used to tell his friends, 'Was I born just like that? My mother had to do penance to have me.' Elsewhere he said that he was indebted to his mother for the breadth of his wisdom.

Bhubaneshwari's complexion was fair, her voice melodious, her every movement aristocratic. She was highly intelligent and skilful, pleasant but spirited. She sought to inculcate lofty values in her son. She told him, 'Remain pure. Maintain your self-esteem, and never hurt another's. Remain calm always, but be firm if necessary.'

As the son of such an extraordinary mother, Vivekananda could unreservedly say, 'One who does not worship his mother can never truly grow.'

This may be hard to understand, but the ideal cannot be neglected in our country. One foreign devotee who studied the lives of the monks of the Ramakrishna Mission found that most of them had been strongly influenced by their mothers. In contrast, the influence of the fathers was far less significant.

More than anyone, Bhubaneshwari Dasi knew her son's strengths and weaknesses. She once said, 'From childhood, Naren has had one grave weakness. Once he gets angry, he cannot be controlled. In his anger, he used to destroy all the utensils and furniture in the house.' Naren's two sisters, Haramani and Swarnamayee, were often completely exasperated by his tantrums. If they tried to catch him, Bilu would run into the garbage heap and making faces call out, 'Now catch me! Catch me!' Swami Vivekananda admitted to his disciples in later years, 'I was extremely naughty when I was young. Would I have been able to tour the world penniless, though, if it had been otherwise?'

There was another aspect of Bhubaneshwari's character that made a lifelong impression on Vivekananda: her self-control. He revealed, 'My mother once fasted for a full fourteen days.' Vivekananda inherited this strength from his mother and maintained it to the very end. Sometime before his death, on the advice of his ayurvedic physician, he abstained from drinking water for twenty-one days, much to everyone's amazement.

One may find in the various memoirs penned by Vivekananda and his brothers hundreds of sketches of the happy times that the family shared. I love this joyful aspect of Vivekananda's early life. Here we meet a Vivekananda who cherished and upheld the closeness of the family unit. To cite one incident: he was delighted to be the best man at the wedding of Sri Ramakrishna's devoted disciple, Ramchandra Dutta.

Reminiscing about the time when they were all young, that far-off golden age when happiness flowed uninterrupted in the family, Mahendranath wrote in his memoirs, 'Towards the end of one's life, all the childhood memories come flooding back. What we used to be fond of then, what we ate or felt, I would like to experience it once again. I would like to taste once more dumplings made of ground lentil.' The same thing happened to Swamiji in his final days. He was then at Belur Math. He said to the monks: 'Assemble everything for me. I will fry *phuluri* (fried balls made of chickpea flour).' The monks gathered together everything he requested—a pot, cooking oil, powdered gram and so forth, even the phuluri-seller's wooden seat. Like a phuluri-seller, Swamiji sat with his dhoti folded above his knees and, frying the flour balls in oil until they were done, started calling out heartily: 'Come, come, those who want to buy, come!'

Bishwanath's illness and sudden demise ushered in an era of endless trials for his wife and Narendranath. One could almost call it an ordeal by fire. By this time, the problems with the relatives had already started. Even though we cannot be sure as to the details of these problems, we do know that the poisonous atmosphere of the joint-family system had exasperated Bishwanath to the point of moving with his family out of the ancestral home at Gourmohan Mukherjee Street. This happened a year before his death. With his wife and children he moved to a rented house at 7, Bhairab Biswas Lane. When he returned after some time to the ancestral home, it is believed that Taraknath was none too pleased.

As an only child, Bhubaneshwari Dasi had inherited some property from her father, Nandalal Basu, namely, her father's house and a four-cottah piece of land (one cottah = 66.8 square metres). Bishwanath also received a garden house from his maternal grandfather. Their sons would inherit these properties.

But then something disturbing happened. This is what is stated in Bhupendranath's memoirs: 'One day, Bishwanath's middle maternal uncle appeared out of the blue and told him something in private. Listening to his advice, our father willed away his property to this uncle. We heard this from our mother who fully agreed with his decision. For had he not done so, this property, which had been given to him by his maternal grandfather, would surely have been usurped by his rapacious paternal uncle gradually. Around the same time, all the co-owners of the ancestral dwelling house of the Basus located at Madhu Roy Lane were trying to sell it off and Bishwanath was made to sign over his rights in favour of that paternal uncle. Our mother argued with him for a long time. She begged him to consider that if he gave everything away to his uncle, she and her children would have nothing to fall back upon.'

There is some doubt regarding the actual date of Bishwanath's death. According to the Calcutta Corporation records, he died on 23 February 1884. Yet, according to Bhubaneshwari's application to the high court, he died on the day after. The Corporation records, however, do confirm that he passed away at the Gourmohan Mukherjee Street house. He had suffered from chest pain followed by a heart attack during the night, although the death register curiously only mentions diabetes as the cause of death. The records from the burning ghat bear Narendranath's signature, in English. He was at a friend's house when he received the news late at night and it is probable that he went directly to the burning ghat. (There is usually a small government office to record deaths at cremation grounds.)

Bhupendranath reveals a most intriguing detail: Bishwanath 'was to have gone the very next morning to choose a bride for his eldest son.'

Bhupendranath's book describes various concerted attempts by Narendranath's parents to arrange for his marriage. After his father's death, one of his friends—an attorney of the Calcutta high court—even proposed that if Narendranath married his granddaughter, he would bear all the expenses of the lawsuits.

There is a striking similarity in the way Bishwanath and Narendranath, father and son, died. Each faced a crisis around nine o'clock in the evening and died of a heart attack. The news of Bilu's death reached his mother the next morning from Belur Math. When she wanted to know 'the cause behind the sudden death of her eldest son', Bhupendranath told her, 'The same as with father.' This news left both mother and grandmother inconsolable.

Bhubaneshwari was born in 1841. She married Bishwanath when he was sixteen and she ten. During the course of their married life, she bore him ten children. She had to endure the deaths of several of them in their infancy. She lost her husband when she was forty-three and was faced with the prospect of having no money to raise her children. At the same time, she was enmeshed in a destructive and costly legal battle and was about to be ousted from the ancestral home. The son who could have helped her support the family became a monk, one daughter took her own life and, at the age of sixty-one, Bhubaneshwari was faced with her beloved eldest son's death. How much grief can a mother possibly bear?

We know that Swami Vivekananda's untimely death put a final end to all his sufferings. The fact that he tried his utmost to overcome life's obstacles and rise above his sufferings while he was on earth is a source of profound inspiration for all those who find themselves in similar unfortunate circumstances. Here is one who walked barefoot along a road strewn with thorns. How bloody the journey was, and yet Vivekananda's example encourages us to try to win life's arduous battles. He wrote on 2 September 1899, 'Life is a series of struggles and disillusionments ... The secret of life is not enjoyment, but education through experience.' To his devoted disciple and dear friend Ajit Singh, the Maharaja of Khetri, he said that life is a constant attempt to express oneself and fulfil one's goals against all odds.

ॐ

Before I describe how the family could have been brought to such financial ruin, let me pause in my narrative to look at a few more scenes of their happy home life. Mahendranath explicitly mentions that his older brother took snuff from a young age and one could smell the snuff on his mosquito net; pigeon flying was a favourite pastime enjoyed by all members of the family; Narendranath used to entertain his little brothers by casting shadow puppets on the wall with his fingers; and he was fond of playing a form of cricket which in Bengali is called *batomball* (known elsewhere in India as *gilli-danda*). When a schoolteacher dashed his younger brother's head against the wall, Narendranath wrote a letter of complaint to the school superintendent, Brajendranath Dey, and the teacher was justly reprimanded.

As a youth, it was Narendranath's habit to get up very early each morning. Bhubaneshwari once told Swami Akhandananda that however late he went to bed, her eldest son never slept late in his life.

In those days, it was customary for barbers to visit large families on a regular basis to shave the gentlemen. We know, however, that at Belur Math Swami Vivekananda used to shave himself. He could use a razor efficiently without the help of a mirror. He often joked about the reason he developed this skill. While in the United States, he had once visited a barber's shop, but the barber refused to shave him because his white clients would have boycotted the shop if it became known that a black man had been shaved there.

Another typical Bengali scene: two cots were attached to form one large bed. There Bilu, Mahendranath, their sister, mother and grandmother would all rest together. Bishwanath was absent at that time and Bhupendranath not yet born.

Bishwanath's mother's family was Vaishnava (worshippers of Lord Vishnu in his various forms, especially as Rama and Krishna), while his father's family was Shakta (worshippers of the goddess known as Durga, Kali or Shakti). Both influences were present in his family. As long as

Bilu's great-grandmother was alive, she would wake the children up very early every morning and regale them with tales of Lord Krishna. It was from her that Mahendranath developed the habit of not eating before he had watered the tulsi plant. He also refrained from touching some varieties of lentils, spinach and onion—foods from which strict Vaishnavas abstain. During these years, under the influence of Raimani, cauliflowers were also banned in Bhubaneshwari's family and, on occasions, cow dung had to be tasted. This was a normal Hindu practice at the time and had medicinal value as well as ritualistic significance.

Narendranath however did not always strictly follow these traditions as evidenced by the incident that occurred when the family was travelling to Raipur to join Bishwanath. Mahendranath elaborates, 'They cooked meat at Ghoratala. I would not eat it. Then my elder brother came and put a piece of meat in my mouth and pounded on my back so that I would be forced to swallow it. "Eat!" he commanded. Then what did I do? I ate it. What else can a tiger do when it tastes blood?'

It was his mother's training that influenced Swami Vivekananda most deeply and formed the foundation of his character. Bhubaneshwari told her eldest son, 'Do what you think is right, regardless of the outcome. For this, you may sometimes face hardships or suffer injustice, but never swerve from the path of truth.' It was because the mother herself led her son in the path of immense courage that we got this brave sannyasi in our midst. The homeless Vivekananda became the prophet of his age because he abided by his mother's will and refused to bargain with truth.

In one of his lectures abroad, Vivekananda declared that he had inherited his mother's purity, as well as her capacity to love selflessly and unconditionally. He added that everything he had been able to accomplish in his life, all his good deeds and actions, were through her grace. He has also referred many times to his mother's exceptional self-control, something which he had never encountered in any other woman.

cs

Narendranath took three university examinations: the entrance examination, First Arts Standard (FA, which later became Intermediate Arts or IA) and Bachelor of Arts. I want to express my immense gratitude to those scholars who were able to retrieve Vivekananda's results from the university records and, for curious readers, I reproduce them below. Interestingly, his results were not at all spectacular. The great figure, who later toured America and England and achieved resounding success everywhere because of his brilliant eloquence in the English language, scored only a 47 per cent in English at the entrance level, a 46 per cent in the FA and a 56 per cent in his BA. He passed with only a second class in both his FA and BA examinations.

Entrance Examination

English	47
Sanskrit	76
History	45
Mathematics	38
TOTAL	206 out of possible 400

First Arts Standard

English	46
Sanskrit	36
History	56
Mathematics	40
Logic	17/50
Psychology	34/50
TOTAL	229 out of possible 500

Bachelor of Arts

English	56
Sanskrit	43
History	56
Mathematics	61
Philosophy	45
TOTAL	261 out of possible 500

I hope that students who are disappointed with their grades will draw assurance and inspiration from the results of this man who eventually became an incomparable writer and speaker, wonderfully eloquent in both Bengali and English, and one of the greatest philosophers of our time. As we can see, there is very little correlation between university grades and the grades one achieves in the great examination that is life itself. It is also worth reflecting here on the nature of our examination system and its ability to judge the real merit of a person.

ॐ

This splendid boy, Narendranath, brought up in a happy and contented family, received two massive shocks almost at the same time. The first was spiritual—his encounter with Sri Ramakrishna. The second was external—the financial devastation of his family in the wake of his father's sudden death. The sole earning member was now gone. Narendranath was only twenty-one and reading law at the university. As the eldest son, he had no one, save himself, to turn to for financial support.

He was faced with a large family and its associated expenses, and with no possibility of earning a livelihood! Taking advantage of this opportunity, the members of the extended family started their legal proceedings. Bhubaneshwari was forced to leave her husband's family home along with her helpless children.

Describing the menace of the joint-family system, Bhupendranath, Swamiji's youngest brother, said towards the end of his life: 'Those who shout themselves hoarse over the sanctity of the system know precious little, indeed, about how the system actually works or else they just choose to ignore the feuds, squabbles, bitterness, injustice and tragedy that seem to be inherent in it ... As a matter of fact, the joint-family system is completely outdated in a commercialized and industrially advanced society and there is really no reason to continue with it.'

After Bishwanath's death, nobody came forward to help his grieving family. Bhupendranath comments on this sad truth in his writings: 'Even though we had plenty of relatives, spread out all over Calcutta, none of them cared to come and see us now that Bishwanath Dutta, attorney-at-law, Calcutta high court, was dead and gone ... Friends and family decided to forget our very existence and we were left to fend for ourselves.'

The truth was that towards the end of his life, Bishwanath had grown somewhat lax in the supervision of his legal practice. The friend in whom he had entrusted the affairs of the office, seized this opportunity, borrowed money from various quarters in Bishwanath's name, and then embezzled it.

Not long after his father's funeral, Narendranath realized that the family was in dire financial straits. His younger brothers were mere children and could not be expected to assume any responsibility. Swami Vivekananda gives us a heart-rending description of those days: 'Even before the mourning period was over, I began running around for a job. Dizzy from lack of food, I walked from office to office, barefoot, in the blazing sun, carrying my application papers ... But to no avail. I was rejected by everyone. This early experience taught me that unselfish sympathy is very rare in this world; there is no place here for the poor or the weak. Even those who, only a short time ago, would have considered themselves fortunate to do me a favour, now turned away reluctant to help, though they could easily have done so had they wished. When I faced this, I felt sometimes that the world was the handiwork of the Debil. One day is etched in my memory above all others. I was walking from one place to another in the hot sun and my feet had blistered. Utterly exhausted, I sat down in the shade of the Ochterlony Monument [now called the Shahid Minar] on the Maidan. A couple of friends were there with me, or perhaps they met me there. In order to console me, one of them sang:

Bahiche kripaghana Brahma-niswas pabane
(Here blows the compassion-filled breath of Brahman.
It is His breath we feel in the wind.)

When I heard that song, I felt as if someone was beating me violently on the head. Thinking of the pitiful condition of my mother and brothers, I was filled with resentment and despair. "Be quiet!" I told them. "That fanciful nonsense is all right for people whose nearest and dearest are not starving, people who have never had the last morsel of food snatched away from them, people living in the lap of luxury being fanned by the *punkah*. For them this song may be beautiful. Before this song rang true to me, too, but now in the face of heartless reality, it is nothing but relentless mockery." I dare say my friends were terribly hurt by my words. How could they possibly understand the grinding poverty which made me utter them?'

In a similar vein, Vivekananda is reported to have told Mahendra Nath Gupta (known also as M. or Master-mashai):, 'It is because of all my suffering that I have reached this condition. Master-mashai, you have not suffered this pain. Yet I know that if one has not undergone suffering, one cannot fully surrender to God.' Mahendra Nath Gupta was a prominent householder disciple of Sri Ramakrishna who later wrote a biography of him entitled *Sri Sri Ramakrishna Kathamrita*.

Vivekananda poignantly describes his own personal sufferings and sacrifice on behalf of his family: 'Waking up early in the morning, I would secretly find out that there was not enough food for all of us, so I would inform my mother, "A friend has invited me for lunch." Then I would go out, so that the others would get a larger share. On such days, I had very little to eat, sometimes nothing at all. I was too proud to tell anyone. I had a few wealthy friends but on their own they did not try to find out how I was doing ... On rare occasions, one or the other of them would ask, "Why do you look so pale and sad today?" Only one friend ever discovered how things really stood—and that was not from me. Having learnt of our plight, he used to send money anonymously from time to time to my mother. I will remain eternally indebted to him.

'Some of my childhood friends, who had degenerated in their youth and had resorted to unscrupulous means to earn money, now became aware of my poverty and tried to drag me into their company. I noticed that those among them who had fallen on hard times, as I had, and had been obliged to adopt ignoble paths to sustain their livelihood, actually had genuine empathy for me. But I would not be pulled in that direction. Even Mahamaya, the great enchantress, took advantage of my reduced circumstances and tried to ensnare me with various temptations. A certain well-to-do lady had been infatuated with me for a long time. At the earliest opportunity, she sent a proposal inviting me to put an end to my poverty once and for all by accepting her along with her riches. Disgusted, I sternly rejected the offer. When another woman approached me with a similar proposal, I told her, "Look, you have wasted your life selling the pleasures of the flesh. Now death looms before you. Have you done anything to prepare yourself? Shun these worthless desires and call upon God."

At one time, a few so-called friends of his urged Narendranath to take up drinking and deceived him into visiting the house of a prostitute. After taking her leave, he went around telling everybody, bitterly, 'Today I have entertained myself with women and alcohol.' He even went home and told his mother the same thing.

We learn from his biographer Pramathanath Basu: 'One evening, a few of his friends wanted to take him with them to a garden house in the suburbs of Calcutta. There the guests listened to music and sang. Narendranath also participated. Later, when he felt a little tired, his friends indicated an adjacent room where they begged him to take rest. He lay down, and was resting by himself, when a young woman entered. She revealed her profession and also that she had been sent to him by his "friends". Narendranath immediately prepared to quit the room. He told her, not unkindly, "Please forgive me. I have to go now. I wish you well. One day, when you come to realize that it is a sin to lead a life like this, you will surely find a way to get out of this mess."'

And so life flowed on for Narendranath. He later confessed in his memoirs, 'In spite of all these sufferings, I never lost faith in the existence of God, nor did I doubt for a moment the truth of the saying, "God is merciful." Every morning, I remembered Him as soon as I woke up and I got out of bed repeating His name. Then I resumed my search for a job. One day, as I was getting out of bed, my mother overheard my prayer from the next room and called out bitterly, "Keep quiet, boy! You have been repeating the Lord's name since you were a child. What has He ever done for you?" These words hurt me terribly. Stunned, I asked myself, "Does God really exist? And, if He does, does He listen to our fervent prayers? Why do I pray so much and get no answer? Why is there so much woe in His benign kingdom? How can He truly be compassionate when His creation is so full of evil?"'

There is more along these lines. Narendranath continues, 'It was against my nature to do anything secretly. So it was not surprising that now I began to tell people rather aggressively that God does not exist. Moreover, I added that even if He does exist, it is no use invoking Him because it produces no results. Of course, soon rumours began to spread that I had become an atheist and that I was consuming alcohol, mixing with people of loose morals and did not even hesitate to visit houses of ill-repute.

'The stories floating around in our neighbourhood were not favourable either. A neighbour complained to Sharat Chandra [later Swami Saradananada], "There is a young fellow living in that house. I have never seen such a conceited fellow! He is too big for his boots— and all because he has a BA degree! When he sings, he even strikes the tabla arrogantly and struts around smoking cheroot before all the elders of the neighbourhood."'

Vivekananda often told his disciples in America that, in spite of having a BA, he failed to secure a job and earn even the most basic fifteen rupees a month. This will undoubtedly serve as an eye-opener for those who believe that the job market in Calcutta in those days was very lucrative.

Narendranath moved from door to door in search of employment. At last, his situation came to the attention of Master-mashai (M.) who was then the headmaster of the Metropolitan Institution (now Vidyasagar College) at Sukia Street. This institution had been established by Ishwar Chandra Vidyasagar in 1872. It was on Master-mashai's initiative that Narendranath was invited to teach at the main branch of the school. Subsequently, when another branch was opened up in Champatala at Siddheshwar Lane, Narendranath was appointed headmaster there.

Vidyasagar's son-in-law was the secretary of the school and, as fate would have it, the hapless Narendranath found disfavour with him. This gentleman and his cohorts instigated the students of classes IX and X to circulate a petition against Narendranath which said: 'The new headmaster cannot teach.' The person who came into this world to teach was himself castigated by his students for failing to teach them properly!

On seeing the petition Vidyasagar immediately ordered Narendranath's dismissal. He did not investigate the matter further, merely sending the message, 'Tell Naren not to come here any more.' Barely three months had passed since Narendranath had taken up the post, but there was nothing he could do. He had to bow down. Yet he harboured no bitter feelings against Vidyasagar. He only praised him as the great social reformer.

Among those who personally witnessed this unfortunate turn of events at the Metropolitan School was the respected Swami Bodhananda of the Ramakrishna Mission. He was, at that time, a student in the junior school. He remembered that Narendranath used to come to school wearing an *alkhalla* (loose cloak), a *chapkan* (loose, long robe), a pair of trousers and a six-foot-long *chador* (scarf) around his neck. Often he used to carry an umbrella in one hand and the relevant textbook in the other.

After losing his job, Narendranath appealed to Shibnath Shastri for a teaching post at City School. Alas, Shibnath Shastri paid no heed to this request. It would be relevant to mention here that at this time Sri M. himself had been at the receiving end of Vidyasagar's ire. Vidyasagar had suggested that Master-mashai's frequent visits to Sri Ramakrishna, who was then very ill, had made him negligent in his duties and his students had not fared as well in their examinations as Vidyasagar had hoped for. As a self-respecting headmaster, Master-mashai resigned from the school on hearing the first hint of this reproach.

Master-mashai told Sri Ramakrishna what he had done and Ramakrishna responded, 'You have done the right thing. You have done the right thing. You have done the right thing.' Very rarely did Sri Ramakrishna talk so candidly on the subject of his disciples' livelihood.

Fortunately, the learned Master-mashai did not have to remain unemployed for long. Sir Surendranath Banerjea soon invited him to teach at his newly established Ripon School.

The Monk as Man

But what about Narendranath's future? It is believed he was able to secure a humble post near Gaya in the record office of a zamindar. However, he did not report to work. We may assume it was because he had already decided to become a monk. A full year had elapsed since his father's death. It was now March 1885.

CB

Across the years critics have questioned if Narendranath was inclined by nature to be a monk or if he was driven to it by want.

Did Narendranath work for some time after leaving the Metropolitan School? It is a subject of debate. One high court source cites him as saying, 'With Aghornath Chattopadhyay's help I worked in a college after leaving Metropolitan Institution.' Another high court source, however, quotes Narendranath as saying around the same time, 'I am unemployed.'

We can form a reasonably accurate picture of the severity of the family crisis from a few isolated incidents gleaned from a variety of sources. On one occasion, Sri Ramakrishna Paramahansa of Dakshineshwar begged his disciple Sharat Chandra Chakrabarty to go and visit Naren. Sri Ramakrishna told Sharat, 'Naren is of Kayastha caste; his father was a lawyer; he lives in Simla.' With this information Sharat went to Naren's house at Gourmohan Mukherjee Street on his way home from college one day. It was in the summer of 1885. Sharat describes the scene thus: 'On a worn-out bed, there was a worn-out mattress. On the mattress there were two or three torn pillows. To the west of the room, a grimy mosquito net hung from a peg. From the joists hung a torn *punkah* (a hand-pulled ceiling fan).'

Naren was lying on the bed. He was down with a severe headache and was taking camphor. Since his father's death, Naren had been suffering from frequent bouts of headache. Sharat spoke to Naren for a short while, addressing his future gurubhai as Naren-babu.

The family's legal problems were then at their peak. Sri Ramakrishna advised him, 'Pursue the lawsuits hard. Be tenacious. Hiss, but do not bite.' Poor Narendranath—his mind was not on the lawsuits at all. Helplessly, Bhubaneshwari tried her best to make him focus on doing the needful. She even visited Sri Ramakrishna at Cossipore with her youngest son, Bhupendranath, to beg Sri Ramakrishna to use his influence on her eldest son. Bhupendranath, who was only six at the time, describes their visit:

'Mother took me to Ramakrishna's room. He was reclining on a bed in a large room and leaning against a cushion. As we entered, he said, "The doctor has asked me not to talk, but I have to talk to you. I am glad you have come. Please take Naren back with you. Girish and the others have dressed him up in the garb of a monk. I objected to it. I told him, 'Naren, how can you do this? Your mother is a widow and your brothers are very young. How can you become a monk?'" After that, mother, Narendranath and I set off for home. On the way, in the horse-carriage, mother repeated to Narendranath what Ramakrishna had told her. Narendranath's comment was, "He asks the thief to steal and advises the householder to remain alert!"'

&

Following Bishwanath's death, Bhubaneshwari took up the awe-inspiring role of the ten-handed Durga who destroys all evil. Her management skills will always remain a source of wonder to all householders. Doing the impossible, she reduced her regular domestic expenses from a thousand rupees to thirty rupees a month and started selling her jewellery.

Swami Saradananda describes her with awe: 'Following the loss of her husband and her subsequent reversals of fortune, qualities such as patience, tolerance and a kind of spirited courage seemed to flower within her ... She was never sad, not even for a day ... Her jewel of a son was contemplating renouncing the worldly life entirely; he was unsuccessful in almost all his pursuits and had failed to get a job. The way in which Bhubaneshwari calmly handled her duties in such a difficult time inspires our respect.'

After his father's death, the stressed-out Naren suffered from frequent blinding headaches. He often took camphor for relief. Narendranath's mother used to don a silk sari to perform her daily puja. When the sari got torn, she asked Naren to buy her a new one. Having no means by which to procure a silk sari, he went away, his head bowed. When Sri Ramakrishna came to hear about it, he asked a disciple for a new silk sari and then gave it to Naren, saying, 'Please take this sari to your mother so that she can wear it during her worship.' Naren would not accept the gift and so Sri Ramakrishna sent the sari to Bhubaneshwari through someone else.

In the time period between Sri Ramakrishna's death and Vivekananda's commencement of his itinerant life, there were some who, out of sympathy, did help him out financially. Master-mashai mentions in *Kathamrita* that somebody gave Narendranath a hundred rupees; however, the name of the donor is not disclosed. From Mahendranath's later writings, we gather that this donor was Master-mashai himself. This sum helped to pay for Narendranath's family's expenses for three months.

Another compelling incident took place during the same period. One day, at Cossipore, Narendranath related the following incident to Master-mashai, 'This morning as soon as I got home, everybody started rebuking me. They all said, "Your law examination is approaching and yet you are just fooling around! You are not conscientious."'

Master-Mashai asked, 'Did your mother say anything?'

Naren replied, 'No, she was simply urging me to eat. They had cooked deer's meat. Although I did not feel like eating, I took some ... Then I went to grandmother's house to study in the study room. As I was turning the pages of my book, a terrible fear came upon me, a kind of dread. I began to feel that studying itself was a terrifying thing. Suddenly, my heart began to beat faster and I started to weep. I had never wept so bitterly before in my life. I tossed the books aside and started to run. My shoes got torn ... I ran along the roads of Cossipore to reach the Master. How that term "conscientious" depressed me! Shankaracharya had spoken about three things that can be received through good fortune and *tapasya* [spiritual discipline]: a sense of common humanity, the desire to be free and the company of great souls. I realized that I already had those three things. I am a human being. Through the power of tapasya, I have experienced the desire to be free. And, through the power of tapasya, I have come to know such a great man.'

During the period after Sri Ramakrishna's passing away, the young disciples established a math at Baranagore. Here they embarked on their difficult spiritual journey. But Narendranath was still in a crisis: household duties clashed with his duties as a monk. 'If one is not spirited and fearless, one cannot fulfil both,' he observed. Knowing that there was no money to pursue litigations, his close brother disciples Shashi (Swami Ramakrishnananda) and Sharat (Swami Saradananda) told him, 'Naren, you do not have money. The lawsuit is very costly. The two of us can teach in a school in Bally (Howrah, West Bengal) and earn some money. We will come and live in the monastery so that we can set this money aside. This money will be of use to you.'

Though they had very little themselves, these two selfless brother monks were deeply concerned about Naren's family. Their circumstances in Baranagore were pitiful. The young monks did not have beds but only a few coarse mats made of bulrushes and one torn carpet. The disciples used to sleep with their arms folded under their

The Monk as Man

heads; they placed bricks under the mats for pillows, they did not wear saffron robes, nor did they have shoes or any proper clothes. Despite this poverty, how powerfully their love for their master and for each other shone through!

Somehow Narendranath managed. Kedarnath Das came forward to help him continue his litigations. Because he was in the *khor* (straw) business in Bagh Bazar, Kedarnath was nicknamed 'Khoro Kedar'. On his own, he offered Naren a sum of one hundred rupees.

Then Narendranath borrowed five hundred rupees from Balaram Basu. This money had actually been donated by Sri Ramakrishna's disciple, Suresh Mitra, towards setting up the math. Naren had to borrow this money when the litigations were at their peak. He was able to repay the loan after a year and a half by selling some of his share certificates to Prasaddas Baral of Burra Bazar. Mahendranath and Sharat Maharaj went to Prasaddas Baral's office with a letter from Narendranath's lawyer, Atul Ghosh, to receive the money. It is said that this same money was used for the marble flooring in the prayer room at Belur Math.

The role of the two gurubhais, Rakhal Maharaj (Swami Brahmananda) and Sharat Maharaj (Swami Saradananda), is unforgettable. They offered Narendranath constant assistance and support during his family crisis. When Narendranath's relatives tried to oust Bhubaneshwari and her children from the ancestral house after her husband's death, Rakhal—whose father was a zamindar—came with his men to safeguard Narendranath's interests. Ananga Maharaj (Swami Onkarananda) has described several episodes that occurred during this phase. The researcher Shankari Prasad Basu was a great favourite of Ananga Maharaj.

Again, it was Rakhal Maharaj who took the responsibility of caring for Swami Vivekananda's mother and his family after his death. Swami Vivekananda had entrusted him with this responsibility, saying, 'Rakhal,

I am not well. I may leave this world soon. Please take care of my mother and the family. Help Mother go on pilgrimage. This is your responsibility.'

Once family quarrels begin, they never cease. The proof is in the eighteen chapters of our Mahabharata. These quarrels do not spare the dead, nor do they hesitate to drag a monk away from his chosen path to the courtroom. And, if these quarrels do go to court, there are two things that cannot be kept track of: time and money. So the litigations involving Vivekananda's family reached out with their bared fangs and gripped the second half of his brief life.

ଙ୍ଗ

Bhupendranath says that after Swami Vivekananda left home, there was nobody to help Bhubaneshwari. To verify this statement, one has to go through the accounts of the litigations. Although there are fleeting references to them in the various biographies of Swami Vivekananda, to date the facts have not been fully explored. Bhupendranath states that he cannot accept some of the conclusions drawn by certain biographers. Then again, Bhupendranath himself may not have been in possession of all the facts. For example, he did not have many of Swami Vivekananda's letters written to his non-Indian and non-Bengali friends and disciples, some of which were subsequently collected by Marie Louise Burke and reproduced in her wonderfully researched book, *Swami Vivekananda in the West: New Discoveries*. One has to read a few thousand pages of this six-volume book in order to obtain a comprehensive understanding of Swami Vivekananda.

This much we do know: Swami Vivekananda fought like the ten-armed Goddess Durga in order to have justice meted out to his family. Alas, whatever the goddess's disadvantages may have been in the field of battle, bad health was certainly not one of them. In this respect,

Swami Vivekananda was very unfortunate. He was plagued by ill health over the next few years. Those who dare to dream big have to pay a heavy price in this country. I fully believe that those who are presently struggling against poverty, as well as those who are fated to do do in the future, will feel less lonely if they only ponder on Swami Vivekananda's difficult life.

଼

An aged lawyer has been able to pass on to me certain privileged legal information about the Dutta family. Because of the confidential nature of this information, we will call him 'Chitragupta'. He possesses details of the lawsuits and the precise nature of Swami Vivekananda's testimony in the courts as a witness.

Before we consider Chitragupta's information, let us refresh what we already know. Bhubaneshwari used to travel to the high court in a palanquin. Bilu preferred to go on foot, and he often reached the high court sooner than his mother. From the existing legal papers, we can trace Bhubaneshwari's signature in Bengali. Rarely does one come across such exquisite handwriting.

In 1952, the barrister Sudhirchandra Mitra made extensive inquiries in the high court regarding the possibility of obtaining legal information concerning Swami Vivekananda's father, Bishwanath. The then chief justice, Phanibhushan Chakrabarty, helped and in fact sent some relevant documents to Sudhirchandra.

Since the lawsuits spanned several generations, we must realize that we are looking at a series of lawsuits and not merely one case. Therefore, we will have a better understanding of them if we study the genealogy of the Dutta family and a list of the cases that were filed before the various courts. We can then understand who stood to benefit financially, those who were unmarried or childless, those who had only daughters and no son to continue the family line, etc.

Let us go back to Ramsunder Dutta. We know the names of his five sons. The eldest, Rammohan, had two sons and seven daughters. His eldest son, Durgaprasad, who eventually became a monk, was Swami Vivekananda's grandfather. Rammohan's second son was named Kaliprasad. Kaliprasad in turn had two sons, Kedarnath and Taraknath. Taraknath was therefore Vivekananda's paternal uncle. The legal battle which so deeply affected Swami Vivekananda was initiated by Taraknath's wife, Gyanadasundari. Taraknath and Gyanadasundari had one son who died in infancy and six daughters. At a later point, after Gyanadasundari had lost everything, she surrendered her future welfare completely to Bhubaneshwari's son, Vivekananda.

Bhupendranath writes: 'The legal contest was fought between Bishwanath Dutta's wife and the wife of the late Taraknath Dutta. The name of Swami Vivekananda was not mentioned in this case. Ultimately, Aunt Gyanadasundari lost her case and her house had to be auctioned. Towards the end of her life, however, she appealed to Swami Vivekananda for succour and he helped her by offering a large sum in cash.'

We shall see that, despite Swami Vivekananda's generosity, the problems with this particular aunt did not cease there. On the contrary, he was cheated of even greater sums of money. For this reason, the problems multiplied and the case continued, even though Gyanadasundari was old by this time. Bhupendranath tells us that Gyanadasundari later confessed that she was goaded to fight the case by certain family members. The housing authorities also levied an additional 5,000 rupees tax in the midst of all this trouble.

There is substantial evidence to prove that this uncle and aunt used to frequently torture Bhubaneshwari and her family. In consequence, Bhubaneshwari 'had to suffer from the beginning of her married life ... she bore with infinite patience all the tyranny meted out to her and her husband.' It came to such a pass that she possessed 'only one

The Monk as Man

sari, while the other daughters-in-law of the house had many'. Sadly, it took Bishwanath a long time to realize the ordeals to which his wife was being subjected. Finally, he said, 'How is it that I earn so much money and yet my wife does not get to eat a full meal?'

It is not surprising that for many of today's generation, the problems in the joint-family system seem inscrutable. If the husband has a good job, why should his wife own only one sari and not be able to eat a proper meal? When the husband has a house, why does he have to appear in court constantly to establish his claim to it?

The joint family was the curse of nineteenth- and twentieth-century middle-class Bengali society. And it was unavoidable. The well-to-do were expected to live with their extended family under one roof. The earnings of any one member were shared by all. This translated into food and other household expenses. Legally speaking, although the members of a joint family had their rights and interests in the common property, the assets remained undivided. Hence, partition suits for division of property often dragged on for forty or fifty years before a final settlement was negotiated.

From these lengthy procedures, the lawyers of Calcutta were naturally able to stuff their pockets well. These suits did not end in the lower courts. Appeals were filed in one higher court after another. In this context I should mention that often helpless, childless widows sold their rights and interests in the joint-family property to other co-heirs.

I shall first present a gist of the case against Bhubaneshwari as laid out by Bhupendranath and then add a few enlightening details. He writes, 'Bhubaneshwari Debi bought a share of the undivided ancestral house in her name from a young widow while she was living with Kaliprasad and his family. But after our uncle Taraknath's death, aunt Gyanadasundari forcibly ejected Bishwanath's family from the house and then filed a suit in the court.'

It is a brief summary and, in order to better appreciate Vivekananda's anguish, it is necessary to look at it in more detail. We see the Dutta family embroiled in more than one case. An exact time frame may help us understand this more simply. Let us begin when Swami Vivekananda was only fourteen years old.

1 SEPTEMBER 1877

Bhubaneshwari buys the portion of the house belonging to Bindubasini, the wife of Madhab Dutta, the second son of Radhamohan. Does she buy it with her husband's money or does Taraknath buy the property in Bhubaneshwari's name? This was the question hotly debated in the courts. It should be noted however that the practice of buying property in another's name, known in Bengali as *benami*, was a standard practice in those days.

1880

Another coparcener, Shachimani Dasi (Gourmohan Dutta's granddaughter), brings a suit against the partition of the property. Bhubaneshwari Dasi is one of those against whom this suit is brought. The eminent attorney, Robert Belchamber, is appointed commissioner with the task of dividing the property. He does so on the basis of the evidence brought before him, but that does not end the dissension. It goes to the courts.

AUGUST 1885

Following Bishwanath's death in February 1884, Taraknath claims the rights to the property bought in Bhubaneshwari's name.

25 DECEMBER 1885

An altercation takes place between Taraknath and Bhubaneshwari over the issue of demolishing an old wall in the house in order to repair one of the bathrooms. Narendranath's mother insists that he take part in the conflict.

25 FEBRUARY 1886
Taraknath dies.

JULY 1886
Taraknath's widow, Gyanadasundari, files a suit against Bhubaneshwari in the high court.

11 AUGUST 1886
Bhubaneshwari Dasi applies for a letter of administration claiming the right of inheritance to the property. Her letter is dated only five days before the death of Sri Ramakrishna. This action is necessitated by the fact that Bishwanath died intestate. The letter of clearance is obtained the next day. How fast the operations of the courts were then! In all these legal papers, we can see Narendranath's signature alongside that of his mother's.

16 AUGUST 1886
Sri Ramakrishna passes away.

EARLY 1887
Gyanadasundari initiates her lawsuit. It is conducted by the eminent English barrister, Mr Pugh.

8 MARCH 1887
Narendranath is now living at Baranagore Math. Under cross-examination, he states, 'I am unemployed.'

14 MARCH 1887
Gyanadasundari loses the cases and elects to appeal again to the high court.

10 NOVEMBER 1887
A judgement is handed down by the division bench comprising three judges of the court. Gyanadasundari once again loses.

1888

Bhubaneshwari wants the house to be partitioned according to the terms Shachimani sought and in accordance with the suggestions made by Robert Belchambers.

23 NOVEMBER 1888

Bhubaneshwari obtains legal rights to her share of the property.

28 JUNE 1902

The various litigation suits have now been in process for more than fourteen years, and yet the case has not been concluded. Swami Vivekananda now comes to Calcutta for one final time, the last Saturday of his life, and endeavours to put an end to them, once and for all. He is successful, but is compelled to give the coparceners some financial compensation.

4 JULY 1902

Swami Vivekananda leaves his mortal body.

&

On 4 July 1889, Swami Vivekananda had written to Premadadas Mitra, his friend and correspondent in Benares (now Benaras), 'My mother and two brothers live in Calcutta. I am the eldest. My younger brother is studying for the First Arts, and the youngest is but a child. They were once wealthy, but since my father's demise, they live in abject poverty. Sometimes they have to go without food altogether. Compounding this hardship is the fact that some of our relatives took advantage of their helpless condition and ousted them from our ancestral house. Although it is true that my mother brought a lawsuit in the high court and recovered part of the property, she and my brothers are penniless.

Had the litigations continued, I cannot even imagine what would have happened to them … Now, however, the lawsuit has come to an end. So I will stay here in Calcutta for a while to settle matters. Please bless me that after this, I may leave this place for good.'

Another message was sent to Premadadas by Vivekananda just ten days later, on 14 July. In it he declares, 'Most of my problems have been taken care of. I have engaged a broker to sell a piece of land. Hopefully it will be sold soon. When that happens, I will be relieved and will be able to come to Benares to be with you.'

Bhupendranath informs us: 'There is something in the biographies of Swamiji that is not quite accurate. People assume that because Bhubaneshwari won the property settlement, Swamiji was now relieved of his financial burden. However, barristers need to be paid their fees and, in this case, they demanded immediate payment. When they were finally paid, this writer (Bhupendranath) was present and kept the receipts.'

೦೮

Swami Vivekananda's hardships as a monk, how he fought against financial hurdles right up to his death, how he was forced to bow down his proud head to fulfil his filial duties—this complex saga, while not unpublished, has been given very little weight or publicity.

But without this information, how can we ever hope to comprehend the magnanimity of Swami Vivekananda or understand why he was unwilling to shirk wordly responsibilities? The great Vivekananda showed us ordinary mortals how to overcome wordly obstacles in the path to salvation. He is worshipped by the poor of the world, the poor of India and the poor of Bengal because of the unbelievable struggles that marked his life.

When the litigation started with Shachimani in 1877, Bhubaneshwari travelled by a hackney carriage with her husband to the high court. While climbing into the carriage, she asked Naren if he would like to accompany them, but he declined.

At that time, she testified before the court that she had bought properties worth five hundred rupees each from Bamasundari and Bindubasini. They were the widows of Radhamohan's sons, Bholanath and Madhabchandra. Bhubaneshwari had acquired these properties on 1 September 1877.

On the basis of the report of the Commissioner of Partitions Robert Belchambers, Justice Arthur Wilson awarded a one-fourth share of the property to Shachimani. This lawsuit determined with utmost precision the boundaries and portions in which the homestead was to be divided. My source Chitragupta reveals that this disposition of the property cost the phenomenal sum of 2,892 rupees—in spite of the fact that no dividing walls were ever erected! The co-heirs all paid for their respective portions, even though some family members tried to prove after Bishwanath's death that it was Taraknath who had paid for Bhubaneshwari's portion.

As Bhubaneshwari became entangled in myriad financial and legal problems, Narendranath got increasingly preoccupied with Sri Ramakrishna. This became a source of disappointment for Bhubaneshwari. One day, she reprimanded her son, 'What are you doing, Bilu? You are only roaming around like a vagabond. You have no idea how I am managing, how I am trying my best to make both ends meet.'

Narendranath answered, 'Mother, who am I to look after the family? The one above will take care.'

Sri Ramakrishna had a householder disciple, Ramchandra Dutta, who was related to Bhubaneshwari. He had been nursed by her as an infant and after his mother died, she had raised him. A distressed Bhubaneshwari asked Ramchandra , 'Will Bilu ever come back?' The devoted Ramchandra assured her, 'How can he do without you?'

The Monk as Man

Narendranath was living in Baranagore when he heard about Gyanadasundari's lawsuit against his mother. It was filed only a month before Sri Ramakrishna's death. Aunt Gyanadasundari claimed that the property bought by Bhubaneshwari had actually been paid for by Taraknath, even though it was in Bhubaneshwari's name. At this time, the main adviser to Gyanadasundari was one of her sons-in-law. An attorney by the name of Nimai Basu submitted Bhubaneshwari's response in writing: 'My husband used to send money regularly from afar. This is my personal property.' Narendranath confirmed that his mother's signature in English on the document was in fact genuine.

When Narendranath learnt that the court hearing was scheduled for a later date, he went on a pilgrimage. But he did return on time. There were quite a number of witnesses in this case. Vivekananda himself gave evidence in court on 8 March 1887.

According to Swami Gambhirananda (1889–1988), Bhubaneshwari was represented by the barrister W.C. Bonnerjee. Some details about the trial have emerged. Mr Pugh, the barrister for Gyanadasundari, cross-examined Narendranath closely with the aim of establishing the family's indigence. He first asked how old Narendranath was. Narendranath replied that he was around twenty-three. Mr Pugh then asked Narendranath the nature of his occupation. Narendranath's reply was that he was presently unemployed. He added that he had been appointed headmaster of Metropolitan Institution about two years earlier, in 1885, but had resigned after three months. After that, he had worked for some time in a college in a position offered to him by Dr Aghornath Chattopadhyay.

Mr Pugh's next question was whether it was correct that Narendranath had not lived in the ancestral house for a long time. Narendranath said that he used to live there with his mother after his father's death. While he was not always there in the period contested in the trials, he was residing there at the time of his uncle Taraknath's death.

Next came a most unusual question: 'Have you become somebody's *chela* [disciple]?' Narendranath was visibly offended. He replied that he knew what a disciple was, but he could not understand Mr Pugh's insinuations. He emphasized that he had never been a chela to a begging sadhu.

Mr Pugh pressed further. He wanted to know if Narendranath had ever helped with raising donations for religious events. Narendranath answered that he had never accepted contributions for Sri Ramakrishna.

Then Narendranath turned the tables. He asked the barrister if he himself knew what the word chela meant. At this, Mr Pugh was more than a little discomfited.

On another day at the court, Narendranath informed that he had had altercations with Taraknath twice. Subsequently, he had never had the occasion to meet Taraknath, although he had come to the house on two occasions before his uncle passed away. His mother had also returned to the old house. Narendranath mentioned that at this time, they observed that his mother's room was still untouched. Likewise, the room that he and Mahendranath had shared. But there was yet a third room that his family had once occupied and that had been demolished by Taraknath.

In his biography of Vivekananda, Swami Gambhirananda says that the English judge observed aloud that Narendranath would make a fine lawyer. Mr Pugh, the barrister for the other side, shook Narendranath's hand and said, 'I agree with the judge.'

After a long hearing, Justice McPherson of the high court gave his verdict: It had been clearly established that Bishwanath used to send money to his wife regularly. Therefore, the onus was on Taraknath's widow to prove that Taraknath had purchased the property in Bhubaneshwari's name. Since Gyanadasundari had not presented any account books to the court, she failed to furnish the necessary proof. Moreover, the existence of a letter written by Taraknath further worked against Gyanadasundari. In this letter to one of his relatives, Taraknath states that he had not bought the property and that it belonged to Bhubaneshwari. Another point in Bhubaneshwari's favour was that she had once executed a power of attorney in favour of Taraknath, empowering him to register the property with the Calcutta Collectorate, and he had done so.

In 1887, the division bench of the appellate court, comprising Chief Justice Arthur Wilson and Justice Richard Tottenham, awarded their judgement in favour of Bhubaneshwari. Gyanadasundari lost the case on 10 November 1887. But do lawsuits end so easily? We shall see that they continued to haunt Swami Vivekananda until the very end.

ଓଃ

Let us take help from the books written by Shankari Prasad Basu to put these problems into perspective. Swami Vivekananda paid 6,000 rupees for the portion of the house that he purchased from his aunt Gyanadasundari. Of this amount, he was compelled to borrow 5,000 rupees from the treasury of the Ramakrishna Math.

However, researcher Shankari Prasad Basu tells us that this sale was not negotiated with good intent. For Gyanadasundari was conniving all the while to cheat her nephew. By 6 August 1899, her motives became clear and Swami Vivekananda wrote in a letter to Mrs Ole Bull, his *'dhira mata'* (calm mother) in whom he had ample trust, 'As to mental worry, there has been enough of late. The aunt whom you saw has a deep-laid plan to cheat me, and she and her people contrived to sell me a house for 6,000 rupees or £400, and I bought [it] for my mother in good faith. Then they would not give me possession, hoping that I would not go to court for the shame of taking forcible possession as a Sannyasin.'

More litigations ensued and they lasted quite a few years more.

Once again, Swami Vivekananda was obliged to borrow money from the treasury of the math. The above-mentioned loan of 5,000 rupees plus this additional loan added to his anxieties. The only money he could call his own was what his friends and admirers gave him from time to time. Along with that, he had earned some extra money by writing books or articles and he did receive some reimbursement for his lectures abroad. Shankari Prasad reassures us that 'at the end, Swamiji was able to repay all the money that he had borrowed.'

Certain members of Swami Vivekananda's family, who had recorded the events of those years, did not recall the vital fact that Swamiji had purchased portions of the ancestral home for his mother. It was Shankari Prasad's research that uncovered this little-known detail and he had good reasons to feel uncomfortable about disclosing it. He writes, 'I think Swamiji helped Taraknath Dutta's widow financially on condition that she would return the portion of the house that belonged to Bhubaneshwari.' But here again, Swamiji became a victim of fraud.

In order to understand Swami Vivekananda's distress and to comprehend the nature of the obstacles that stood in the path of his spiritual progress, it was necessary to talk at length about the various lawsuits. Without discussing these openly, it would have been extremely difficult to establish just how conscientious Vivekananda was with regard to his family.

Shankari Prasad's account of the buying and selling of portions of the ancestral home is supported by a footnote in Swami Gambhirananda's book entitled *Yuganayak Vivekananda*: 'From other sources, it is learnt that Swamiji bought a one-fourth portion of the house at 2, Gourmohan Mukherjee Street from Amritalal Dutta on 2 December 1898, and bought the land and house at 3 Gourmohan Mukherjee Street from Bishweshwari Dasi on 29 January 1899. He gifted both properties to his mother on 27 May 1899.'

Alas, the litigations continued to cast long shadows. On 4 March

1902, just a few months before his death, Swami Vivekananda wrote to Sister Nivedita from Benares: 'I have spent the little money I brought from Europe in feeding my mother and paying her debts. What little remains, I cannot touch, as that is the expense for the pending lawsuit.'

Swami Brahmananda's diary narrates very poignantly the painful resolution of the whole story. Swami Vivekananda returned to Calcutta, where the family litigations were taking place, on Saturday, 28 June 1902. He went to dine at his sister Swarnamayee's house with a few friends. His relative and coparcener Habul Dutta came to visit him there and, of his own accord, talked about winding up the litigations. Swami Vivekananda said he would give a thousand rupees more if they could bring the dispute to a close. They reached an agreement. Swami Brahmananda then went to the office of the attorney Paltu-babu with Habul. There they drafted a letter noting down the legal conditions. This letter was then sent to the attorney N.C. Basu, who was acting for Habul Dutta. A letter of reply was received agreeing to the conditions.

Such speed is extremely unusual in Indian legal matters. It is perhaps clear that Swamiji had the feeling that his days were numbered and he could not wait any longer.

The fee of four hundred rupees for the attorney Paltu was paid by Swami Vivekananda on 2 July, two days before his death, as per the stipulation of Habul Dutta and Tamu Dutta. Vivekananda did everything in his power to fulfil the terms of the contract that had been drawn up.

಄

It is a mistake to think that money can ever be the basis of the relationship between a mother and a son. We last saw them coming home together from Cossipore in a hackney carriage, with Bhupendranath seated between them. On the way, Bhubaneshwari was relating to her eldest son what Sri Ramakrishna had told her.

We have yet another scene from 16 August 1886. Narendranath came home from the cremation ground after the obsequies of Sri Ramakrishna and gave his clothes to his mother for washing. Unknown to her, some of Sri Ramakrishna's ashes were tied to the garment. The next day, he asked his mother about the ashes. Bhubaneshwari said that she had found some ashes and had thrown them away. 'Alas, alas!' cried Naren. 'Those were Ramakrishna's bones.'

After the first phase of litigation was over, Narendranath retired to the math and was not often seen outside. Then, as a wandering monk, he set out on a pilgrimage to various parts of India. Bhupendranath writes of those years: 'He did not keep a close connection with his family during that time. He would visit his mother occasionally, when he happened to be in Calcutta. Nobody had seen him in a saffron robe at home until he came back from Europe in 1897.'

☙

Mother Bhubaneshwari was, indeed, unfortunate. All three of her sons caused her endless pain. Vivekananda fell ill at the monastery in Baranagore before the onset of summer in 1887. On hearing this news, the helpless widow immediately rushed there with her youngest son. But Vivekananda had made a rule barring women from entering the monks' quarters. When he saw his mother entering without notice, he said, 'I was the one who made the rule and it is for me that the rule is being broken!'

There would be no news for months on end of the wandering monk Vivekananda. We do not have any letters written by him to his mother. She had to bear all her tragedies alone.

On a Sunday morning in May 1891, Bhubaneshwari received a letter from Simla informing her that Jogendrabala had taken her own life. Her daughter was only twenty-five years old. A grief-stricken

Mahendranath went to the Baranagore monastery to communicate this news. Yogen Maharaj, Baburam Maharaj and Girish Chandra Ghosh after conferring with one another decided to send a telegram to Saradananda to beg Vivekananda to return to his mother, who was overwhelmed with grief. The telegram was sent from Howrah station to Saradananda.

Then the two monks went to Raghumani Dasi's house at Ramtanu Basu Lane where Bhubaneshwari lived. Bhubaneshwari was weeping inconsolably when they arrived. Baburam Maharaj sat there, mute with grief, and it fell on Yogen Maharaj to try to console her. The monks returned to Bagh Bazar around nine o'clock that evening. The news of Jogendrabala's suicide eventually reached Swami Vivekananda at Almora. Vivekananda, too, was plunged into great sorrow. How painful was the struggle to sever his ties with his family!

Mahendranath records the scene as it was later described to him: 'The telegram overwhelmed my brother. Deep inside his heart, a struggle waged. In the end, the monk won. A weeping Vivekananda told Saradananda, "You keep links with Bengal, you forward letters to me and cause trouble ... You always pester me. I do not want to be in touch with anybody, and you want to maintain relations with all!"'

A suicidal family line? Once, in Balaram Basu's house, Swami Vivekananda remarked to Yogen Maharaj, 'Do you know why we Duttas are so talented in our thinking? Ours is a family with a history of suicides. There have been many in our family who have taken their own lives. We are eccentric. We do not think before we act. We simply do what we like and do not worry about the consequences.'

In a humorous vein, Niranjan Maharaj attributes the brillance of the Dutta family to something else entirely. He once told Mahendranath, 'Do you know why Naren is so intelligent? Because he can smoke a hookah! You cannot be brilliant if you do not smoke a hookah. Just start smoking and you will be as sharp as Naren!'

After coping with his sister's suicide Swami Vivekananda again left on his wanderings. Once again, he cut off all links and started his journey, finding even more inaccessible mountains and caves for solace.

From time to time, he returned to Baranagore quite unexpectedly, passed a few days in the company of his gurubhais and then left again. Each time he would say, 'This is my last visit. I will not be back.' From 1891, he travelled the length and breadth of India. Mostly he was alone. During his wanderings, he preferred not to keep any contact, even with his gurubhais.

But did Vivekananda really want to erase his mother, completely and cruelly, from his mind? Was he ever able to do so?

Curiously, we have more than 550 letters by Swami Vivekananda written during his wandering days, but not a single one has been preserved that is addressed to his mother. Was Bhubaneshwari silent on her side too? Did she never write to her Bilu? It is scarcely believable; the mind refuses to accept it. If only her letters could be found, they would reveal so much more about the monk and his relationship with his mother.

To some extent, however, Swami Vivekananda's feelings for her surface even through his letters to others. For example, on 29 January 1894, he wrote from Chicago to Sri Haridas Viharidas Desai, the dewan of Junagadh, 'You had been to see my poor mother and brothers. I am glad you did. You have touched the only soft place in my heart. You ought to know, Diwanji, that I am no hard-hearted brute. If there is any being I love in the whole world, it is my mother ... So on the one hand, my vision of the future of Indian religion and that of the whole world, my love for the millions of beings sinking down and down for ages with nobody to help them, nay, nobody with even a thought for them; on the other hand, making those who are nearest and dearest to me miserable; I choose the former. "Lord will do the rest." He is with me, I am sure of that if of anything.'

On another occasion, the sannyasi himself declared that it was only because he had inherited his mother's purity and her capacity for selfless love that he was able to contemplate such a revolutionary role for himself. Whatever good he had done in his life was only through the grace of his mother. Bhubaneshwari imparted much more to this illustrious son of hers than a basic felicity in the English language—not just bookish knowledge but also moral depth. She used to tell him, 'It is a sin to cast morality aside, no matter what difficulties one encounters in life.'

This gives us a unique insight into Swami Vivekananda's frame of mind during his itinerant years. No matter where he was, he could not altogether free himself from worrying about his mother. At one point, he wrote: 'When I was staying in Manmatha-babu's house in Madras, I dreamt one night that my mother was no more. I felt heartbroken. At that time, I was not writing letters to the math very frequently, let alone letters to my family members. When I told Manmatha-babu what I had dreamt, he immediately sent a telegram to Calcutta and inquired after my mother's welfare. My friends in Madras were then working to hasten my journey to America, but I did not want to leave these shores without some knowledge of my mother's well-being. Manmatha-babu understood my predicament. He told me that he knew a man who had occult powers. He had, by rigorous ascetic practices, acquired the power to tell a man's fortune—good and bad, past and future. This occultist assured me that my mother was well. He also told me that very soon I would have to go far away on a spiritual mission.'

At a certain point during his travelling days, Vivekananda cut off all ties with everyone—family and gurubhais alike. After he parted from his gurubhais in Meerut, there was no news of him for some considerable time. Then one day a letter arrived at Baranagore, but it lacked a signature. It contained a request that a certain medicine which could be found in the house of the 'armless' Habu be sent to him. The letter was shown to Mahendranath who confirmed beyond doubt that it was his brother's handwriting.

Then, for a few years, there was no news of Swamiji until another unsigned letter arrived, this time from Jaipur. Much later, a few letters started coming from H.H. the Maharaja of Khetri, Ajit Singh. The letters that Vivekananda wrote prior to this phase of complete withdrawal show that he was in a very depressed state of mind. Mahendranath mentions one letter that is particularly distressing. In it, Swami Vivekananda writes: 'I have not found God. Even though I tried very hard, I could not get enlightenment. However, this has increased the love in my heart. I feel love for everybody.'

☙

In these long years, did Swami Vivekananda try to fulfil his duties towards his mother and family, or did he fail to do so? This question will forever remain hidden behind the veil of history.

Then, in the year 1891, a new era began.

On Thursday, 4 June, H.H. the Maharaja of Khetri, Ajit Singh woke up at 6.30 a.m. In the early evening, he spent half an hour with Maharaja Pratap Singh of Jodhpur. Then came a sannyasi, one who was proficient in Bengali, English and Sanskrit. They talked on a wide range of subjects, dined together and, at eleven o'clock, the sannyasi took his leave. That sannyasi was Swami Vivekananda.

This was the first chapter in their long relationship. It would not be an exaggeration to say that Swami Vivekananda won Ajit Singh's heart. Undoubtedly, the Maharaja also touched Swamiji's heart. On this first visit to Khetri, Vivekananda stayed for almost five months—from 4 June to 27 October. It was his longest stay at any one place during his itinerant years. In fact, according to Swami Prabhananda, he stayed at Belur Math—the monastery he himself established—for a total of only 178 days.

Swami Vivekananda visited Khetri twice more in his life, once in

April 1893 just before his departure for America and again in 1897, after he returned from the West. Sometime during his second stay at Khetri, hearing about Swamiji's family concerns, Maharaja Ajit Singh took the decision to lighten his financial burden.

Mahendranath Dutta writes, 'Khetri's Maharaja used to send 100 rupees to Swamiji's mother on a regular basis. The money was sent every month via Sharat Maharaj, Yogen Maharaj and Mr Sandel. He specially requested that this arrangement be not discussed with others.'

The letters that are now stored in the Khetri archives reveal that the king wrote frequently to the members of Swami Vivekananda's family from 1892 onwards, and also received letters from them in return. To cite one instance: There is a letter from Mahendranath to Maharaja Ajit Singh dated 28 February 1893 from 7, Ramtanu Basu Lane: 'Anxious as I am not receiving your Highness' any letter for a long time ... I have got news of my brother some fifteen days ago who is now in Madras.'

In his subsequent letter to the maharaja, dated 22 March 1893, Mahendranath includes a list of books he has recently read. He says, 'I have sent up my younger brother (Bhupendranath) to the well-known Metropolitan Institution, one of the best schools of the town and he is prosecuting his studies well. We received news of our elder brother. Got news of my brother who is now at Madras living with Baboo Monmath N. Bhattacharya, the Assistant Controller of province.'

Those who imagine that in his second visit to Khetri (April 1893) Swamiji's primary concern was to discuss the assistance that his family needed, may not be entirely correct. On this occasion, Swamiji stayed at Khetri for three weeks—from 21 April to 10 May.

At this point we will not concern ourselves with the unparalleled contribution of the Maharaja of Khetri to Swami Vivekananda's tours abroad. We shall only look at the ways in which Swamiji tried his utmost to help his mother and his family.

Beni Shankar Sharma has said in this connection: 'Swamiji never made one feel that everything related to the family is undesirable or he did not sacrifice his love for his mother on the altar of asceticism. On the contrary, one finds that he was prepared to sacrifice everything— ambition, leadership and fame—for his mother.'

According to this same writer, when Ajit Singh took up the responsibility of bearing the expenses of Swami Vivekananda's tours abroad, he decided to provide for Swami Vivekananda's family as well. This entailed the payment of 100 rupees every month for their sustenance. The maharaja undoubtedly realized that his duty was to free Swami Vivekananda from his worries regarding his family before his tour abroad.

On 2 June 1893, just two days after Swami Vivekananda's departure for the United States, Mahendranath wrote to the maharaja from Ramtanu Basu Lane: 'I have the honour to receive your Highness' letter on the 31st May and to express my acknowledgement of a receipt of a half note of Rs 100. I have informed the contents of the letter to Swami Ramakrishnananda and to my mother and my grandmother. Mother and my grandmother have both given their consent to my brother's tour around the world.'

Soon (13 June) we find Mahendranath writing again to the Maharaja of Khetri: 'I am in receipt of your Highness' letter together with a half note of Rs 100 … I have heard from Swamy R. and Swamy Sharat Chandra that my dada has gone to Burma. He shall then go to China or some such place … both my mother and grandmother have expressed their "ashis" to your Highness' family.'

On the same day that this particular letter was dispatched, Swami Ramakrishnananda wrote to the Maharaja: 'Mahendranath has received your half of Rs 100 which you had sent.'

In a letter to the maharaja dated 20 July 1893, Swami Shivananda thanks him profusely for supporting Swami Vivekananda's family and then inquires, 'It is rumoured that Vivekananda has started for England. if it be so, do you know what would be his address there?'

Maharaja Ajit Singh's financial assistance was a closely guarded secret. Initially, even the king's Munshi, Jagamohanlal, remained unaware of it. We have an interesting story about the method of money transfer from Rajasthan to Bengal from a letter written by Jagamohanlal (now apprised of the situation) to Mahendranath on 6 July 1893. He writes: 'I am serving under H.H. the Maharaja of Khetri who has been pleased to confide in me and to acclaim so with all your known affairs ... I am desired to enclose herewith the first half of a currency note no. V/41 62743 worth one hundred rupee by way of support for your family expenses and shall be glad to send the other half on receiving an acknowledgement.'

Mahendranath replied to Jagamohanlal on 31 July 1893 from Calcutta: 'I am glad to learn that you accompanied my brother on his journey from your place to Madras and back again to Bombay and reached him up to the steers. There is no news of him in Calcutta ... A rumour was circulated the other day that he has reached Chicago ... As for your enquiry to Swamy R. about my studies, I am glad to say that up to this time I have worked well and keeping up good progress with the class and that professors are quite satisfied with me.'

He adds, 'Received a half C. Note of Rs 100 but in future if there be any occasion of sending here C. Note, please do that by registered letter as the post office men have suspected it and will possibly open the letter and appropriate it to themselves as they have given me sly hint to this.'

Swami Ramakrishnananda used to write to Khetri's maharaja and munshi, care of the government office address of Baikuntha Sanyal. In a letter dated 10 February 1894, for example, Swami Ramakrishnananda gives Jagamohanlal some long-awaited news: 'He is still at Chicago and is doing well ... saw Mahendranath the other day, he with his mother and youngers and other family members is doing well. He is luckily engaged with his studies ... His exam will fall on the 26th prox.'

Recently, I had the good fortune of looking at the transcripts and degree certificates of Mahendranath's various examinations. They show that he received a first in the entrance examination, but a third each in the FA and BA examinations. In those days it must have taken him great courage to go to England and read law with a third division in BA.

Towards the last decade of the nineteenth century, a regular arrangement of hundred rupees per month was no pittance. As I mentioned earlier, an educated clerk in Calcutta used to earn fifteen rupees a month. Those who were fortunate enough to earn the grand sum of fifty rupees would celebrate. According to some historians, the sum of one hundred rupees was the equivalent of 10,000 rupees today, while others put the value as high as 20,000 rupees. It is, indeed, remarkable that a disciple should be so generous towards his teacher's family. In the years since then, Bengalis have expressed their devotion to the Ramakrishna Math by offering financial contributions, but honestly, they have not been as overwhelmingly generous as the maharaja. We must also keep in mind the fact that the title 'Maharaja' does not necessarily signify that Khetri was a large kingdom.

Unfortunately, even with this largesse of a hundred rupees a month, and also taking into account the fact that litigation was not as costly in those days as they are now, the family was unable to put an end to the continuing legal crises that besieged them.

We should also note the strict condition of secrecy that the maharaja insisted upon. For him, his financial assistance was a private act; he did not want it to be publicized. He began sending the monthly stipend in 1891 and continued it until his death on 18 January 1901. His unparalleled generosity over this ten-year span came to light only eight decades later, when none of the principal recipients was alive: Bhubaneshwari died in 1911, Swarnamayee on 16 February 1932, Mahendranath on 14 October 1956, Bhupendranath on 25 December 1961.

The Monk as Man

Swami Vivekananda, however, did express his debt to the maharaja in public on 17 December 1897. This was after he had returned from his first visit to the West. Vivekananda declared, 'It would not have been possible for me to do what little I have done for India but for my friendship with Khetri's Maharaja.'

There are more revealing facts about Swamiji's dependency on the Maharaja of Khetri. I shall touch upon several poignant incidents that occurred towards the end of Swami Vivekananda's life later, in the context of his mother. But before that it will not be out of context to enquire about his concern for his mother while in America and Europe.

 C8

Swami Vivekananda was initially surprised to learn that in the United States sons often refer to their mothers by their names. He was even more surprised to discover that it shocked American ladies to be addressed as 'mother'. He commented, 'Later on, I understood the reason: because that would mean they were old.'

Swami Vivekananda frequently mentioned his own mother while he was in the United States. He would often recite the stories and poems he had heard from her during his childhood, while lying next to her on the cot. A reference to his prodigious memory would make him recall that she, too, was blessed with the same capacity. 'Yes,' he would say, 'my mother had this kind of memory as well; if she heard the Ramayana once, she would be able to recite it by heart.'

He recalled that his mother's voice was very sweet. She used to sing songs of Krishna to herself. It was her practice to read for a few hours in the afternoon and again for a few hours in the evening by the kerosene lamp. There was no electricity in those days.

We even have a physical description of Bhubaneshwari in her later years: 'She was strong; her eyes were large and oval-shaped. Strength, firmness and an indomitable spirit emanated from her.' It seems that only a mother like her could have borne a son like Swamiji. The three brothers resembled their mother in many ways.

Manmathanath Gangopadhyay has written, 'Swamiji had his mother's eyes. The depth of his eyes, however, cannot be described.'

Above all, Swami Vivekananda's mother had faith in herself. Even in the midst of the deepest crisis, she never allowed that flame to be quenched. Though it may be slightly out of context here, it is worth recalling Swamiji's illuminating observation: 'The history of the world is the history of men who had faith in themselves. That faith summons the divinity within ... Death comes only when a man or a nation loses faith in itself.'

Sometime in July or August 1908, a group of women offered a written felicitation to Bhubaneshwari Debi in the home of Sir Nilratan Sarkar at 61, Harrison Road (now Mahatma Gandhi Road). Bhupendranath was in jail at that time. After his release, on 24 Sraban 1314, he told his mother, 'You never received much recognition for being Vivekananda's mother. But for being *my* mother, you even got a public reception!'

Later, Bhupendranath admitted that his remark was made in jest. His mother did become widely known abroad through Vivekananda. In 1894, Swamiji delivered an inspiring lecture in Boston entitled, simply, 'My Mother'. He was referring to the Divine Mother, but he explained how the human mother was related to the divine. Some members of the audience were so enchanted with this lecture that on Christmas that year, they sent a card to Bhubaneshwari with a picture of the child Jesus lying on his mother Mary's lap. It was accompanied by a letter in which the writers drew certain parallels between the lives of the two sons and their mothers.

The letter runs: 'Today is Christmas, the birth of Lord Jesus. At this auspicious time, when we celebrate and rejoice over the gift of

Mary's son to the world, we felicitate you because we have your son in our midst. He says that whatever service he has been able to render to men, women and children was through your blessings. It is your nobility of spirit that is reflected in your son's work. In appreciation and admiration, we offer you our gratitude.'

Not only did Swami Vivekananda lavish praise on his mother, he relied on his mother's judgement as well. Her opinion mattered greatly to him. When Pratap Mazumdar, for example, viciously denounced him, declaring, 'He is nothing but a cheat and a fraud. He comes here to tell you that he is a fakir,' Swami Vivekananda wrote a most poignant letter to Isabelle McKindley. It is dated 26 April 1894:

'Now, I do not care what they even my own people say about me— except for one thing. I have an old mother. She has suffered much all her life and in the midst of all she could bear to give me up for the service of God and man; but to have given up the most beloved of her children—her hope—to live a beastly immoral life in a far-distant country, as Mazoomdar was telling in Calcutta, would have simply killed her.'

It is, indeed, fortunate that around the same time as Pratap Mazumdar was spreading these slanders, the Christmas card and letter arrived from the United States to soothe Bhubaneshwari's anxieties— the letter that said that he had been able to do so much in America only by virtue of his mother's blessings.

A few years later, again in America, we find Swami Vivekananda once more praising the selflessness, tolerance and forgiving nature of his mother: 'Our mothers are great! We want to die with our head on her lap ... To bring me into the world, she underwent great penance. For years before my birth, she kept her body, mind, food, clothes and senses pure ... So she deserves to be worshipped.'

In 1896, Swami Vivekananda's family problems escalated once more. At that time, his beloved gurubhais, on his request, were taking care of his family. Only a great soul like Vivekananda could shoulder both the responsibilities of his family and the duties of monkhood in this way.

Now the focus turns to London. Swami Vivekananda writes to Sara Bull on 5 June 1896 that his brother Mahendranath has been in London for the last two months. He wants to pursue a career as a barrister. We get to know further details from Mahendranath himself. He writes, 'Sharat Maharaj (Swami Saradananda) went to London from Calcutta by ship in March 1896. The present writer went to London to read law after a week.'

It is not clear to what extent Swami Vivekananda supported Mahendranath's decision to read law, although Mahendranath does write that he and his brother were on good terms. He says, 'Swamiji asked for the *Bachaspati* dictionary, so everybody helped to pool in Rs 100 to buy the dictionary and sent it to the present writer.'

Swami Vivekananda was then experiencing a number of difficulties in London because of his new surroundings. His brother's presence not only added to his worries, but also compounded his difficulties and even created some unpleasantness. It seems that Mahendranath troubled his older brother considerably. Our only consolation is that were it not for Mahendranath's stay in London, his invaluable three-volume book on Vivekananda in London would not have been written.

We know that in their first encounter after a gap of many years, Mahendranath found it difficult to recognize his brother. This was Swami Vivekananda's second visit to London, while Mahendranath was a stranger to the city. Swamiji seemed aloof though he lovingly presented Mahendranath a gold pen at the time. Mahendranath later sent this pen to his younger brother in India, but it failed to reach Bhupendranath because it was intercepted by the postal employees. After this first meeting, Swami Vivekananda took a five-pound note from his pocket and sent it to his brother via his disciple Krishna Menon.

Mahendranath also records one curious piece of advice that Swami Vivekananda gave him. Apparently, he came to Mahendranath's room one day and said, 'Ensure that you do not have dirt under your nails. Clip the nails. I keep small instruments in my pocket for that purpose. Always remain clean, otherwise people will be repelled by you.'

What my nation wants is pluck and scientific genius. Swami Vivekananda, for his part, reveals his hopes for his brother in his letter to Mrs Bull on 5 June 1896: 'So I want Mohin to be an electrician. Even if he fails in life, still I will have the satisfaction that he strove to become great and really useful to his country ... In America alone there is that something in the air which brings out whatever is best in every one ... I want him to be daring, bold, and to struggle to cut a new path for himself and his nation. An electrical engineer can make a living in India.'

Swami Vivekananda was confident that the Maharaja of Khetri would support Mahendranath. He added, 'I myself have 300 pounds and am prepared to give Mahendranath all of it ... You want to send me money but I will not be able to accept it.' Immediately after this, he expressed concerns about his brother's health. 'He is getting bouts of "jungle fever" (malaria) every fifteen days. The boy is very good.'

In later years, Mahendranath formed a close friendship with the famous Bengali painter Nandalal Bose (1882–1966). From Bose's memoirs, we understand that, 'Swamiji was not happy with Mahim going to England, probably because of the financial strain it imposed. Mahim-babu remained in London for one and a half or two years. Due to the dearth of money and a feeling that his brother did not care for him, he decided to return to India on foot. Most of the journey he did on foot ... He traversed through Europe, Northern Africa, West Asia, Greece, Iran, Syria, Russia, Bulgaria ... After six years of travelling, he finally reached Calcutta in 1902.'

When Swami Vivekananda last saw his brother in 1896, he himself was thirty-three years old, Mahendranath was twenty-six,

Swami Saradananda was thirty, J. J. Goodwin (Swami Vivekananda's stenographer) was twenty-five and John P. Fox (an American admirer of Swami Vivekananda) was twenty-three. After Mahendranath quit the shores of England, he kept in touch with no one except John P. Fox. He became a detached, restless traveller and, for the next six years, did not even write a letter to his mother.

The year following his departure, Mr Sturdy wrote to Miss Macleod, a devotee of Swami Vivekananda, 'I do not know anything about Mahim. He has disappeared completely. He has not left an address, so I have returned his letters to the post office.'

Swami Vivekananda definitely suffered on his brother's account. Mahendranath did not want to abide by his wishes and become an electrical engineer. Then, when Mahendranath was ill with a high fever, Henrietta Müller turned him out of her house. This upset Swami Vivekananda greatly. It seems that in the autumn of 1896, Mahendranath was moving from one lodging house to another and was not doing very much.

While reminiscing with J. J. Goodwin at a later stage, Mahendranath himself acknowledged that Swamiji had wanted to send him to America with Swami Saradananda and Goodwin. Swamiji had said, 'There are many more things to be learnt in New York than in London.' Swami Vivekananda was enamoured of American science and technology, but they did not hold any attraction for Mahendranath.

In Mahendranath's memoirs, he reports that Goodwin had tried relentlessly for several days to coax him to accompany him to America. Sometimes through gentle coaxing, sometimes by scolding and sometimes by joking and teasing, he tried his best to fulfil Swamiji's wish and persuade Mahim to change his mind. Goodwin would growl like a lion, roll his fists and say, 'Come with me to America or I will break your face!' But each attempt proved unsuccessful. It seems Mahindra was too proud even to ask Swami Vivekananda for the money to purchase a steamer ticket home to India and so he was faced with no other choice but undertake the arduous journey back on foot.

Akshay Kumar Ghosh, a young Bengali asking for help, wrote to the Maharaja of Khetri from London on 13 January 1899 to advise him, 'The thirty pounds that you have sent to Mahendranath is with Mr Sturdy. We have not heard anything from Mahendranath for the last nineteen months.'

On 7 July 1898, Bhupendranath Dutta wrote to Khetri's Jagamohanlal from Calcutta: 'I have not written to you for a long time. We have news that my brother [Mahendranath] is now in Turkey. From there, he will go to Persia, Tibet, Mongolia and perhaps even to see the Great Wall of China. We got this news from an American, Mr Fox.'

Even as a sannyasi, Swami Vivekananda could not free himself from the various problems engulfing his family, and Mahendranath's fickleness only increased his worries. He asked Fox to convey to Mahendranath the following poignant message: 'Kindly tell Mohin that he has my blessings always. And what he is doing now is surely much better than being a lawyer, etc. I like boldness and adventure and my race stands in need of that spirit very much. Only, as my health is failing and I do not expect to live long, Mohin must find the right way and take care of Mother and our family. I may pass away at any moment. I am quite proud of him now.'

The letter suggests that in London their relations may have become strained, although in Mahendranath's own writings, we find only reflections of his deepest love and respect for his brother. Times had undeniably been rough for Swami Vivekananda in England and, dependant as he was on the generosity of others in a foreign land, he had been as affectionate and generous to Mahendranath as he possibly could. However, strict conditions had been placed on the use of the money he was given and it seems that Swamiji was unable to be as forthcoming with it as he would have wished.

At a later date, Swami Vivekananda wrote an angry letter to Mr E.T. Sturdy when he and Miss Müller accused Swamiji of indulging in luxuries: 'You and Miss Müller were in charge of the house at St George's Road. My poor brother was ill there and Miss Müller drove him away ... Every penny of the money you have given me for my work is still untouched. In front of you I had to send my brother away, perhaps to his death. I have not given him a farthing of the money which was not my own.'

ଔ

Swami Vivekananda left England on 16 December 1896 to return to India. His steamer went via Colombo, Sri Lanka. He reached Calcutta on 19 February 1897. He immersed himself quickly into the work of setting up the monastery at Belur and then he set out to tour the whole of India.

He hardly had time to breathe. September 1898 found Swami Vivekananda in Kashmir. Letters reached him care of Justice Rishibar Mukhopadhyay. Unfortunately, Swami Vivekananda fell ill there and remained incapacitated for two weeks. When he felt a little better, he wrote candidly to H.H. Maharaja Ajit Singh on 17 September:

'I am in want of funds. Though the American friends are doing everything they can to help me, I feel shame to beg from them all the time, especially as illness makes one incur contingent expenses. I have no shame to beg of one person in the world and that is yourself. Whether you give or refuse, it is the same to me. If possible send some money kindly.'

The maharaja immediately took steps and did the needful. A grateful Vivekananda responded from Belur Math on 15 December 1898, with a receipt for the money order of 500 rupees and a note:

'I am a little better now. Don't know whether this improvement will continue or not.'

Despite the maharaja's swift intervention, Swami Vivekananda grew increasingly restless. His continued illness brought with it the fear of unanticipated expenses. His concerns for his family were also growing. In his letter to Maharaja Ajit Singh of 22 November 1898, he says: 'I want to live with my mother and get my younger brother married to prevent extinction of the family.' One can assume that here Swami Vivekananda is echoing his mother's fears. Yet, strangely enough, Swamiji had once written that if Mahendranath were to get married, he would turn him out. According to Shankari Prasad Basu, of the two, Swami Vivekananda probably considered the youngest one to be more suitable for marriage. One has to remember also that all this while there was no news of Mahendranath.

The next sad, private letter from Swami Vivekananda to H.H. Maharaja Ajit Singh brings tears to one's eyes, even after a hundred years: 'Your Highness, … As you know already, I have been ailing since my return. In Calcutta, your Highness assured me of your friendship and help for me personally and [advised me] not to be worried about this incurable malady … After trying these two years a different climate, I am getting worse by the day and am now almost at death's door. I appeal to your Highness's generosity and friendship. I have one great sin rankling always in my breast, and that is [in order] to do service to the world, I have sadly neglected my mother. Again, since my second brother has gone away, she has become awfully worn-out with grief. Now my last desire is to be of some service to my mother, for some years at least. I want to live with my mother and get my younger brother married to prevent extinction of the family. This will certainly smoothen my last days as well as those of my mother. She lives now in a hovel. I want to build a little decent home for her and make some provision for the youngest, as there is very little hope of his being a good earning man. Is it too much for a royal descendant of Ramchandra to do for one he loves and calls his friend? I do not know who else to appeal to. The money I got from Europe was for the "work", and every penny almost has been given over to that work. Nor can I beg of others for help for my own self. About my own family affairs, I have exposed myself to your Highness; none else shall know of it. I am tired, heartsick and dying. Do, I pray, this last great work of kindness to me, befitting your great and generous nature ... P.S. This letter is strictly private. Will you please drop a wire to me whether you will do it or not?'

The king came to the rescue with a telegram of reassurance. On 1 December 1898, the ailing Swami Vivekananda sat down to reply to the noble king of Khetri from Belur:

'Your telegram has pleased me beyond description, and it is worthy of your noble self. I herewith give you the details of what I want.

The lowest possible estimate of building a little home in Calcutta is at least ten thousand rupees. With that it is barely possible to buy or build a house ... fit for four or five persons to live in.

As for the expenses of living, the 100 rupees a month your generosity is supplying my mother is enough for her. If another 100 rupees a month be added to it for my lifetime for my expenses—which unfortunately this illness has increased, and which, I hope, will not be for long a source of trouble to you, as I expect only to live a few years at best—I will be perfectly happy. One thing more will I beg of you—if possible, the 100 rupees a month for my mother be made permanent, so that even after my death it may regularly reach her. Or even if your Highness ever gets reasons to stop your love and kindness for me, my poor old mother may be provided [for], remembering the love you once had for a poor Sadhu.'

What we can make out from this is that it was not possible for Maharaja Ajit Singh to afford 10,000 rupees for a new house. That is perhaps why Swami Vivekananda bought a portion of the ancestral home from his aunt for the lesser price of 6,000 rupees. Shankari Prasad notes that he borrowed 5,000 rupees from the treasury of the monk for this purchase.

ଔ

Once again, let us focus on the itinerant Vivekananda. In 1899, he made preparations to go to the West for the second and last time. On 19 June, the day before he boarded the ship *S.S. Golconda*, Swamiji brought Bhubaneshwari and a few relatives to Belur Math. People gathered in the corridor adjacent to the prayer room to listen to the songs sung by Swamiji. At his mother's request, Swami Vivekananda sang a few songs dedicated to Kali and Shiva. When evening fell, he brought his mother back in a hackney carriage to Simulia, and himself went to the house of the late k- in Bagh Bazar.

On 20 June 1899, Swami Vivekananda boarded the steamer in Calcutta. His travel companions were Swami Turiyananda and Sister Nivedita, his spiritual daughter and disciple. During their voyage, Sister Nivedita used to write regularly to Miss Josephine Macleod and Mrs Sara Bull. On Tuesday morning, 28 June, when the steamer was approaching the shores of Ceylon (now Sri Lanka), Sister Nivedita wrote to Josephine Macleod:

'I did not ... tell you how he spoke of his mother and of the anguish he had caused her and his determination to come back and devote the rest of his life to her. "Don't you see?" he cried. "I have got the true *vairagyam* [renunciation] this time! I would undo the past if I could— I would marry—were I 10 years younger—just to make my mother happy—not for any other reason. Oh what ailed me, all these years? That mad frenzy of ambition—and yet"—with a sudden change to self-defence—"I was not ambitious! Celebrity was thrust upon me!"

"Of course, Swami!" I said——"You never had a bit of that meanness. But I'm awfully glad you're not 10 years younger!" And he looked at me and laughed.'

On 16 August 1899, Swami Vivekananda sailed for New York from London. In December, he was occupied with giving lectures in Los Angeles. Thoughts of the litigation suits back in Calcutta were not far from his mind, however. Swami Vivekananda wrote to Sara Bull on this topic two days after Christmas: 'I am much better in health. I have started work already and have sent to Saradananda some money——Rs 1,300 already——as expenses for the lawsuit. I shall send more, if they need it ... Mr Leggett has got a little over £500 I had with Sturdy on account of Raja-Yoga and the Maharaja of Khetri. I have now about a thousand dollars with Mr Leggett. If I die, kindly send that money to my mother.'

Compare this new found urgency with what he had written to Mrs Bull four years earlier, on 25 April 1895: 'You may do anything you please with my affairs, I will not even murmur.'

Far from India, on foreign shores, this ailing son worried about his mother no end. In the first month of the new century, on 17 January 1900, Swami Vivekananda wrote again to Sara Bull from Los Angeles. This time he reported: 'I have been able to remit Rs 2,000 to Saradananda, with the help of Miss Macleod and Mrs Leggett. Of course, they contributed the best part,' he said, 'the rest was got by lectures.'

He adds, 'Well, I came here principally for health. I have got it; in addition, I got Rs 2,000 to defray the law expenses. Good, it is becoming clearer to me that I lay down all the concern for the Math and go back to my mother. She has suffered much through me. I must try to smooth her last days. Do you know, this was exactly what the great Shankaracharya himself had to do! He had to go back to his mother in the last few days of her life! I accept it; I am resigned. I am calmer than ever. I have forebodings that my mother has not very many years to live ... leaving my mother was a great renunciation in 1884. It is a greater renunciation to go back to my mother now. Probably the [Divine] Mother wants me to undergo the same that She made the great Acharya do. Is it? The only difficulty is the financial part.'

The subject of Acharya Shankara's life and teaching arouse little interest in Bengal now. He renounced the world at a very young age; he also left the world very young. According to some, he was only thirty-two when he passed behind the curtain of eternity. His mother's name was Vishishta. When Shankara sought her consent to follow the life of an ascetic, she said, 'Son, if you go away, who will look after me? Will the relatives perform my funeral rites while you are still alive?' Her voice was choked with tears.

Shankara begged her, 'Please give your consent willingly and allow me to leave home. I assure you, wherever I am, I will come home and perform your funeral rites. Usually a monk cannot do this, but I will do it for you.'

Years later, while he was teaching in the village of Sringeri, in Karnataka, *Jagadguru* (teacher of the world) Shankara felt the taste of mother's milk on his tongue and realized that his mother was soon going to leave the mortal world. He immediately returned to his birthplace, Kaladi village in Kerala.

His mother's words upon seeing him again were, 'My dear son, why are you so late?'

Acharya Shankara silently began to attend to his mother. Full of affection, his mother inquired whether his mission had been successful. Shankara continued to remain silent as he served her. Gradually, in his presence, his mother forgot her pain and accepted death peacefully.

After her death, the self-seeking relatives harassed Shankara. They challenged his right to perform the funeral rites of his mother. They said to him, 'What! Why are you sitting beside her dead body? A monk has no right to perform funeral rites ... So, now that you have realized how arduous the life of a monk really is, you have come back to be a householder! You want to place fire in the mouth of your dead mother at her cremation ... and want to own property! But you have been ousted from the *Veda-marga* [the path of the Vedas], you no longer belong to our caste because you are a monk and you live outside your native land. You have committed a grave sin for, even though you are a Namboodri Brahmin, you have left Kerala. We will never allow you to put fire in your dead mother's mouth!' (It is a Hindu ritual that allows the soul to move on.)

Shankara replied, 'You have never taken care of her. I will perform the rites.'

The pyre was prepared. But where was the fire to burn the dead body? No one came forward to offer fire. So Shankara rubbed flint on his mother's right hand to produce a flame and then he cremated her.

When the king of the region, Raja Shekhara, heard reports of this cruel treatment of Shankara, he punished the relatives. Shankara was born around AD 780 and is presumed to have died in AD 812.

There is an old adage which says that one nightingale does not herald the spring. We see the incomparable love that the sage Shankara had for his mother. If we only try to search for others who have expressed such profound love, it may be easier for us to understand Vivekananda. A similar example can be found in the person of Sri Chaitanya as well. We can observe many parallels with Vivekananda, as recorded in the book *Chaitanya Charitamrita* by Krishnadas Kabiraj. A few glimpses from the life of the Mahaprabhu should suffice:

'After renouncing the world, Lord Sri Chaitanya lived in Nabadwip, West Bengal. Once his mother came to visit him. As soon as he saw her, Sri Chaitanya prostrated himself before her. Shachi Debi took her son in her arms and started weeping. Both mother and son were overwhelmed with emotion. It pained Shachi Debi to see his shaven head. She stroked him tenderly, gazed at him with unspeakable love, and kissed him again and again. Tears filled her eyes and prevented her from seeing him clearly. And she wept as she said, "Nimai, please do not be as cruel as Bishwarup [her eldest son]. He, too, became a monk and did not return. Please do not do that. I will die if you do.'"

Sri Chaitanya wept as he said, 'Mother, please listen to me. This body has been given to me by you; it is not mine. You have raised me. I will not be able to repay my debt to you even if I were to be born a million times. I may be a monk, but I will never be able to forget you.' In this way, Sri Chaitanya consoled his mother Shachi and paid his respects by touching her feet. Later, after circumambulating her, he departed for Nilachal.

At one time, Sri Chaitanya met with the esteemed scholar Sribasa of Puri, who became his devoted follower. Sri Chaitanya embraced Sribasa and told him, 'Please give this food and cloth which you have offered me to my mother. I have followed the path of asceticism and neglected her greatly. May she forgive my sins. Tell her that it is a son's duty to attend to his mother. I have behaved like a mad man. Perhaps Mother will not take offence at her mad son. Please tell her what I have said. She will be happy. It is her wish that I remain in Nilachal. I will sometimes go visit her and pay homage to her.'

Sri Chaitanya used to send his dear friend Jagadananda to Nabadwip from time to time. Jagadananda would console the sad mother by giving her news of her son. The author of *Chaitanya Charitamrita* asks, 'Who else has loved his mother like the Lord? He is the best among sons. He is forever attending to her, even though he is a monk.'

Swami Vivekananda used to say as well, 'One who cannot truly worship one's mother cannot grow.'

The episode when Swami Vivekananda went to see his mother after returning from the West in 1897 has been dealt with in one of the three articles that was published anonymously in *Brahmabadin* in 1911, the year of Bhubaneshwari's death. At that time, where had the patriot, the orator, the saint disappeared? Vivekananda became his mother's boy once more. He placed his head on his mother's lap and wept. Then he asked her to feed him and take care of him.

Could Swami Vivekananda hear death's approaching footsteps? On 17 January 1900 he wrote to Mrs Bull from America saying that he was returning to his mother and had henceforth chosen to follow the path shown by the great Shankaracharya. On 7 March 1900, he went on to describe how he would raise the money to support his family in India: 'The thousand dollars I have in New York will bring Rs 9 a month; then I bought for her a bit of land which will bring about Rs 6; and her old house—that will bring, say, Rs 6. I leave the house under litigation out of consideration, as I have not got it. Myself, my mother, my grandmother, and my brother live on Rs 20 a month easy. I would start just now, if I could make money for a passage to India, without touching the 1,000 dollars in New York.'

About his mother, he went on to say: 'All my life I have been a torture to my poor mother. Her whole life has been one of continuous misery. If it be possible, my last attempt should be to make her a little happy. I have planned it all out.'

Five days later, he wrote to Swami Brahmananda asking if the compound wall had been raised at Belur. He added, 'If I can, I shall build a small house there and serve my old grandmother and mother.'

From another letter (18 May 1900), however, it appears that Swamiji had by that time given up the idea of a little house by the Ganga for his mother because he did not have the money. He discloses the details of his financial situation at that time. 'Mrs Sevier gave me 6,000 rupees for the family—this was distributed between my cousin, aunt, etc. The 500 rupees for buying the house was borrowed from the math funds. Do not stop the remittance you send to my cousin, whatever Saradananda may say to the contrary. Of course I do not know what he says.' Swami Vivekananda then clearly states that neither he nor his mother had ever used the math's money for their personal expenses.

At the first Durga puja celebrations held at Belur Math, the divine mother, Sarada Debi, gave Swami Vivekananda an important role to play in the ceremony. Swami Vivekananda did not forget Bhubaneshwari during this sacred festival. Sri Ma's memoirs testify to that. We get a delightful picture of Swami Vivekananda's mother happily plucking an aubergine here and a chilli there from the Belur Math gardens. 'My Naren has done all this!' she proclaimed, unable to hide her pride. An embarrassed Vivekananda corrected her: 'Do you think *your* Naren has done all this? No, no, the One who does everything has done it. Your Naren is nothing.'

ભ

The year 1900 marked Swami Vivekananda's last experiences on Western soil. On 24 October, he travelled from Paris to Constantinople (now Istanbul) with his foreign friends. From there, he journeyed via Athens to Cairo with the singer Emma Calvé, Josephine Macleod and a few others.

During this time, Vivekananda's extremely trusted gurubhai, Swami Saradananda, wrote to Mrs Sara Bull, 'Whatever funds Swamiji had borrowed from the monastery's treasury, he has repaid in full. He has also sent extra money for the lawsuit.' This lawsuit was probably the one against Gyanadasundari Dutta. As we know, she took the money, offered assurances that she would comply with the legal agreement, but ultimately refused to part with the property. Swami Saradananda also reported that Swamiji had included some additional money for the monastery.

ભ

The sudden turn of events that took place in Cairo is described in the last chapter of this book. But for now we shall look at the evening of

9 December 1900, when Swami Vivekananda returned to Calcutta, without prior notice, and hastened to Belur Math. Reaching it after dark, he climbed the locked gate of the monastery and made his way to the place where the monks were having their evening meal. With great joy, he sat down with his gurubhais to eat *khichudi*, a preparation made with lentils, rice and vegetables all cooked together. Those who saw him that evening perhaps did not realize how the son had ignored all concerns for his health to return home.

After returning, Swami Vivekananda saw at once the poverty in which his mother was living. On 15 December 1900, he wrote to Mrs Ole Bull from Mayavati in the Himalayas: 'The remittance you send to my cousin should henceforth be sent to me direct, the bills being drawn in my name. I will cash them and send her the money. It is better the money goes to her through me.' It is not clear why Sara Bull would send money to the cousin in the first place. Possibly this large-hearted monk had promised to offer some money to his aunt's daughter.

After his return from Mayavati on 24 January 1901, Swami Vivekananda's visits to his mother and grandmother grew more and more frequent. He would go to Calcutta to visit them, and his mother would come to Belur Math as well. She would arrive and call out, 'Bilu-u-u.'

Sometimes he would send gifts of fruits and vegetables to their home.

Much was made of Swami Vivekananda when he first went to his grandmother's house on Ramtanu Basu Lane after returning from abroad. His presence made everybody happy. Swami Vivekananda was especially fond of his grandmother and had grown extremely close to her during his student days. Raghumani Dasi was supposed to have been even more beautiful than her daughter. Even though by this time she was greatly advanced in years, she was still radiant. She would prepare a variety of curries for her grandson. Sometimes he would turn up with a group of friends. How much he appreciated her traditional Bengali dishes is discussed in the next chapter.

Even when he was a grown man the bond between grandson and grandmother was strong enough for her to be able to ask her world-renowned grandson, 'Now that you have completed everything you wanted to do, why don't you get married?' Swami Vivekananda would laugh at this suggestion.

One day, when Swamiji went to visit his mother and grandmother, he arrived just as they were finishing their meal. As a gesture of love, he wanted to eat something out of his mother's dish, but his mother had almost finished her portion—only one *sajne danta* (green stem) remained. Not listening to their protests, he ate the danta with great relish.

✿

By now, it was clear to Swami Vivekananda's gurubhais and devotees that his health was deteriorating. He himself was eager to make use of what little time he had left. He had two goals: one was to firmly establish the Ramakrishna Mission, and the other was to disseminate Sri Ramakrishna's teachings. At the same time, he was involved with training a new generation of monks. These were not simple goals and they were met by obstacles at every step. However, the infinite love and loyalty of his gurubhais was a great support to Swami Vivekananda in his pursuit of these lofty endeavours. The history that they created through their silent contribution to the spiritual life of India is yet to be fully recognized.

From early 1901, Swami Vivekananda embarked on a number of pilgrimages to one holy place after another. These sacred places were not always easy to reach and, quite often, his various illnesses got worse along the way. Still, he did not stop.

The Maharaja of Khetri, Ajit Singh, died in a fall on 18 January 1901, the day that Swami Vivekananda left Mayavati Ashrama. This untimely and somewhat mysterious death of his dear friend and devotee was very painful for Swamiji, more so because the one person on whom he had depended the most was no longer there to support him. But he had to move on.

Swami Vivekananda wanted to undertake a pilgrimage to East Bengal (now Bangladesh). A pilgrimage was nothing new for him; what was new this time was that he was travelling with his mother to fulfil her cherished desire. The virtuous son was eager to be of service to his mother.

Unfortunately, he was not well enough to commence the journey immediately. At the beginning of the year, on 26 January, he wrote: 'The moment I land in Bengal, especially at the Math, the asthmatic fits return! The moment I leave, I am better ...'

Then came his joyful declaration: 'I am going to take my mother on a pilgrimage next week. It may take us months. This is the wish of a Hindu widow. I have brought only misery to my family all my life. I am trying to fulfil this one desire of hers.'

At around the same time, Swami Vivekananda had also intended to take his mother to the south of India, but ultimately his ailing body proved to be an insurmountable obstacle.

As it turned out, they could not leave for East Bengal the following week; they left instead on 18 March. Swami Brahmananda wrote in his diary: 'Swamiji, Nityananda and five others are going to Dacca (now Dhaka) this evening.'

Bhubaneshwari's inclusion in this party came about in the following way. Upon hearing that her son planned to travel to East Bengal, she went to Belur Math one day and asked the swamis to tell her son to bathe in the Brahmaputra River. (A particular conjunction of the planets made this a very auspicious for bathing and over 100,000 pilgrims were gathering for the sacred ritual.) Swami Vivekananda immediately sent a telegram inviting his mother to join him for the trip.

In a letter written on 29 March 1901 to Sara Bull, Swami Vivekananda states, 'My mother, aunt and cousin came over five days ago to Dacca as there was a sacred bath in Brahmaputra river.' In the same letter, he informed that he was taking his mother and her companions to Chandranath, 'a holy place at the easternmost corner of Bengal' (near Chittagong).

A disciple of the master asked Swami Vivekananda in Dacca, 'Why has your health deteriorated when you are so young? Why did you not take care of your health?'

Swami Vivekananda responded, 'I had no sense I had a body when I was in America.'

While he was in Dacca, Swami Vivekananda indicated clearly that he would not live long, but no one took his remarks seriously at the time. He said that he would live for only another year. During his remaining time on earth, his only wish was to take his mother to a few holy places and that is why he was going to Chandranath and Kamakhya, in Assam. Swami Vivekananda asked if anyone else wanted to travel with them. Only those who had a regard for women could come, he emphasized.

Swami Brahmananda's diary supports this account and states that Swami Vivekananda's mother and cousin also accompanied him to Kamakhya. However, in Dacca and Shillong, Swami Vivekananda's illnesses took a turn for the worse.

On 12 May 1901, the party returned to Calcutta. In Swami Brahmananda's diary, we read: 'Sunday. Swamiji, Gupta, Swamiji's mother, cousin, aunt, Ram-dada's widow Krishnapreyashi Dutta, came back from Shillong.'

Krishnapreyashi was the widow of Sri Ramakrishna's devoted disciple, Ramchandra Dutta who had died on 17 January 1899. She herself would not live long. She died due to tuberculosis on 1 April 1902. Ramchandra and his wife had lived at 11 Madhu Roy Lane and Naren had been the best man at their wedding. Mahendranath later wrote about Krishnapreyashi, 'She had a high regard for my mother. Such a calm, courteous and mild-mannered lady is rarely found.'

Was the aunt mentioned in Brahmananda's diary the same aunt, Gyanadasundari, who was at the centre of the lawsuits? Possibly so. Swami Vivekananda was an unimaginably kind person. He did not distinguish between friends and foes. He once said to Swami Brahmananda, 'If in this hell of a world one can bring a little joy and peace even for a day into the heart of a single person, that alone is true; this I have learnt after suffering all my life ...'

The beauty of Assam enchanted Swami Vivekananda. He wrote to Mary Hale on 5 July 1901: 'I have been touring of late in Eastern Bengal and Assam. Assam is, next to Kashmir, the most beautiful country in India.' Unfortunately, the Assam Tourism Board seems to have missed this priceless quote!

His health was declining by the day, but that did not prevent Swami Vivekananda from travelling. In August, he went to Darjeeling with Mrs Banerjee and a cousin. Who was this cousin? It turns out her name was Priyambada Dasi. An element of confusion exists about this name because there were two Priyambadas in Swami Vivekananda's circle. Bhupendranath mentions a Priyambada who was a poet. She has been identified as Priyambada Basu. At that time, it was customary for a woman to write 'Dasi' after her given name. Even Swamiji's mother would sign her name as Bhubaneshwari Dasi.

It appears that the Priyambada who went with Swami Vivekananda was Priyambada Ghosh of 123, Manicktala Street. She was like a dear sister to Swami Vivekananda, as well as his devoted disciple. She used to come to Belur Math often and bring all kinds of dishes for Swamiji, most of which would be consumed by those serving him!

This is, perhaps, the right time to mention another cousin whom Swami Vivekananda was extremely close to. This was a distant cousin from Barojagulia named Mrinalini Basu. Vivekananda went to visit her in the second week of June 1902, shortly before his death. Her father was the village zamindar Sarbeshwar Sinha. Her husband had become a monk and since then she had lived with her son in her father's house. On the occasion of Swami Vivekananda's visit, she offered him a basket of *jamun* fruits (roseapples). Swamiji had diabetes and, upon returning to the Math, he happily fermented these jamuns to make vinegar.

Although it seems that at this stage of his life Swami Vivekananda was intimately involved in the lives of his relatives, he remained detached from all familial bonds. Once, his devotee Sharat Chandra Chakrabarty brought up the name of a very prominent householder disciple of Sri Ramakrishna's named Suresh Mitra. Swami Vivekananda had once borrowed the 500 rupees that Suresh Mitra had donated for the establishment of the math. Sharat Chandra Chakrabarty accused Swami Vivekananda of neglecting this most generous disciple in the twilight of his life. He said to Swamiji, 'I heard that you did not keep in touch with him much, you did not even go and see him before he died.'

Swamiji answered, 'We could only do so if we were allowed [by the relatives]. It is a long story. But, know this for certain, that among worldly people it matters little to your relatives whether you live or die. If you succeed in leaving back some property, you will find that even in your lifetime it sets up a quarrel in your household. You will have no one to burn you on the pyre, not even your wife or sons. This is samsara.'

Even though Swami Vivekananda was, by now, critically ill and encumbered with numerous problems, he was consumed by anxiety about who would look after his mother after he was gone. I believe that at this time Swamiji was in Dacca. He met with his mother on 25 March in Narayanganj. A few days earlier, on 20 March, he had expressed his worries to Mrs Bull: 'Mohin, my brother, is in India, in Karachi near Bombay, and he corresponds with Saradananda. He writes to say he is going to Burma, China, etc. The traders who lure him have shops in all those places. I am not at all anxious about him.' And then

Vivekananda's devastating comment: 'He is a very selfish man.'

This is in stark contrast to Swami Vivekananda's earlier praise of his brother to John P. Fox. We must remember that by now Swami Vivekananda was acutely aware of his own impending death and he wanted to be assured of his mother's well-being afterwards. Perhaps he could predict that soon after his death, Bhupendranath would become involved in the struggle for India's independence and would leave home. Then who would look after their mother?

It would be pertinent at this point in our narrative to read out a letter written by Mahendranath on 24 April 1902 from Srinagar to Gupta Maharaj (Swami Sadananda) in which he reluctantly admits some responsibility. Mahendranath writes: 'From what I hear, I have to look after Mother. She is not doing well at all. Now I have to work and earn, so that I can provide for her.'

We know that around 1903 Bhupendranath became secretly involved with other Indian revolutionaries. Could it be that his brothers knew about his affiliations even earlier? Was it because Mahendranath was away that Swami Vivekananda acted with such urgency to end the lawsuits and all the strife that went with them?

Over the next few months, we find Swami Vivekananda thinking of his mother constantly. He wrote to Swami Brahmananda from Benares on 21 February 1902: 'If Mother and Grandmother desire to come to Benares, send them over. It is better to get away from Calcutta at this time of the plague.'

What about Swamiji's health? During this period, he became so ill that his legs swelled and he found it difficult to walk. His body got hypersensitive and hurt if pressed. Although it was the peak of summer, his *kabiraj* (ayurvedic physician) advised him not to take water or salt for twenty-one days. Using his phenomenal willpower, Swami Vivekananda obeyed these injunctions to the letter. And despite his health, he would at this time stand by the fire and cook food in the Western style.

Some of his childhood friends once reminded him, 'When you were young and we asked you to get married, you used to say, "I won't get married. Just see what I will become!" Now you have fulfilled our expectations.'

Swami Vivekananda answered them, sarcastically, 'Yes, I have surely done that! You can see I don't get to eat properly and how hard I have to work! What can I say? Comfort is not in my destiny. As soon as I lie down on the mattress, I start getting asthmatic attacks. It is only when I lie on the floor that I feel better.'

In the last phase of his life, Swami Vivekananda lost the use of his right eye because of diabetes. In a later chapter, I shall provide the reader with a list of all the different ways in which this disease can assail a person, but for now, let me move on to the last phase of my research on Swami Vivekananda's mother.

On 19 June 1902 Swami Vivekananda went to Calcutta to visit his mother, grandmother and other relatives. One can assume that here they had the initial discussions about the lawsuits that would be concluded in his sister's house a week later—Saturday, 28 June, the last Saturday of Swami Vivekananda's life. On 22 June, Swami Vivekananda's mother and grandmother came to Belur Math to visit him. It rained throughout that day.

For the new generation of readers, I would like to record a touching episode that had taken place in April, just a few weeks earlier. Miss Macleod writes in her memoirs: 'One day in April, he said, "I have nothing in the world. I haven't a penny for myself. I have given away everything that has ever been given to me." I said, "Swami, I will give you fifty dollars a month as long as you live." He thought a minute and then said, "Can I live on that?" "Yes, oh yes," I said, "but perhaps you cannot have cream." I then gave him two hundred dollars, but before four months had passed, he was gone.'

We can glean more details from Swami Brahmananda's diary. It emerges that Miss Macleod sent Swami Vivekananda another sum after April. Out of that money and other offerings that he had received, Swami Vivekananda gave 100 rupees to his mother and fifty rupees to his sister. It is quite possible that following the death of the king, the money from Khetri was no longer being sent.

☙

A very poignant account of the day Swami Vivekananda cast off his mortal body is preserved in Sister Nivedita's letters. These beautiful and poetic letters shall forever remain an integral part of the literature on Sri Ramakrishna and Swami Vivekananda. We also have Bhupendranath's description of that day to refer to.

Strangely enough, the Bengali version of Bhupendranath's book on Swami Vivekananda and its English translation, *Swami Vivekananda: Patriot–Prophet*, differ vastly. Each one contains material not to be found in the other. In the English version, for example, Bhupendranath has given his mother and grandmother a very central role in all the legal dealings. His grandmother sold her '4 cottahs of rented land situated on Balaram Dey Street to fight the lawsuit brought against [them] by [their] aunt.' He expresses sadness that his mother's sacrifices were never recognized: 'She was no more than an object of curiosity to some among the associates of Vivekananda.'

By collating the information from both versions, we may reconstruct the series of events surrounding Swami Vivekananda's death. On the morning of 5 July 1902, Swami Vivekananda's personal attendant and would-be monk Nadu (Haren) brought the news of his death to the family. Bhupendranath gave the news to his mother and his grandmother. His mother wanted to know 'the cause behind the sudden death of her eldest son'. He answered, 'The same as with father.' The two women were overwhelmed with grief.

Bhupendranath recalls that 'a lady from the neighbourhood came and tried her best to console them.' Nadu had asked Bhupendranath to contact the Mitras of Simla Street (his sister Swarnamayee and her husband). 'On arriving at my sister's house, I found that my brother-in-law already knew what had happened.'

Then Bhupendranath and Nadu went to Belur Math. Bhupendranath saw that Swamiji's body had been laid out on a cot. Around him were gathered all the swamis of the monastery, as well as Atul Chandra Ghosh and Sister Nivedita. After a while, his mother arrived with her grandson, Brajamohan Ghosh. 'She wept bitterly,' he writes.

In the English version of Bhupendranath's book, it is written that the swamis asked Bhupendranath to take his mother away. Sister Nivedita saw Bhubaneshwari off with tears in her eyes. In the afternoon, Girish Chandra Ghosh came when the pyre was being lit and Nivedita asked him, 'Why did they send Mother away?' In the Bengali version of the book, we read, 'The matter was explained to her' (that is, Bhubaneshwari). In the English version, it says that it was explained to Bhubaneshwari that the Swamis were required to observe 'certain codes of conduct'.

On the last Saturday of his life, Swami Vivekananda had visited Sister Nivedita at her home in Bagh Bazar. Afterwards, he went to his cousin's house for a dinner invitation that he was obliged to accept. There he sat down, in a state of considerable anxiety to find a solution to the family litigation. The coparcener Habul Dutta was there and on his own, began talking about winding up the lawsuit. Swami Vivekananda could not let go of this opportunity. He said that he would pay a thousand rupees more if that would put an end to the strife. The co-heirs Habul Dutta and Tamu Dutta agreed.

Next, Swami Brahmananda went with Habul to the attorney Paltu's office. Their attorney, N.C. Basu, was sent a letter with all the conditions duly stipulated. Accordingly, N.C. Basu sent a letter back agreeing to the conditions. On 2 July 1902—two days before Swami

Vivekananda's death—Paltu was given 400 rupees (as part of the demands of the coparceners) and the money was taken from Shantiram. Thus, the legal problems of the family finally came to an end.

After Swami Vivekananda's death, Sister Nivedita expressed a measure of surprise that he had been able to tidy up matters so effectively. He had sent her a message that the litigation had ended amicably and that he had no regrets.

Swami Vivekananda—at once eldest son and monk—had sought to resolve his mother's problems, as far as was possible for him, before he died. We have seen how he tried his utmost to abide by her wishes and keep to his word: he visited holy places with her and also took her to Kalighat in Calcutta. Moreover, to ensure that after his death his mother would have no problems, he requested his gurubhais to take care of her.

Swami Brahmananda became like a son to Bhubaneshwari Dasi. After Swami Vivekananda's demise, he took up the responsibility of consoling the grief-stricken mother. At the beginning, he used to come and spend time with her every day and, till the very end, visited her regularly and shared her grief. 'He often ate food cooked by her and even tried to help in domestic matters. Apart from her financial affairs, he also had to take responsibility of the legal matters related to the ancestral property that were still not fully resolved.'

After a few years, when Bhubaneshwari was better able to cope with her grief, Swami Brahmananda sent her to Puri on a pilgrimage. As long as she lived, until 1911, he used to help her and render her service like a true son. His own diaries attest to this.

ର

How Swami Vivekananda's foreign disciples and friends tried their best to protect and serve the members of his immediate family is also a long story.

Bhupendranath was interned for his revolutionary activities. To save him from the wrath of the British overlords, Sister Nivedita—who was not wealthy herself—offered to pay the bail of 20,000 rupees. But Bhupendranath says that he did not have to use her money. He had raised the bail from Dr Prankrishna Acharya and his cousin Charuchandra Mitra, who had put up 5,000 rupees each.

Bhupendranath writes that when he 'bade goodbye to Sister Nivedita before going to jail, he requested her to look after his mother in his absence. My mother told me that Sister Nivedita had fully kept this request. Her words to my mother were, "Bhupen has asked me to look after you."'

It is believed that Sister Nivedita secretly supplied Bhupendranath with the information that when he was released from jail, if he did not leave the country immediately, the British could indict him on other accounts. Bhupendranath wrote that his mother 'helped [him] with the necessary money so that he could leave the country under an assumed name.' Three or four days later, he boarded a ship bound for the USA via Europe. There is reason to believe that a friend of Sister Nivedita's helped him with his passage. Thankfully, his mother was not left alone. Mahendranath had come back to Calcutta within fifteen days after Swami Vivekananda's death to return to 3, Gourmohan Mukherjee Street at Swami Saradananda's request.

Even while Vivekananda was alive, his beloved gurubhai, Swami Brahmananda assisted him greatly in the responsibility of looking after his mother. Swami Ramananda and the renowned Dr Tapas Basu have drawn my attention to the following touching episode which was related by Swami Hariharananda to Brahmachari Akshay Chaitanya:

'Immediately after returning from America, Swami Vivekananda gave some money [10,000 rupees] to Swami Brahmananda and said, "Rakhal, please go and give this money to my mother." Swami Brahmananda protested, "You should give it to her!" Then Swami

Vivekananda explained, "No, you do it please. If I give the money, everybody will say, God knows how much money he has given to his mother and brothers! What has he given to the Math?"'

If you would like to know who took care of Bhupendranath in the United States, I would advise you to read carefully the lives of Sister Nivedita, Sara Bull and Josephine Macleod.

The respected swamis of Belur Math took care of Swami Vivekananda's mother and grandmother as long as they were alive. They took Bhubaneshwari with them to visit holy places. One such pilgrimage was to Puri in 1911. Unfortunately, she fell ill after returning from Puri and contracted meningitis. She was treated by Dr J. Kanjilal, but did not recover. Bhubaneshwari Dasi died of meningitis on 15 July 1911 at the age of seventy. We do not know what her dear son, Bilu, thought in heaven, but her exiled son, Bhupendranath, dreamt in New York that his mother had died.

Mahendranath was present at the cremation, as was Sister Nivedita. She had been a constant presence by Bhubaneshwari's bedside during her last days and was able to offer much consolation to her.

On 28 July 1911, Sister Nivedita wrote to an English friend, Mr Radcliffe, the erstwhile editor of *The Statesman*, to report the death of Swami Vivekananda's mother. She mentioned that she had seen Bhubaneshwari a few hours before her death and had been to her cremation.

Swamiji's grief-stricken mother remained on earth for nine long years after her son passed away. Who looked after her? According to Beni Shankar Sharma, the promised sum of 100 rupees a month still came regularly from Khetri, although the Maharaja was no longer alive. This is not impossible, but doubtful.

In a distant country, Swami Vivekananda's foreign disciples took responsibility of Bhupendranath. Even after his mother's death, Josephine Macleod tried her best to bring him back to India and help him establish himself there. Once, she even wrote to Rabindranath Tagore asking him if he could offer a job to Bhupendranath. Tagore replied to her from Illinois, saying that he had offered a job to a former freedom fighter before and it had almost led to the closure of his university. So Tagore was helpless. He advised Bhupendranath to teach in America until the rulers of his country, the British, changed their policy.

Sister Nivedita's letter to Josephine Macleod on 16 August 1911 is a touching testimony to those who, out of their deep love for Swami Vivekananda, silently bore the responsibility of his family: 'Your ten pounds came, but you may know that by this time Swamiji's mother is dead ... I have kept it safely in the bank, and await your instructions. The sister is still there—and as expenses of illness and death are always considerable, I fancy you will wish this last offering to be paid, as before ... The grandmother died two days later, at sunset. So Swamiji has gathered His own to Him once more.'

Why would Sister Nivedita refer to 'His own'? Possibly, she guessed right. The monk whom the world knew as Vivekananda could renounce money and women, but not his love for his family. Like Adi Shankaracharya and Sri Chaitanya, he did not care what the world thought of him.

All his life, Swami Vivekananda paid homage to his mother and acknowledged his debt to her. That is why he is unique, and perhaps that is why he is so passionately worshipped even today—by men and women, mothers, children, sons, sisters and brothers.

Certain incidents about Swamiji's life had been presented in this chapter in the belief that one cannot know a man unless one knows his mother.

CHAPTER TWO

Emperor, Monk and Cook in One

In India, over the last one hundred and fifty years, who has empathized the most with the plight of the starving masses? The answer is simple. Swami Vivekananda. He was even prepared to sell the precious land earmarked for his monastery to save his destitute and starving countrymen from death. During the famine in the Punjab, he announced to Sakharam, Ganesh and another gentleman, 'I assure you, as long as one dog in this land remains hungry, my sacred duty is to provide it with food. To do anything else would be sinful!' To a certain Vedanta scholar who wished to engage him in debate, he said, 'Learned Sir, first do something for those who are dying of hunger, then come to me for a discussion on Vedanta.'

I had the good fortune to study in a school that bears Swami Vivekananda's name. As a result, since 1942 till today, I have been able to explore an aspect of his life that is seldom discussed or publicized. A senior student at the school, Patla-da, told me once many years back that the depth and extent of this topic could only be compared to the Atlantic Ocean. The topic was: 'Vivekananda and Food'. Patla-da was doubtful if it would ever be possible to do justice to this subject, even if one devoted a lifetime of study to it. He argued that it would take at least 390 years to appreciate the revolution Swami Vivekananda had brought about in only thirty-nine years!

When I heard this, I was crestfallen. I told Patla-da, 'I cannot do it then. You said it would take at least 390 years.' Patla-da countered with a swift rebuke: 'Have you learnt nothing after all this time? Remember what Confucius said, "The journey of a thousand miles begins with a single step." Incidentally, Swami Vivekananda had once prophezied that the Chinese would one day dominate the world. That age is not too far away!'

Patla-da further encouraged me by saying, 'I firmly believe that only someone who hails from a family of Brahmin priests would have the courage to undertake a study entitled "Vivekananda and Food". The reason? You have, by virtue of being a Brahmin, a unique three-in-one experience: you are accustomed to fasting, you are used to taking half the requisite amount, and you are also used to hearty meals.'

And so I begin. At our school, food was generally distributed on special anniversaries associated with Sri Ramakrishna and Swami Vivekananda. There was a particular way of distributing prasad to the devotees called 'standing prasad'. This had been introduced by Swami Vivekananda himself. Here one receives the prasad in a shallow earthenware dish or in a packet and one consumes it standing—hence the name. Patla-da usually had a major role to play in the prasad distribution. He never concealed his preference for certain kinds of offering over others. Thus when we repeatedly began to receive *bonde* (a sweet made of chickpea flour and sugar), Patla-da took a stand.

He managed to procure data concerning Swami Vivekananda's personal likes and dislikes. Armed with this information, he said to me, 'Please tell the headmaster that Narendranath went to Dakshineshwar to meet Sri Ramakrishna in the hope of having plenty of *rasgolla*s (a sweet made of curdled milk, and soaked in syrup) and not bonde!' According to Patla-da, bonde was the favourite sweetmeat of Bankimchandra Chatterjee. It was Bankimchandra who penned the immortal *'Bande Mataram'* (Mother, I bow to thee). When he was later arrested by the police and detained at the Howrah police station for insurgency, the irrepressible Patla-da declared, 'I never shouted "*Bande Mataram*"! I said, "*Bonde kheye matha garam*" (agitated by eating bonde).'

When I duly informed our headmaster, Sudhanshushekhar Bhattacharya, about Swamiji's preferences, he said, coolly, 'Swami Vivekananda did not like sweets. He liked chilli peppers. It will bring tears to your eyes if I arrange for his favourite food.'

Over the years, Patla-da grew obsessed with gathering information about Swami Vivekananda's culinary preferences. He decided that if he ever became a monk, he would take the following name: Swami Bhojananda (the bliss of feasting). He came to learn that the Ramakrishna Order does not impose restrictions on what one eats. One is required to renounce only money and women. At Dakshineshwar Sri Ramakrishna loved to feed people. This tradition was carried on by his foremost disciple, Swami Vivekananda and, fortunately, it continues to this day. I have yet to come across a monk belonging to the Order who does not enjoy distributing food at the drop of the hat.

ఇ

Coming back to my boyhood friend, Patla-da. I gave him a notebook to record all his discoveries about the nature of 'bhojana yoga' (the yoga of eating) in the Ramakrishna Order. Patla-da's practice was to write down short questions in the notebook and then supply short answers. One memorable day, he gave me a quiz. He said, 'You will get two big *jibhegaja*s (a sweetmeat made of layers of refined flour dough fried in oil and then sugar-coated) if you can tell me which country can express these three ideas in a single word: emperor, monk and cook.'

I had no ready answer. Patla-da tried to console me with a jibhegaja and then gave the answer himself: 'India! The word is 'Maharaj' (literally, a great king). It is only in this sacred land of ours that an emperor is a Maharaj, a monk is a Maharaj and a cook is a Maharaj! Swami Vivekananda was a king among men, he was a monk and he was also the world's greatest cook. I have yet to gather more evidence to support my theory but I believe he is the only Indian who had the courage to cross the seven seas to reach America and Europe and promote Vedanta and biryani.'

Eventually, Patla-da graduated from Howrah Vivekananda School, but he did not abandon his fascinating research on this little-known aspect of Swami Vivekananda. He continued to use the notebook, and he kept in touch with me as well.

One day, I complained to him, 'This is an arduous task. I cannot find references to food in any book about Swamiji, nor can I locate any restaurant which he frequented or from which he borrowed his recipes.'

Patla-da rebuked me sharply: 'I can see that by going to so many restaurants, you have only learnt how to eat, my friend! Now you have to learn how to conduct research. How can you find the right restaurant? During the best years of his life, when he was in Europe and the United States, Swami Vivekananda promoted his beloved India. When he was in India, he did not have money to enjoy good food. After his father's death, he did not even have enough to eat and, at times, was forced to go without food altogether. Later, when he returned from his tours abroad, he worked so hard that he ruined his health. Towards the end of his life, following the strict orders of his kabiraj, he could not take even a sip of water for twenty-one days, let alone think of sweetmeats!'

I could see no way forward. 'How can I write about someone who could not afford to eat, and yet whose gurubhai once complained to the physician that a *barfi* (sweetmeat made of condensed milk cooked with sugar) had made him ill?'

Patla-da was familiar with the incident. He provided me with additional details. 'The doctor's name was Shashi Bhushan Ghosh. He lived in Bagh Bazar. Swami Vivekananda wrote to him from Almora on 29 May 1897 about this incident. Be patient and find out what he said about this famous barfi. He told his dear friend, "I ate one-sixteenth of a barfi in Lucknow, and Yogen says that this is what made me ill in Almora." He urged the doctor not to pay heed to what Swami Yogananda had written. "Please don't listen to Yogen," he emphasized.'

Patla-da did not allow me to be dissuaded by all these conflicting stories. 'Have courage,' he said. 'Begin from the beginning, like me! "Morning shows the day"—you know that, don't you?'

'Then you are saying that I shall forever remain ignorant and slightly addle-headed?' I queried.

Patla-da corrected me, 'Oh, we are not discussing your life or mine! We are only concerned with Swami Vivekananda's life. What I am urging you to do is write a great six-volume book on "Swami Vivekananda and Contemporary Eating Habits". You will soon find that like *Sri Sri Ramakrishna Kathamrita*, it is selling like hot jalebis!'

Patla-da returned to the subject of our discussion. He was then studying somewhere near Kankurgachi (an old suburb of Calcutta), and often visited the Yogodyan (the Ramakrishna Math, also in Kankurgachi), as well as the Advaita Ashrama in the Himalayas and Belur Math. The old monks loved him. He pursued his secret research and jotted down data in his notebook. Patla-da knew a few of the monks who had actually seen Swami Vivekananda. He asked them, 'When did we first catch a glimpse of the rebellious side of Vivekananda?'

'Only Thakur (Sri Ramakrishna) knows,' they would reply piously.

'But Naren had not met Thakur at that stage,' Patla-da objected. He went on to tell me, 'Let me describe what happened. Naren was only five years old and living in his ancestral home at Gourmohan Mukherjee Street in Simulia. One day he fought a battle with his mother and the battlefield was the dining room. They fought over whether it was more appropriate to drink water holding the glass in the right hand or the left. Narendranath's right hand was dirty and he did not want to make the glass dirty by holding it in that hand. However, in those days, it was not customary to hold the glass in the left hand. Needless to say, Naren prevailed and his row with his mother changed the practice of holding a glass in Bengal. Nowadays, mothers get upset if their children hold the glass in their right hand! Have you realized the implications? Can you appreciate its significance? A mere five-year-old altered our tradition. If we had been there, you and I, we would have declared that this boy would one day revolutionize the history of table manners and eating habits in our country!'

⅓

Patla-da created a precedent among our circle by taking the decision to go abroad to earn his living. Before he left, he offered me some sound advice on how to conduct research on Swami Vivekananda's life. He told me, 'One approach will not suffice. You can approach the subject in 108 different ways. You can, for instance, divide his thirty-nine years into various phases: childhood, adolescence, youth and middle age. In each phase, Swami Vivekananda depended on one kind of food or another. You could undertake a chronological account of his eating habits from the fifth year of his life onwards till he left his mortal body on 4 July 1902!'

After a pause, he continued, 'There are other ways to approach the subject. For example, the criterion vegetarian and non-vegetarian may be helpful. Incidentally, it may be worthwhile to consult his horoscope in this connection. It appears that he was fated to cause controversy! But as I said, vegetarian or non-vegetarian may be a criterion. Then again, if you do not like this classification, there is another approach which could be fruitful: which cuisine did he like——Bengali, nawabi or sahebi (Western)? Each one has several subcategories. Under Bengali, we have Bardhamani and Dhakai. Nawabi can be divided into Lahori and Lucknavi. Sahebi into American, French, German, Italian and Spanish.'

Patla-da looked at a piece of paper he was carrying and said, 'This is just the beginning. Then we have to ask, what kind of environment did he enjoy while eating? Did he enjoy eating at home, or did he enjoy the kind of atmosphere, say, at Hrishikesh's street stall, or the one at a luxurious American hotel?'

'Enough, Patla-da!' I interjected. 'What varieties of food did he *not* try during his thirty-nine years?'

'Alas, you will forget everything when I am away,' Patla-da retorted in a forlorn tone. 'Just use your head and try to gather all the information you can. Unlike Swami Vivekananda, we two were not born with fabulous memories. Just keep asking the basic questions: Eastern or Western? Hot or mild? Fruits or roots? Ice cream or kulfi (homemade Indian ice cream)? Chilli peppers or peppercorns? Asparagus spears or the stalks of *dengo*? These are not trivial questions. One may find references to the Vedas, the Ramayana, the Mahabharata, the Bible and the Koran for each.'

I obediently took down whatever Patla-da said, but he had not yet finished.

'Swami Vivekananda was not afraid to face philosophical questions such as this: Which is better, overeating or starvation? Please note this. As Swamiji was preparing to leave the world, he said that starvation is better than overeating. The next moment, however, before he could be questioned, he announced, "It cannot be denied that to be half-fed is better than to be starved!"'

There was no stopping Patla-da: 'We have to work together, you and I, for quite some time. People may have become famous for eating and feeding others, but how many of them invented hundreds of recipes? It was only possible for Swami Vivekananda because he was many things at once—a rich man's son, a mendicant and a compelling orator. Sometimes he was able to partake of a mouth-watering buffet in a first-class hotel, at other times he had merely rice with *telakucho* (a small variety of arum) on a *kachu* leaf. Sometimes there was no food at all. Now the question is, when and where did he fast, and for how long? Where was it that he had nothing to eat, even though hunger was gnawing at his insides? Was it in Calcutta, or in north India, or in America, the land of plenty?'

Patla-da added, 'Please do not be afraid.' Possibly, he feared that by this time my eyes would jump out of their sockets! 'If you can find out which foods were his favourites,' he went on, 'and which experiences led him to say fearlessly that in order to be a good monk, one had to be a good cook, both of us will make our mark in the world!'

Patla-da then told me of his decision to go abroad and added, 'I am taking this notebook with me. I will send you more data on Swami Vivekananda the cook. Please carry on, and enlighten everyone on this fact that it is only in India that the word for cook and God is the same: *thakur*. I will come back!'

Patla-da has not returned. He still lives abroad, but continues to carry on with his research. Over the years, he has sent me quite a few notebooks filled with material on the topic. I have also been able to gather some information from various sources—Swami Vivekananda's writings, his letters and lectures, as well as from accounts written by others. It has taken me a long time to assemble all these facts a hundred years after his death. Even then, I feel probably that we do not know everything on the subject.

Before one meal is over, it is time to prepare for the next. But in between we have to make some time to tell the waiting guests that food is ready. Come, let us explore the great man Vivekananda in a new role altogether and be amazed, as we have been.

Bhubaneshwari's parents were devout Vaishnavas. Not only were they vegetarians, but it was a regular practice among them to nibble the holy basil leaf before the first meal of the day. These Hindu traditions influenced the non-vegetarian Dutta family of Simulia.

Here is one episode. One day, Naren was unwilling to eat any vegetable on his plate because they had come into contact with the fish. So he began arguing with Swarnamayee, his elder sister, who was serving the meal. Overhearing the row from the bath, Naren's father Bishwanath expressed his irritation with his son. He said, 'His forefathers ate snails and oysters and now he is acting like a Brahmin and will not touch fish!'

Bishwanath was something of a gourmet and was also pretty fond of cooking. Frequently, he used to enlist the services of a Muslim chef to prepare certain dishes at home.

Narendranath's innate organizational abilities first found expression in the domain of cooking. He set up a club with the local boys called 'The Greedy Club'. This was long before he dreamt of setting up the Ramakrishna Mission. Possibly, it was his first step on the path to serving man and God!

Another incident: Narendranath, Mahendranath, their mother and sisters were travelling to Raipur to join Bishwanath. On the way, in Ghoratalao, they cooked some meat. Mahendranath was a vegetarian, thanks to his grandmother's influence. He writes, 'I would not eat it. Then my elder brother came and put a piece of meat in my mouth and pounded on my back so that I would be forced to swallow it. "Eat!" he commanded. Then what did I do? I ate it. What else can a tiger do when it tastes blood?'

Even as a youth, Narendranath was open to foreign influences. He bought old volumes on French cooking. According to him, it was the French who had first taught a semi-civilized European society to cook civilly. The fact that, as Swami Vivekananda, he would one day heap praise on the French and their civilization has its roots in his love for French cuisine. The French are a highly creative race and those who come into contact with them tend to absorb this propensity to create. In Narendranath's case, we can notice this in the extensive research on cooking that he did as the founder of the Greedy Club. The following recipe for *bhuni-khichuri* was invented by him at the time: An egg is beaten well and poured over rice. Then one adds peas and potatoes to cook *bhuni-khichuri*. Some experts admit that this recipe is superior even to pulao (a preparation with rice). Bishwanath often used to have *kalia* (a variety of curry) and pulao cooked in his house. His son went one step further and, through cooking, brought together the East and the West.

Rakhal Chandra Ghosh became a member of this eating club. He later became known as Swami Brahmananda and was the first president of the Ramakrishna Order. He was deemed protector of the math during crises. As a youth, he practised wrestling and developed a hearty appetite. He used to eat half a seer (approximately half a kilo) of *kachuri*s (fried bread made of flour and pulses) after his exercises. Kachuris, at that time, cost six annas (6/16th of a rupee) a seer. Naren also loved kachuris, along with *singara* (a salted stuffed snack), khichuri and pulao. He was also very fond of jibhegajas.

Narendranath Mukhopadhyay, the district judge, narrated an enchanting tale about Naren's fondness for sweet jibhegajas. When Naren was very young, he used to often come to visit this gentleman. He continues, 'The snack-seller, Kailash, brought all kinds of snacks in a large pot every day to sell to the boys. Some of them bought two pice (2/64th of a rupee) worth of snacks, some got four pice worth, while some as much as two annas' worth ... They ate happily. Swamiji belonged to a different level altogether; he was on par with his uncle Gopal Chandra Dutta ... Jibhegaja happened to be his favourite. One day he was unhappy with the amount that he had been served.

So he took one piece, touched it with his tongue and dropped it into the pot. Then he laughed and said to us all, "Please, do not take any jibhegaja, any of you. All the pieces have now come into contact with the one I dropped!" Thus he claimed the whole pot! He was always making fun.'

Kachuri and various sweetmeats feature in stories about the Cossipore garden house as well, where Sri Ramakrishna breathed his last on 16 August 1886. Naren's gurubhai, Shashi (Swami Ramakrishnananda), once spotted Mahendranath Gupta and Naren in Cossipore and eagerly went to Phagu's shop to buy them *luchi*s (a kind of fried bread), kachuri and a few sweets. In another story, Naren went to the hostel of the singer Pulin Mitra where he was offered kachuri. He liked it exceedingly and shared some with Pulin.

Swami Vivekananda had changed his mind about Indian food, however, by the time he returned from the West. Not only did he express strong displeasure about certain kinds of Indian food in his lectures, but also wrote: 'This dyspepsia that you notice in every home ... Why? ... [It is] due to the taking of impure food from the bazaars. Those who live in the villages do not, as a rule, suffer from indigestion ... Why? They do not have luchis, kachuris and other such poisonous foods!'

He could have stopped there, but did not. He went on to further criticize: 'Fried food is sheer poison. The sweet vendor's shop is the house of death. In a warm country, the lesser oil and ghee taken, the better it is. Butter is much more easily digested than ghee. Flour has nothing in it; it only looks snow-white; all the nutrients of wheat are in unrefined flour. That is nutritious ... In the delicacies of the sweetmeat shops, there is hardly anything nourishing. You get only poison, poison, and more poison! Earlier, people rarely used to eat these! Now those who live in cities, and especially those who come from villages to live in towns, are great sinners in this respect, as they take them every day

… If you are hungry, throw away all sweets and fried stuff into the ditch and buy a pice worth of *murhi* (puffed rice)——that is a cheaper and more nutritious food!'

Realizing that a single isolated rebuke will not eradicate long-entrenched beliefs, the social reformer and patriot Swami Vivekananda once more expressed himself vehemently: 'To be rich in our country and to be lazy have come to mean one and the same thing … One who eats fluffy, nice, round luchis is a dead man! … Those who have money feed their children kachuris and sweets! It is demeaning to let them have only rice and chapatis, is it? Why will the children not be like animals with distended stomachs if they are fed like that? The English people are so robust, they work so hard day and night and their native place is a cold country, yet even they feel afraid to touch such food. And look at us. We must have luchi, kachuri and food fried in ghee or oil! Formerly, village zamindars in Bengal would think nothing of walking twenty or thirty miles … nowadays their children come to Calcutta and put on airs, are myopic and wear glasses, eat luchis and kachuris from the bazaars, hire a carriage to go from one street to another, and then complain of diabetes——and their life is cut short. This is the result of being "civilized Calcuttans."'

☙

Once Patla-da returned to Howrah on vacation. We had a long discussion about Swami Vivekananda's cautionary attitude against kachuris. Patla-da said, 'This attitude, this antipathy, towards kachuris was a late development. Swami Vivekananda cooked and ate kachuris in London even in 1896. Once, he went down to the kitchen in the basement of the house in which he was staying. He melted butter, made kachuris with mashed potato inside and also concocted a spicy potato curry to go with it. Then he came back upstairs to the dining room.'

'Terrific, Patla-da,' I applauded. 'Unless one presents contradictory facts about great men, one cannot satisfy readers.'

Patla-da had not finished his tale. 'Alas, something dreadful happened. The housemaid's name was Miss Cameron. Swami Saradananda told Swami Vivekananda's brother Mahendranath, "Please, set a few kachuris and a portion of the curry aside for Miss Cameron, otherwise, she will be upset." While they were eating, Miss Cameron arrived and asked if they had cooked and kept anything for her. She especially eyed Saradananda suspiciously, whom she alleged only knew how to eat and put on weight! This spirited lady was then offered two kachuris and a portion of the spicy curry. At first, she was nonplussed. How should one eat a kachuri? She tried it with sugar, but did not like it. Then Saradananda advised her to try it with salt, which she did. Then, something terrible happened. She tasted the curry. Her eyes began to water and her throat burned. The poor lady screamed and slapped her cheeks. To her, it seemed like the curry was made of chilli peppers cooked with peppercorns. "Oh, poison, poison!" she cried. One assumes that this English rose never dared to ask for kachuris or spicy curry again!'

Patla-da asked me to note down his next words: 'Love towards all, hot *chai*, fragrant tobacco and very hot chilli peppers—regarding these four Swami Vivekananda knew no limits.'

'Don't worry, I will give you my notebook,' he said. 'Nobody will appreciate it anyway in a foreign land.'

Patla-da's collection of facts and information astounded me. My eyes grew as round as *chhanabara*s (posset cakes). And I am not being discourteous here. Sri Ramakrishna himself mentioned posset cakes once. He referred to Shibnath Shastri's devotion to God as 'posset cake in syrup'.

'But, Patla-da,' I protested, 'even if I present an abridged version of all that you have in your collection, it will surely come to at least 737 pages!'

'Naturally,' said Patla-da, serenely. 'Do not forget that the scope of the subject is immense. Viewing Swami Vivekananda from various perspectives can be very tough indeed. If you try to take all of them into account, I dare say, you will take thirty-nine years more! So it is better to order them chronologically; then you will not face problems writing a summary. The first phase can be the "happy eating" phase: Narendranath's father was still alive and Narendranath had just been introduced to Thakur Sri Ramakrishna in Dakshineshwar. At this meeting, Thakur brought butter, sugar candy and a few pieces of *sandesh* and affectionately fed them by hand to Naren. Narendranath said afterwards, "I told him, 'Why don't you give me the food and I will distribute it among my friends and we can all eat.' He never listened."'

Sri Ramakrishna also shared his smoking hookah with Narendranath.

Someone raised the objection, 'Narendranath eats in hotels!' Sri Ramakrishna rebuked the informer: 'What is that to you? ... Even if Naren eats in a hotel, and you eat boiled rice and ghee, you can never be like him!'

It was not in Narendranath's nature to conceal the truth. Once, he ate in a hotel and immediately came and confessed to Sri Ramakrishna: 'Thakur, today in a hotel, I have eaten what we Hindus consider inedible.'

'You have not committed a sin,' Thakur assured him.

It is a fact that Narendranath was very fond of dining out. He prophesied, 'One day, in Calcutta, shops selling *chops* (crunchy fritters with pieces of meat, vegetable or egg as stuffing) and cutlets (fried pieces of meat or vegetables coated with breadcrumbs) will flood every street and the bend of every alley, the way *paan* shops do now.'

Mother Sarada Debi, Sri Ramakrishna's consort, gives us an insight into the way Narendranath cooked. She writes, 'When I cooked for Thakur in Cossipore, I boiled the meat in water, adding a few bay leaves and a small quantity of spices. I cooked it until it was as tender as cotton ... Naren could cook meat in a variety of ways: he used to mince it and then fry it; he used to cook it with mashed potatoes—what is it called?' Possibly she was referring to meat cutlets.

The second phase of Narendranath's eating, according to Patla-da, began after his father's death. This phase is characterized by starvation and undernourishment. It continues up until Khetri's 'dewan' Jagamohanlal sees him off in Bombay on the steamship to America.

After Narendranath's father died, he faced abject poverty. He said, 'Waking up early in the morning, I would secretly find out that there was not enough food for all of us, so I would inform my mother, "A friend has invited me for lunch." Then I would go out, so that the others would get a larger share. On such days, I had very little to eat, sometimes nothing at all. I was too proud to tell anyone.'

It was impossible for Swami Vivekananda to ever forget those days of privation. Shortly before his demise, he told his disciples, 'How painful those days were! One day I fainted on a veranda of a house by the roadside as I had eaten nothing. I came round when it rained. Then, on another day, I had to do odd jobs in Calcutta for a whole day and could get nothing to eat. Finally, I returned to the math at ten or eleven in the evening and ate there. And this is not the only time that this has happened.' (One assumes that he is referring to the monastery at Baranagore. Narendranath's gurubhais were also suffering there.)

One day a sannyasi came to the monastery at Baranagore. His name was Hirananda. He asked, 'How do you manage?'

'People give alms,' replied Narendranath.

Hirananda had with him six annas. He gave them to Narendranath and said, 'Let this money be used today.'

Narendranath did not want to accept the offering. He said, 'It is not necessary. We have rice enough for today and tomorrow.'

Nonetheless, it was a harsh life that the young boys led. It could not possibly have been easy for them. Starvation or undernourishment was the norm at Baranagore.

Some of these incidents of great hardship have been recorded. One day, four gurubhais went out collecting alms and came back empty-handed. They could not offer food to the deity on that day, nor did they have anything to eat themselves. So they sang devotional songs to God.

Swami Premananda tells us, 'Some days we had only rice for our meal, on other days we had nothing. We had no utensils. We ate our food off leaves. But if we tried to pluck a few gourd or banana leaves from a nearby garden, the gardener would drive us away. So we each placed our portion of rice and boiled telakucho leaves on a *mankachu* leaf and ate it. But because of the mankachu leaf, our throats itched as we ate. Finally, we found a way of dispensing with the dreaded mankachu altogether: we placed the rice on a cloth which we spread out on the floor and then all of us ate from the same cloth. We had it with a curry which we kept in a bowl. It was made with salt and chilli peppers.'

It is obvious that the experiences of Baranagore stood Swami Vivekananda in good stead during his itinerant days. He wrote in a letter, 'I go about from house to house shamelessly and eat like a crow … I have decided not to beg any more. How does it benefit the poor if they have to feed me? If they get a handful of rice, they can feed their children instead.'

It was not that Swami Vivekananda was offered food everywhere. He wrote from a place near Khandwa in Madhya Pradesh: 'The people here are uncivilized and inhospitable. If you ask for a handful of rice, they refuse; if you seek shelter, they drive you out. I fast and do not even drink water every day, then eat very little to keep myself alive.'

On his way from Brindaban to Giri Govardhan, Swami Vivekananda resolved not to beg at all. He decided that he would eat only such food as he would be offered without asking for it. On the very first day, he felt pangs of hunger in the afternoon. It began to rain. Wearily, Vivekananda continued on his way. Then he heard somebody calling out to him. Swami Vivekananda began to run. The man, who was approaching from behind, started to run as well. He drew abreast of Swami Vivekananda and offered him food. Thus Swamiji's resolve was not broken.

Swami Vivekananda remained firm in his decision not to beg. As a result, he was often compelled to go hungry. Once he had gone without food for two days when a rich man's syce called out to him, 'Have you eaten?' Swami Vivekananda replied that he had not. The syce kindly offered him a few pieces of chapati and some hot chutney. The chutney was so hot that Swami Vivekananda began to have a severe stomach ache; his stomach had become sensitive from not having eaten for two days. The syce felt miserable. At that moment, a man was passing by with a basket on his head. Swami Vivekananda asked him what he was carrying. The answer was tamarind. Swami Vivekananda begged him for a little tamarind, ate it and his stomach ache subsided.

On another occasion, Swami Vivekananda and Swami Akhandananda were wandering in the vicinity of Almora. He had not eaten and was utterly exhausted. Three kilometres from Almora, he fell down on the ground. Swami Akhandananda ran to and fro, looking for someone to help. Near a graveyard, he noticed a Muslim fakir. The fakir gave Swami Vivekananda a piece of cucumber, and saved his life. Swami Vivekananda later admitted, 'I never craved for food more.'

At Hathras railway station, on his way to Haridwar, Swami Vivekananda happened to meet the assistant station master, a gentleman by the name of Sharat Chandra Gupta (later Swami Sadananda). Noticing the monk, Sharat Gupta asked him, 'Swamiji, are you hungry?'

'Yes,' came the answer.

'Please come with me to my house,' said the kind soul.

'What will you feed me?' asked Swami Vivekananda.

By way of reply, Sharat Gupta recited a verse in Urdu:

'O dear one, you have come to my house.

I will cook my heart with spices and offer it to you.'

In California, Swamiji used to narrate these stories from his itinerant days to his disciples. How many times death stared him in the face because of starvation and exhaustion! There were times when he could not move one step ahead for want of a handful of rice. He sought shelter under the shade of trees. His austerities took him to a point when he could no longer speak, or even think clearly. Yet he had no fear of death. There was something within him that had not been born, that would not die, that had no sense of hunger or thirst. He felt that Nature could not grind him to death; Nature was his instrument. He used to pray, 'O Lord of lords, O Supreme, do express Yourself in and through me. Do establish yourself in the kingdom of my heart! Arise, awake! Never stop!' At this time, his prayers and meditation were his only modes of sustenance. He used to say that it was because of his fervent prayers that he was still alive.

A man who is not afraid of starvation is afraid of nothing. Once, Swami Vivekananda was roaming by himself in northern India. He was downcast. A suspicious police officer pestered him and wanted to imprison him. Neither did Vivekananda make any objection, nor was he frightened by the prospect. He simply said to the police officer, 'Come, take me with you. Right now I do not know if I shall ever eat again. At least I shall be able to eat two proper meals in the police station.'

What was the longest stretch that Swami Vivekananda had to do without food? It seems that he never had to go more than three days in a row. If it was a matter of a day or two, he was accustomed enough to deal with the physical discomfort.

The threat of starvation could not subdue Vivekananda's spirit. He arrived in Meerut in December 1890 and by chance met six of his gurubhais. They stayed for a few days at the garden house of Lala

Nandaram Gupta, located at 259, Rambagh, and transformed the house into a miniature math. A relative of Amir Abdar Rahman offered some money to the monks so that they could make pulao—a rare treat. Swamiji enthusiastically took responsibility for this meal and shopped for the ingredients himself.

At Meerut, Swamiji demonstrated to his disciples the art of becoming a jack of all trades. One moment, he would read the holy scriptures to them; the next moment, he would cook them delicacies. One day, he hit upon the idea of preparing *shikh kebab* for everyone. He arranged for the meat and used branches of a peach tree as skewers. Then after cooking he personally served the guests. However, he himself abstained from eating, saying that his only pleasure was to serve others.

One can easily appreciate the difference between going without food in one's own country and being on the point of starvation on foreign soil. In Marie Louise Burke's famous collection of Swamiji's letters, there is a disheartening telegram which Swami Vivekananda sent from Boston to his dear disciple Alasinga Perumal in Madras in 1893:

Starving. All money spent. Send money to return at least.

The man who, only a few days later, would take the world by storm, was almost facing death abroad through starvation! America is an inhospitable place for the poor. At that time it was a crime to beg in the United States and one could even be imprisoned for begging.

Even after Swami Vivekananda's grand appearance at the Parliament of Religions, his financial troubles persisted. In New York, his American disciple Leon Landsberg (Swami Kripananda) informed Mrs Ole Bull in private that Swami Vivekananda was contributing towards his own rent, advertisements, printing costs and so forth. As a result, 'He starves himself' but works like a giant.

Because Swami Vivekananda had first-hand experience of the miseries of starvation, he could identify with the plight of those who shared the same fate. How anxious he was to ensure that the poor were fed! Before his death, he told his disciple Sharat Chandra that a charitable organization must be set up which would provide food to the needy. 'Then, when we get more money, we shall build a large kitchen. Here, rice will be offered for free, and the place will buzz with shouts of "give, take and eat". The water strained from the rice will flow into the Ganga and whiten the river! I will find peace only when I see such an organization.'

At this point, Patla-da suggested, 'It would be wonderful if you could juxtapose the emperor Vivekananda, who was accustomed to sumptuous feasts, with the sannyasi Vivekananda, who faced starvation. Sometimes, our rajas and wealthy foreigners were eager to serve Swami Vivekananda; sometimes, the same person was begging in the streets. Swamiji had a disciple who believed that it was impossible for monks to get fat. Swamiji responded jokingly that even if he got nothing to eat for five days, his body fat would keep him alive! He was 'insured against damage' in this respect!

We find evidence of this stark contrast in Swami Vivekananda's circumstances throughout his travels abroad. Sometimes he was fed sumptuously, at other times he suffered greatly for lack of food. Sometimes he literally slept on the streets, at other times he stayed with his friends and admirers in their mansions. He stayed in the cheapest hotels, in rented apartments, and also in the most luxurious suites. He subsisted both on mere bread and elaborate banquets. Swami Vivekananda was fascinated by all the various extremities of life in the West. His detailed observations, sent to his gurubhais in north Calcutta, are a travelogue and a treasure of Bengali literature. He wrote of Westerners, for example, 'They are second to none in artistic skill, in gratification of sensual pleasure, in earning money, and in spending money.'

We also have a glimpse of the opulence in America. Once Swami Vivekananda received $500 for a single lecture. A dollar was then the equivalent of three rupees, making his honorarium 1,500 rupees. In an exuberant mood, he wrote, 'I feel very happy here. They love me. Thousands of men and women come to listen to me.'

Again, in the summer of 1894, he wrote to his gurubhais at Alambazar Math, 'Just look at the hotels here! There is one in New York where a room can cost up to Rs 5,000 a day apart from food, etc. This is one of the richest nations in the world—it spends money like water. But, I seldom stay in hotels; I mostly stay as a guest to prominent men.'

Swami Vivekananda describes a formal dinner: 'The dinner is the principal meal. If one is rich, the cook is French and the ways are French. First, you are served salted fish, or fish eggs, or a chutney, or vegetable. These are appetizers. Then comes the soup, then a fruit— according to fashion. Afterwards, one is served fish, followed by a meat preparation, then roasted meat with green vegetables, then more meat, and finally the sweets and ice cream. As one says in Sanskrit, one should end with sweets … As the dishes change, the spoons, knives and forks also change. At the end of the dinner, one is served coffee without milk …

Along with the dishes, the drinks too keep changing for those who drink: sherry, claret, champagne, sometimes iced beverages … They call it a grand affair if, along with different kinds of food, they can offer varieties of wine. They make much of their dinners. One such dinner would render a middle-class householder a pauper in India.'

I know of no other Indian who, towards the end of the nineteenth century, was as conversant with the dietary habits of other nations as the monk Vivekananda was. Let us enjoy another sample from his writings: 'The French style is to take coffee, and a few pieces of bread and butter in the morning; fish and meat, etc., in moderate quantities at about midday, and an elaborate dinner in the evening. The Germans eat a good deal, five or six times a day; each time, they take meat. The English eat thrice, not much in the mornings, but they drink tea or coffee between meals. The Americans also eat three times, and the meals are heavy with a lot of meat.'

Swami Vivekananda noticed that the staple food of the poor in every country was rice. Vegetables, fish and meat were luxuries and used only sparingly, instead chutney served as the side dish.

He observed that the eating habits of the wealthy classes in Europe was the same as that of the majority of people in America. It was the reverse of the fare of the poor. That is, fish and meat was the staple fare, and bread and rice were taken as one would take chutney. He was surprised to find that in America, bread was rarely served. 'If you are serving fish, it is served by itself; when meat is served, it is served alone. Whether meat or fish, you have to eat it without bread or rice.'

Swami Vivekananda also reflects on the method of eating in various countries: 'Sitting cross-legged on a wooden seat, and resting against another piece of wood, the Aryan used to eat his meal out of a single, metal dish placed before him on a slightly raised stool. The same custom persists in the Punjab, Rajputana, Maharashtra and Gujarat. The people of Bengal eat their food from a plate or banana leaf placed on the ground. Even the Maharaja of Mysore eats dal and rice from a leaf placed on the floor ... the Chinese sit at tables ... The Romans and Greeks used to recline on couches and eat with their fingers from tables in front of them. Europeans also use tables and chairs. Earlier, they used to eat with their fingers, but now they use a variety of cutlery.'

Patla-da interjected, 'Just see! He is a genius! With a single brushstroke, he has been able to present the global culture of eating. The moment you read his words, you know that he is not merely repeating the observations of someone else. He has seen it with his own eyes, he has read books on the subject, and is offering it to us like condensed milk—draining the excess water out, as it were! If he had not been a monk, but had instead confined himself to the mysteries of the taste buds, he would have earned enduring fame. Great men are such—they would be successful in any sphere to which they turned their attention.'

Patla-da next advised me to make a kind of grid. 'Divide the whole of his life into a few broad sections: Vivekananda at home, in Baranagore, wandering in India; Vivekananda in the West, in England, as "conqueror of the world" after the tours; and, finally, Vivekananda before his death. Now, for each of these periods, mark out on the grid whether Vivekananda used to enjoy his food and eat heartily or he suffered from lack of food, and you will begin to understand just how much one human being can endure and yet, even with all the disadvantages, feel and think so deeply and with so much goodwill about humanity and its salvation!'

I asked Patla-da, 'How is it possible to find out what Swamiji used to eat or liked to eat, since the man constantly moved about from place to place without a second thought for his own health or financial resources?'

Patla-da retorted, 'Do not be discouraged by that! That is the sign of a dyspeptic community. Since you suffer from chronic indigestion, you are bound to get bewildered!'

Later, after Patla-da undertook his research into Swami Vivekananda's lifestyle in Europe and America, I came to his mind again.

He confessed, 'My friend, think of it! Here in India we merely possessed a few hundred letters written by Swami Vivekananda, and a few lectures which we read about in the Vivekananda school. Nothing else. At that time, the American scholar, Marie Louise Burke, had not yet published her wonderfully well-researched book. How thoroughly she conducted her research, based on letters, memoirs and documents! It is astounding! I have jotted down whatever was pertinent to our subject in your notebook.' It was fortunate, I thought on reflection, that I had given Patla-da such a handsome notebook, without caring for the expense!

Patla-da concluded, 'You can gather details of the phases that cover India later. First, see my notes on the phase that covers America and Europe.'

Since Patla-da resides in England, he naturally began with Swami Vivekananda's sojourns in London. The year 1896 was his starting point. He notes that the nephew of Keshab Sen—a Mr B.L. Gupta—lived in London. Swami Vivekananda once visited their home and Mrs Gupta made him posset sweets in the Indian style.

On another occasion, Swami Vivekananda received a dinner invitation to the house of Henrietta Müller. As she was a vegetarian, they had macaroni soup. The English were, indeed, strange, observes Swami Vivekananda. They were not afraid to add salt to milk! When Swami Saradananda arrived from India, Vivekananda taught him how to hold a soup spoon correctly and drink it from the bowl. When poor Saradananda had trouble holding his knife, Vivekananda would kick him under the table to indicate that it must be held in the right hand. He also advised Saradananda to be careful about displaying his teeth and tongue during eating, to abstain from coughing or making sounds while eating, and to finally, chew softly and slowly.

One day, in London Swami Vivekananda asked his brother Mahendranath, 'What have you eaten today?' He then expressed concern about his welfare and added, 'If you eat the same thing every day, you will feel bored. Ask the cook to make a poached egg or an omelette once in a while. That will change your taste.'

Swamiji's usual lunch was rice and matar dal prepared with a little curry powder, salt and butter. But Saradananda lamented, 'Alas, boiled matar dal here as well!'

One afternoon, around half past one, Swami Vivekananda told

John P. Fox, 'It is the same monotonous fare every day! Let's go and eat in a hotel.'

Another evening fish with cauliflower had been cooked for dinner. Mr J.J. Goodwin, an admirer of Swamiji's, was with him. He refused to eat and asked Swami Vivekananda, 'Why did you eat that fish?' Vivekananda laughed as he explained that the old housemaid had purchased the fish and had he not eaten it, she would have thrown it away.

There was a Mrs Turner who ran a small eating joint in London. She had learnt how to prepare some Indian dishes, so Indians would sometimes dine at her restaurant. One day, Swami Vivekananda quizzed his brother, 'Where have you been?' Mahendranath answered, 'I have been to Mrs Turner's place.'

'What did she cook?' inquired his elder brother.

Mahendranath answered, 'Chapati, a meat dish, two vegetable dishes, mint chutney and *chaler payesh* (a kind of rice pudding with almonds and raisins).'

Then Swami Vivekananda asked, 'Why does she not come here and cook for me one day? It will save me.'

Mahendranath said, 'Perhaps that is not possible. She is not a maid. Why would she come and cook here?'

Then Vivekananda expressed the desire to go and sample Mrs Turner's food, but ultimately that did not happen.

I remarked to Patla-da, 'One finds in the letter of 30 May 1896 that Swami Vivekananda had cooked an entire meal at the house at St George's Road, London. It was an elaborate affair. Perhaps Swami Saradananda had carried spices from home for Swamiji. The day after, in a letter to Mary Hale, Swami Vivekananda raved over the meal. What had he *not* used in the curry! He was still dissatisfied, however, for he lacked a spice—something called by the complicated name of asafoetida. Had asafoetida been used, the curry would have been perfect!'

Patla-da laughed out loud. 'That is the English name for *hing*,' he said. 'The pungent smell of this spice would have made his friend and admirer, Mr J. J. Goodwin, throw up! Did you notice that in the same letter, Swami Vivekananda admits that the dish was cooked in such a way that he himself could not eat it? He writes: "Last night, I cooked a dish. It was such a delicious mixture of saffron, lavender, mace, nutmeg, pepper, cinnamon, cloves, cardamom, cream, lime juice, onions, raisins, almonds, chilli peppers and rice that I myself could not eat it! There was no asafoetida, though that would have made it easier to swallow."'

Cooking is one thing and eating is another. Patla-da will contribute to a whole chapter on Vivekananda the cook. Now he said, 'Swami Vivekananda did not know Mrs Turner, so he did not dare ask her to come over and cook for him. But in America, many eminent and learned women did cook for him at his request. Once he said to Ellen Waldo, "The food here seems so unclean—would it be possible for you to cook for me?" Miss Waldo felt honoured with this opportunity. She went at once to the landlady of his lodging house and obtained permission to cook for him. Swami Vivekananda affectionately gave her a new name, "Haridasi" (servant of God). This devout lady was, indeed, extraordinary. She was an editor, proofreader, stenographer and philosopher all in one.'

✂

Patla-da had painstakingly collected information regarding the different kinds of food Swami Vivekananda could afford at different times of his life, especially his culinary preferences in America. He asked me to take down notes.

In a letter from New York, Vivekananda wrote to Mrs Bull that Miss Hamlin had very kindly sent him a gas stove. He had decided to cook in his bedroom. There was also a common kitchen in the basement of his lodging house and he sometimes used that as well.

What is noteworthy is that Swami Vivekananda loved to treat others, and on these special occasions, it was his custom not to partake of anything himself.

A few days after receiving the gas stove, Swamiji wrote to Mrs Bull again on 14 February 1895: 'Between Mr Landsberg [Swami Kripananda] and me, we cook some rice and lentils or barley and quietly eat it, and write something or read or receive visits from poor people who want to learn something, and thus I feel I am more of a sannyasi now than I ever was in America.'

He wrote to his gurubhais in Calcutta: '*Kalaier dal*? You do not get lentils here, nor do they know much about lentils. But you get greens. There is a variety of spinach which tastes like *nate*, and what they call 'asparagus' tastes like the young stalk of *dengo*. But, alas, Gopal's mother *chachchari* (mixed vegetable) is not to be had!'

There is more: 'These days you get *hilsa* in abundance and one can eat to one's fill. Digestion is never a problem. You also get all kinds of fruits—banana, lemon, guava, apple, nuts, raisins and lots of grapes. Several other varieties come from California. There are plenty of pineapples as well, but no mangoes or lichis.'

In New York, Swami Vivekananda often had dinner invitations to exclusive restaurants, such as the Waldorf-Astoria, the Showells or the Delmonico. These invitations came from the affluent, and Swamiji would call them 'big pockets'.

Here we see someone who had once been obliged to fast for three days in a row in his own country, now going to dinner parties which began in the early evening and ended often after two in the morning! Those who frequent such restaurants, however, cannot be expected to maintain their health. So we find Swami Vivekananda taking the decision to turn vegetarian and avoid all invitations to eat out. In

March 1895, he writes that he will be attending a dinner party, but for the last time.

Let us now move to the next episode in Swami Vivekananda's life: He has become a vegetarian and is staying at the Thousand Island Park. He is fasting regularly with the aim of losing thirty to forty pounds before leaving the place.

There is more in Patla-da's notebook about the incidents in New York. Miss S. Ellen Waldo (a distant relative of Ralph Waldo Emerson) had now taken up the trouble to cook for Swami Vivekananda. Each day she travelled from the far end of Brooklyn to Swamiji's lodgings on 38th Street by a jogging horse cart. It took her two hours . On the days when Swami Vivekananda did not have lectures to deliver, the situation reversed and he travelled to Miss Waldo's house. Then he went up to her kitchen on the top floor of the house and cooked for her. He was no common cook. He experimented endlessly and tried to invent new ways of adding Western spices to Eastern dishes. During the process, he would run excitedly from room to room, like a child. At this time, he used to call Miss Waldo 'Yati Mata'—the mother of the monks.

Patla-da widened his eyes and said, 'During his stay abroad, Swami Vivekananda was not solely getting Vedas and Upanishads from India, but also other things. What exactly those items were can be discovered from one of his letters to Yogen Maharaj who was based in Calcutta. It is dated 24 January 1896:

'Brother Yogen, *arhar dal* (yellow dal), *mung dal* (mung bean dal), *amsatwa* (a cake of dried mango juice), *amsi* (dried raw mango), *amtel* (a preparation with mango), *amer morabba* (mango jam), *bari* (a dried preparation with lentil), spices—everything has reached me ... if you immediately send some of that dal and amtel to Sturdy's address, Highview Caversham, Reading, I will get them as soon as I reach England. Don't send fried mung dal. It probably gets spoilt quickly.'

Armed with these spices and food items from home, Swami

Vivekananda marched through one American city after another!

Another anecdote from Patla-da: Detroit, 18 March 1896. Swami Vivekananda visits a disciple's house and asks permission to cook. He has brought with him herbs, spices, pickles and chutney, all of which have been sent from India. Wherever he goes, he takes these with him. His most precious item is a bottle of chutney which has been sent by an admirer in Madras.

Whenever Swami Vivekananda cooked, the cooking took an extraordinarily long time and the result was very hot. According to some of his disciples, such spicy food was not good for his liver, but he did not agree with them.

At this, Patla-da pronounced solemnly, 'He might have earned love, affection and respect from abroad, but his "Indianness" was intact. I told you that he was promoting Indian cooking. I was right! See what he had written to Swami Trigunatitananda: "What do you mean by the mung dal not being ready? I asked you not to send fried mung! I asked specifically for *chholar dal* (chickpea) and *kancha mung* (not fried). Fried mung gets spoilt and is difficult to boil. If you send fried mung again, it will go down the Thames and your efforts will be in vain! Why don't you read the instructions in my letters properly? Sometimes you even lose the letters! While replying, always have my letter in front of you! You really need some business sense!"'

Not only did the monk promote Vedanta and biryani across the Atlantic, but trade authorities concerned with promoting Indian exports would be pleased to learn that in 1896, Swami Vivekananda also pondered on the question of effective export of spices. Consider what he said on this subject to Trigunatitananda on 17 January 1896. He was writing from New York: 'Please tell Dayal-babu that mung and arhar can be good business options in England and America. Dal soup will have a go if properly introduced. If you can make small packets with the directions for cooking printed on them, and if they can be distributed to individual houses, then it will do well. You can pack the stuff together and send them. Those boris can also be popular. But you have to be enterprising—sitting at home fetches nothing. If somebody forms a company and brings Indian products to this country and England, then he will make great profits.'

Patla-da's comment was, 'So, you can see how seriously Swami Vivekananda took the promotion of both Vedanta and Indian cooking! He was the first to seek out Indian spices and condiments in the West. He often had to make do with their substitutes. If he was looking for chilli peppers, for example, and did not find any, he would settle for Tabasco sauce. Listen to what one American lady has to say on this. Swami Vivekananda was then delivering his brilliant lectures in Chicago. He was being looked after by a kind lady called Mrs John B. Lyons. Her granddaughter, Cornelia Conger, wrote in her memoirs that her grandmother liked to use a little Tabasco sauce in her salad dressing. During a meal, "She handed [Swami Vivekananda] the bottle and said, 'You might like a drop or two of this on your meat, Swami.' He sprinkled it so liberally that we all gasped and said, 'But you can't do that! It's terribly hot!' He laughed and ate it with such enjoyment that a special bottle of the sauce was always put beside his plate after that ..."'

Patla-da's next priceless piece of information was regarding how Swami Vivekananda ate clams. It requires quite a bit of skill to extract the hot clam from its shell, but Swami Vivekananda did not require tutoring. After all, he hailed from the land of snails and oysters!

Once Swami Vivekananda nearly lost his life in a boat accident in the West. He was rowing when he suddenly lost balance and toppled into the river. Fortunately, one of the members of the Bagley family immediately jumped in and rescued him from drowning.

When Swami Vivekananda went to the United States for the second time, he stayed in Pasadena, southern California. His hostess, Mrs Alice

Hansbrough, served him the following breakfast, which he enjoyed immensely: fruit, poached eggs, two slices of toast and two cups of coffee with sugar and cream. She always asked him if he would like a third cup.

During this period, either Swami Vivekananda abstained from smoking cheroots altogether or smoked only a few. At lunch with the Hansbrough family, he would eat mutton (never beef) and an assortment of vegetables. He was partial to peas and preferred fruit, especially grapes, to sweets for dessert.

Patla-da observes, 'I have noticed that wherever Swami Vivekananda was shown genuine hospitality, he always cooked a dish or two. Unlike us, he felt that he must return the favour. Mrs Carrie Mead Wyckoff [Sister Lalita], the sister of Mrs Hansbrough, wrote that Swami Vivekananda not only assisted her in cooking dinner, but often cooked all the dishes himself. Another lady reported that when Swami Vivekananda stayed with them in Nicron Park, he always cooked one meal. Mrs Hansbrough also says that Swami Vivekananda used to be very enthusiastic about making chapatis and curry. When he needed to grind spices, he preferred sitting on the floor. The rising smoke and the butter and ground spices that he was frying made their eyes water. It gave Swami Vivekananda real pleasure to cook for the whole family, this American housewife concluded, but the process itself was at once "elaborate" and "alarming".'

Once, after one of his special culinary efforts, Swami Vivekananda asked Mrs Wyckoff, 'Did you like the dish?' Mrs Wyckoff answered, 'Yes.' 'Is that the truth,' asked Swamiji, 'or are you just saying this for the sake of friendship?' Mrs Wyckoff sweetly confessed that she had said it out of friendship.

Patla-da presented me with a description of a typical dinner of Swamiji's in the Mead household. The time was usually 6.30 in the evening. The menu invariably included soup, fish, vegetables and some typical American pie for dessert. But among this fare, one would notice dishes such as chapatis and curry. By this time Vivekananda was no longer taking coffee after dinner.

On another memorable occasion in northern California, Swami Vivekananda busied himself in the kitchen preparing dinner and simultaneously discussed philosophy, quoting verbatim from the eighteenth chapter of the Bhagavad Gita! Those who were fortunate to be present there would remember that evening all their lives.

As a rule, Swami Vivekananda refrained from eating before his lectures. Perhaps one cannot think clearly on a full stomach! But there were exceptions to this rule. One evening, he dined at the house of a certain Mrs Steele before a lecture. She offered him dates for dessert and Swami Vivekananda enjoyed them immensely. Afterwards, he delivered a scintillating oratory. Mrs Steele was deeply moved by the power of his words and congratulated him. At this, Swami Vivekananda smiled and said that her dates must have been responsible for his performance.

Who else has simultaneously searched for God, promoted the teachings of the Vedas and the Upanishads, analysed so beautifully the deepest feelings of the human soul, *and* devoted such serious attention to culinary pursuits but Swami Vivekananda?

After one historic lecture in Los Angeles, Vivekananda was returning to his lodging with Miss Macleod. He was silent, absorbed in his own thoughts. Miss Macleod assumed that he was engrossed in higher, spiritual thoughts, so she remained silent, feeling it would be inappropriate to interrupt him. Then, all on a sudden, Swami Vivekananda began to speak excitedly like one who had just solved a difficult problem. Now he knew how mulligatawny soup should be cooked! He had just realized that the bay leaves should be added later.

ॐ

Swami Vivekananda was fond both of south Indian cooking and their culture. Yet, from time to time, he would make fun of the Ramanuja and Vaishnava monks who applied tilak to their foreheads. He would laugh at the story that on seeing a devout Vaishnava with tilak on his body, a man mistook him for a tiger and climbed up a tree in fright. 'And their languages!' wrote Swami Vivekananda. 'Tamil, Telugu, Malayalam! You cannot comprehend a word, even after six years of contact. All the world's 'l's and 'd's can only be heard! And that rice with *muragtanni rasam* (hot pepper soup with sour tamarind juice)——the tamarind will make your heart go weak! Those sweet neem leaves, chholar dal, munger dal, the spices! Those baths after a castor oil massage! Those fish fried in castor oil! This is south India.'

I queried, 'So, it is not *mulgathani*, but muragtanni?'

'Correct,' said Patla-da. 'Swami Vivekananda himself offered a footnote. 'Muragtanni is the very hot and sour preparation of arhar dal. *Murag* is "black pepper" and *tanni* is "dal".'

“

Researchers have brought to light the fact that Swami Vivekananda was not only fond of spicy Eastern curries and Western chops or cutlets, but also fruit. One incident testifies to this. It occurred just before he left for America. One day he chanced upon a magician. 'Ask for any kind of food and I will give it to you,' he boasted. He was seated in a tent and his hands were concealed under a blanket. Swami Vivekananda wanted to catch the fellow red-handed, so of all things he asked for Californian grapes. Clearly Vivekananda was partial to these grapes. What is very surprising, however, was that the magician was able to produce them from under his blanket in far-off India! Swami Vivekananda narrated this story to his friends in America.

Vivekananda also praised the grapes that he tasted in England. When his brother Mahendranath came to see him in London in the summer of 1896, Swamiji told him, 'There are fresh black grapes in a glass bowl. Eat a lot of grapes! They purify your blood.'

While Swami Vivekananda was in London, Henrietta Müller, in order to make him happy, arranged for a shipment of mangoes to be brought from India . The shipment took a month to arrive. When they came at last, Swami Vivekananda got busy, like a true expert, in restoring them to their original freshness. He asked Josiah J. Goodwin to fetch ice and place it around the mangoes to make them taste better. By this time, John P. Fox, who was deeply interested in Vedanta, had come over from America. He was seeing mangoes for the very first time in his life. Not knowing how to eat one, he tried to tackle it with a knife and fork. Seeing his difficulty, Vivekananda advised him to eat it with a spoon. Then he entertained his guests with mango stories from India.

We have stories concerning mangoes and Swami Vivekananda in plenty. He liked to refer to them as *anb* rather than the traditional Bengali word *am*. I thought that perhaps anb was specific to the dialect in Calcutta. But, linguists have since told me that anb is, indeed, the correct way to pronounce the word.

There is a variety of mango which grows in Benares called the *langra*. In Swami Vivekananda's time, they used to refer to it as '*langra* mangoes of the Imperial Bank'. Today they call it 'State Bank langra'. Once, one of Vivekananda's disciples went into the garden in winter and found that the mango tree had borne fruit. He discovered two wonderful langra mangoes and brought them away with him.

Another day, Girish Chandra Ghosh and Narendranath got locked in a war of words on the topic of mango. They had partaken of the fruit at Balaram Basu's house in north Caclutta, but it seemed that their experiences had been different. Girish Ghosh recounts, 'The pieces of mango that I got were sweet and the pieces that Naren got were sour. So Naren got mighty angry and spat at me: "*Shala* G.C., you get only sweet mangoes and I get only sour! You shala, you must have made an arrangement with the ones serving!" I said: "We are householders, so naturally we will have all the fun. You, shala fakir, wandering about the streets—what do you expect but dry, sour mangoes!'"

It was quite the norm for G.C. (Girish Chandra) and Swami Vivekananda to exchange this kind of repartee. Alas, Master-mashai was not always present to leave us accounts of their verbal jousts.

There is a wonderful story relating to fruit when Swami Vivekananda was in London. The year was 1896. A famous shop called William Whiteley had the reputation of being the 'universal provider'. Somebody anonymously left some money with the shop owner and asked him to deliver the best fruit every day to Swami Vivekananda. At two o'clock every afternoon, an employee from William Whiteley's would arrive with a large quantity of fruit wrapped up in paper and addressed to Swamiji. Sometimes, Swami Vivekananda would receive fruits a few weeks in advance of their being put up on display! Pineapple, for example, was a rare and costly fruit in London, its cost being as high as a guinea per fruit. Yet, it was delivered to Swami Vivekananda. The best fruit of every season, no matter what the price, was brought to him.

It is not entirely certain who the benefactor was, but the most likely candidate was Josephine Macleod, for it was only after she came to London that the regular fruit deliveries began. It is also worth noting that many of Swami Vivekananda's friends used to frequent William Whiteley's before he started receiving the fruits.

From Mahendranath's memoirs, we learn that Vivekananda was extremely fond of pineapples, but Josiah J. Goodwin did not know how to serve them. So Swamiji came forward to assist him, and soon pieces of pineapple with sugar sprinkled on top were being distributed among everybody.

Another time in London, Swami Vivekananda expressed the desire to eat chilli peppers of which he was inordinately fond. After an extensive search, Krishna Menon found three green chilli peppers in William Whiteley's for the exorbitant price of three shillings. He purchased them and, at breakfast the next morning, Swami Vivekananda ate one after the other. He commented that they had a great flavour, but were not hot at all.

The story of chilli peppers is not yet over. It has to be long, otherwise, according to both Patla-da and me, one does an injustice to Swami Vivekananda. However, before the story of chilli peppers can be concluded, the story of fruit has to be wound up.

We know that Swami Vivekananda loved fruit. Possibly he believed that since all human beings are subject to the laws of karma and acquire *karmaphal* (the fruit of karma), they should literally have access to all kinds of fruits! He told Gopal Chandra Ghosh (Swami Advaitananda), 'Our bones do not rust if we live on fruit and milk.'

Which fruit did Swami Vivekananda like? Some we know for certain: melons, green coconuts, lichis and jackfruit. Once, he visited Master-mashai's house only to have a melon. Others have written that he was very fond of putting sugar and ice into green coconuts and then drinking the water. It is unfortunate that he did not have a refrigerator in which to keep a ready supply of ice! When his disciples asked him which fruit they could offer their guru, he specified lichis. Another time, he wrote a long letter to Christine Greenstidel (Sister Christine) praising the merits of jackfruits in Belur in beautiful, effortless English.

Swami Vivekananda once returned from his cousin's house in Bara Jagulia (in the district of Nadia, about forty-eight kilometres north of Calcutta) with a basket full of roseapples. He was then suffering from diabetes. So he left the juice of the roseapples to ferment in a bottle which was tied to a rope near the kitchen. Once the juice was warmed in the sun, the bottle popped open and Swami Vivekananda announced, cheerfully, 'This vinegar is very good for digestion. All of you must try it every day.'

We also learn about an eccentric doctor who attended Narendranath in his early years. This doctor always carried a small gift with him to offer to the patient. Narendranath was suffering from stones in his bladder. Dr Rajen Dutta came to treat him and brought him *marmelos* (Bengal quince) from the market. In Bengali, marmelo is known as *bel* or *bilwa*, which is phonetically similar to Narendranath's nickname 'Bilu'. Therefore, we may assume that Bilu had a certain fondness for the bilwa fruit.

However much a great man may be fond of fruit, he cannot like them all. In this context, one may say with some justification that Swami Vivekananda did not like guavas. He once said that if he had to dedicate a fruit to God and abstain from it for the rest of his life, that fruit would be guava.

In 1897, he stayed in Almora for a while to improve his health. He wrote to Rakhal Maharaj on 20 May: 'I will go for very light meals at night; I shall eat to the full in the morning and at noon; but at night I will live on only milk and fruit. That is why I am staying in this orchard, "in expectation of fruit". Don't you see that?'

One has to appreciate Vivekananda's sense of humour in the face of acute physical suffering. No wonder he was loved by all.

◌৪

I have not yet taken the opportunity to discuss at length Swami Vivekananda's expertise in the kitchen. I have merely drawn your attention to the fact that he was the only Indian who had the courage and the foresight to simultaneously promote Vedanta and biryani in the West. His dreams are now on the path to fulfilment. The people in the West are more enthusiastic about yoga than we in India. And, very recently, our former overlords, the British, have admitted that chicken curry is now the national dish of England. The servant's food has at last been crowned with glory. In the entire history of India, there is nobody save Swami Vivekananda who can claim the rare honour of introducing Eastern cooking into the Western kitchen. Here was a monk who had renounced everything, who had no desire to run after name and fame, but what a visionary he was! He realized that the teachings of the East could one day reach the hearts of men and women in the West through the kitchen!

Patla-da continued, 'With a single mouth, how can I extol the virtues of the great Swami Vivekananda? Now let us appreciate how he promoted such dishes as khichuri, pulao and biryani. What foresight, resourcefulness and marketing abilities he had in this respect!'

Patla-da then began to read out notes from his notebook. 'Once Naren and his friends cooked bhuni-khichuri. They fried rice with roasted split mung dal and potatoes, then added some sweet-smelling spices, beat some eggs and poured them on the rice, then put ghee, salt and water and brought everything to a boil. When it was cooked, everyone testified that it was very tasty. This account has been taken from Mahendranath's memoirs.'

After Thakur Sri Ramakrishna passed away, it was Swami Vivekananda who decided on what would be offered in Dakshineshwar on his birthday. The dishes included bhuni-khichuri, *alu-kopir dam* (a curry with potato and cauliflower), yoghurt, bonde, etc.

Swami Vivekananda has affirmed that pulao is an ancient Indian dish which existed prior to the conquest of India by the Mughals. Possibly, he was so eager to cook pulao because he wanted to stress that it is an integral part of our ancient Indian heritage.

When Swami Vivekananda returned from his first trip abroad, he went to the house of Balaram Basu. There he declared, 'Nowhere does one get such a variety of vegetable dishes as in Bengal. Rajputana, however, also offers a considerable variety.' A gentleman who was also present on the occasion happened to be the overseer of the Raja of Mahishadal (in the Midnapore district of West Bengal). His name was Shachin Basu. He remarked, 'Rajputana? Maharaj, do they even know how to eat? All their vegetables are cooked sour!'

Swami Vivekananda exclaimed, 'You are talking like a novice ... They were civilized all along! When was Bengal ever civilized? Go to a rich man's house there and your error will be rectified ... And about your pulao: we get references to *palanna* in the ancient book *Pak-Rajyeshwar*. The Muslims imitated us. Akbar describes how to cook Hindu palanna in his *Ain-i-Akbari*.'

In London, Swami Vivekananda was inspired to talk more about pulao: 'Onion is called *palanda; pala* means "meat". Fried onions make the chicken hard to digest. But if the onions are boiled, it is beneficial for the stomach.'

Did Swami Vivekananda change his mind about the benefits of onion later? In Marie Louise Burke's historic book, a student in San Francisco asks Swamiji for his opinion on onions. Swami Vivekananda answers, 'It is not the best food for ascetics.' Then he admits, 'How fond I was of onions once! I used to take long walks in the open air to get rid of the smell in my mouth.'

There are many more stories surrounding pulao. The first time that Swami Vivekananda was leaving for the United States, he decided to cook pulao for everyone who had gathered to see him off in Bombay. Meat, rice, kheer and other ingredients were assembled. Swami Vivekananda picked up some pieces of meat from the stew and ate them with relish. He then set the ingredients on the fire and went into an adjacent room to meditate. When the pulao was done, his friends and admirers begged him to join them, but he replied that he did not feel like eating. 'I wanted to cook for you and have cooked a pot of pulao which cost me fourteen rupees. Now, go and eat it.' So saying, he went back to his meditation.

It has not been possible to determine exactly how many times Swami Vivekananda cooked pulao or khichuri while he was abroad. Ida Ansell describes one incident which occurred while Swamiji and some of his admirers were staying at Camp Taylor in May 1900. They were living outdoor in tents some distance from the city. She writes: 'After the morning talk and meditation, Swami would take an interest in the dinner preparations. Sometimes he helped. He made curry for us and showed how they grind spices in India. He would sit on the floor in his tent with a hollow stone in his lap. With another smooth, round stone, he would grind the spices to a much finer paste than we could with a bowl and chopper. This would make the curry quite hot for us, but Swami would chew red-hot peppers along with it! He would throw his head back and toss them into his mouth with a circular movement of his arm. Once, he handed me one and said, "Eat it. It will do you good." One would eat poison if Swamiji offered it, so I obeyed, but the result was agonizing.' Can memsahibs tolerate such hot chillies! So what if they had come from Bolivia.

For Swami Vivekananda, khichuri or pulao always had to be made very spicy. In Hrishikesh once he had fallen very ill. When he felt a little better, he wanted to eat. His gurubhai Rakhal cooked khichuri for him and put a lump of sugar candy in it. Swami Vivekananda ate the khichuri, but did not enjoy it. Soon, a long thread was discovered in it. In those days, sugar candies sometimes had threads in them. Immediately, Vivekananda queried why there was a thread in the khichuri. So everybody replied, 'Rakhal has put a lump of sugar candy in it!' Swami Vivekananda immediately pounced on Rakhal, 'Shala, Rakhal, this is what you have done! Does anyone put sugar in khichuri? You have no sense!'

When Swami Vivekananda was in Meerut, a certain amir sent him foodstuffs befitting a king. His first impulse was to cook hot pulao.

I asked Patla-da, 'Why were the dishes cooked by Swami Vivekananda invariably hot?'

'Ah, this is what the physicians, psychologists, philosophers and cooks are all trying to find out. Swami Vivekananda never overcame this weakness. He once entered into a competition at Gobinda Basu's house with a monk named Amulya. Amulya consumed a red chilli pepper; Swamiji immediately consumed two. Amulya ate three; Swamiji ate four. They continued like this for some time. Finally, Vivekananda won.'

In Alwar, Swami Vivekananda became close to the Vaishnava monk Ramsanaya. Ramsanaya shared Swami Vivekananda's love for hot food. He used to beg every day and with the money he got he would buy atta. To this he would add salt and chilli peppers to make *tikkar* (a dry, chewy bread). Swami Vivekananda too would join him and survive on this hot tikkar and water alone. Often they would be heard merrily striking the cooking pots with their hands and singing devotional songs.

Swami Vivekananda was once asked, 'Why do you eat so much of chilli peppers?'

He explained, 'I have always been on the move. Chilli pepper has been my sole friend. These days I get a variety to eat, but there was a time when I had to fast.'

Patla-da has proof of the importance that Swami Vivekananda attached to cooking. He used to say to his gurubhais and disciples, 'Whatever you do, it is necessary to concentrate on your work ... One who cannot cook well cannot be a good monk. Unless one cooks with a pure heart, the food remains impure.'

But what about Swami Vivekananda himself? As the scriptures say, we must first practise what we preach.

Swami Vivekananda's gurubhai Hari Maharaj (Swami Turiyananda) has this to say: 'See, Naren works so fast! He wears the turban so quickly ... What one person does in an hour, he finishes in two minutes and at the same time does five or six other things. Such men are rare! Look at the way he peels potatoes or chops vegetables! It appears that the knife has only touched the potato when the skin comes off easily. He never peels away too much either! Amazing! He is always pulsating with life—chopping vegetables, laughing, joking, discussing philosophy, everything is so easy for him!'

An old monk who met Hari Maharaj in Haridwar had this to say about Swamiji: 'I have interacted with so many monks, but have never seen someone like him. He used to make my stomach ache with laughter and laughing he would talk about such deep truths that the spirit of renunciation surged within me even more strongly. I have never seen such a fun monk!'

My time with Patla-da was drawing to a close. He was scheduled to leave for London the next day. He emphasized, 'Please try and understand this first, otherwise, you can never appreciate the Vivekananda who was a lover of food. You must remember that he knew everything about food—its history, geography, chemistry—you name it! There were times when he ate little or nothing. Added to that were his numerous medical prescriptions against eating. But he got boundless pleasure from feeding others. And he was always anxious about those who had not enough to eat. This is our Swami Vivekananda.'

Our next topic of discussion was about which kinds of food one should partake of and which should be avoided. Patla-da said, 'Swami Vivekananda's writings in *Prachya o Pashchatya* (East and West) prove that he pondered deeply on this question. He also discussed it at length with his disciple Sharat Chandra in Belur and their discussion is reproduced in the book *Swami-Shishya Sambad*. The latter is a faithful document on Swami Vivekananda and forms part of the authentic literature on Swamiji in Bengali.

In his writings on bhakti-yoga, Swami Vivekananda refers to the commentary of Bhagavan Ramanuja on pure and impure food. According to Ramanuja, three things cause food to become impure: (1) *jaati dosha*—impurity in the nature of the food itself, like onion and garlic, which excite the nerves and addle your brains; (2) *ashraya dosha*—impurity arising out of contact with an impure person, and (3) *nimitta dosha*—impure because of impurities like worms, hair or dirt in the food. The third has taken on fearful proportions. It can be easily observed that the sweet shops and shops in the bazaar serve adulterated food, and so it is best to avoid them.

Ashraya dosha is the most difficult to avoid and Swamiji had learnt to deal with it when he was away from the math, both during his travels in India and abroad. Many have recorded such instances from his life. He probably had an inner eye regarding this.

The famous artist Charles Neilson once invited Swami Vivekananda to dinner at a Chinese restaurant in Chinatown, San Francisco. The owner of the restaurant was known to Neilson and the Chinese chef even came over and spoke personally to the guests. In order to save time, Neilson had already planned the menu with the chef. When the food arrived, however, Swami Vivekananda would not touch it and rose abruptly from the table because of ashraya dosha. One look at the Chinese chef and Swamiji could, with his inner eye, detect that he was an amoral man. Mr Neilson was extremely disappointed.

On another occasion, Swami Vivekananda was taken to a French restaurant. There he ordered fried prawns. When he returned home that evening, he began vomiting. He said, 'I am getting like my master. I shall have to live in a glass box.' He was referring to the fact that Sri Ramakrishna could not partake of food or drink touched by an impure person.

Another story is far more serious. It is no secret that Christian missionaries in the United States were strongly opposed to Swami Vivekananda and his message. Once, in Detroit, he was invited to a dinner party where some missionaries were present. The meal lasted for a long time and then coffee was served. A cup was poured for Swamiji, but he refused to drink. Much later, he told Swami Birajananda, 'I was about to drink when I saw Thakur. He said to me,

"Do not drink! It is poisoned." I obeyed him. My guru is always with me. Who can harm me?'

On the subject of jaati dosh, Swami Vivekananda offers much valuable advice. For example, he suggests, 'If you are hungry, eat puffed rice, but not kachuris or jalebis. It will be cheaper and fill your stomach as well.'

છ

Swami Vivekananda was extremely fond of lentils, especially kalai. Many a time he appealed to those who were close to him to cook kalaier dal for him. Unfortunately, his gurubhai Swami Abhedananda (Kali Prasad) could not tolerate kalai. It seems he was allergic to it, and would start sneezing if he touched it.

Even though he was fond of dal, Swami Vivekananda advised everybody to take only the watery part of the dal. He said that one must eat dal 'very cautiously, as the south Indians do, that is, one must have only the watery part ... dal is very nutritious, but difficult to digest. Dal made with tender lentils digests easily and is tasty ... boil the lentils, then mash them and mix them with water. If you strain them using a strainer made of wire, the pods will get separated. Then put turmeric, coriander, pepper, chilli pepper, etc.; you will get a very good, easily digestible dal.' This is Swami Vivekananda's special recipe.

Swami Vivekananda believed that the art of cooking and the art of inventing new ways of cooking were one and the same thing. We find him putting this theory into practice many times. Once he was residing in Bodh Gaya. A certain Bengali gentleman sent Swami Vivekananda and his friends two pitchers every morning. One was filled with the juice of the palmyra fruit, and the second with the juice of dates. Swami Vivekananda did not want to waste the latter, so he asked that the rice be boiled with the juice, instead of with water. Quite possibly, that was the first and last date-rice of the world! Those who are curious about the taste can experiment with this recipe in the winter.

Patla-da told me, 'Swami Vivekananda's eating habits were radical! Our ancient scriptures say that milk and meat should not be taken together. But Swami Vivekananda was quite reckless in this regard. He was accustomed to having them together. Again, he was opposed to excessive rice eating. He once explained to Priyanath Sinha when they were eating together in Belur: 'Singhi, one should have concentrated food. It is sheer laziness to stuff the stomach with such a huge quantity of rice and often against our better judgement. We are full from the groin to the throat, as it were, and our whole energy is exhausted in digesting the rice.' About milk, too, he said: 'If one sips milk slowly—as a child suckles milk—it gets digested easily; otherwise, it takes a long while.'

Possibly because he was talking about milk, the thought of ice cream floated into Patla-da's mind. He asked me, 'What is the Bengali for ice cream?' I replied that the English word has now been absorbed into our language, but Patla-da was not at all satisfied with my answer.

He said, 'Very clever! It was Swami Vivekananda who first used the word 'kulfi' for ice cream. There were reasons behind his choice. That very rare object—ice—was brought to the family house in Simulia when it was first introduced in Calcutta. In that pre-refrigerator age, it was customary to keep some kinds of food, especially milk and fruit, in the icebox. Vivekananda also liked putting ice into his green coconut water. Then finally, when he went abroad, he grew fond of ice cream. He was very partial to chocolate ice cream when he was in America.'

It appears that Swamiji was also fond of cream. Once, when he was in America eating with his companions, they inquired if he liked strawberries. Swami Vivekananda answered that he had never seen one. At this, his companions were highly surprised and amused. They pointed out that he had been eating strawberries every day. Vivekananda explained that the strawberries were covered with cream; even stones covered with cream would taste good!

When Swami Vivekananda was staying with the Leggett family, he would frequently excuse himself from the table during the course of the meal and go outside and smoke. They discovered that the easiest way to keep him at the dinner table was to announce, 'There will be ice cream for dessert.' Then Vivekananda would wait patiently for his ice cream like a little boy and consume it with great satisfaction.

Another humorous story is presented by Ida Ansell: 'One evening, Swamiji was talking about the different interpretations of heaven and hell in the Indian scriptures. Usually, after a lecture his devotees would take him ... [out to a] restaurant ... On this particular occasion, it was a very cold night and Swamiji shivered in his overcoat, remarking, "If this isn't hell, I don't know what is." But, in spite of the hellishly cold weather, he chose ice cream, and liked it very much. Just as it was time to leave the café, the hostess had to attend the telephone and asked us to wait. As she left, Swamiji called out after her, "Well, don't be long or when you come back, you will find we have all turned into lumps of chocolate ice cream!"'

There are comedies of errors with ice cream too. Once, after a lecture, he invited eight of his friends to have ice cream. They walked along Powell Street in San Francisco and came to a café. Swami Vivekananda ordered ice cream for everyone. Perhaps the waitress was inexperienced or perhaps she misunderstood his accent. At any rate, she brought them bottles of ice cream soda. Swami Vivekananda did not like ice cream soda and asked her if she would exchange them. So the opened bottles were returned. At this, the manager was annoyed and rebuked the waitress severely. Feeling sorry for the girl, Vivekananda called the manager and said, 'If you scold that girl, I alone will drink up all the ice cream sodas at once!'

Then again, Swami Vivekananda was once heard to have enthused over an ice cream, 'Ah, food for the gods!'

He remained fond of ice cream even when he returned to India. While staying in Mayavati in the Himalayas in the winter, he went into a deep melancholy. Pathetically, he said to Swami Birajananda, 'When I grow old, I will come here, write books and sing.' It was extremely cold outside, the lake had frozen and it was snowing. Birajananda gathered the snow and ice to make a huge ice cream. What simpler way to please Swami Vivekananda than this?

Once or twice, Swamiji even appealed to Sister Nivedita for ice cream, thereby putting her into deep trouble for by that time, Vivekananda had become a diabetic patient.

Patla-da lamented, 'Nobody reads Nivedita's letters with care, yet they are an absolute treasure! There is a reference to ice cream in her letter in May 1899 to Josephine Macleod. She says that the following day, she and S. [Sadananda] were planning to spend five rupees to get Swamiji an ice cream. She admits that it is a little too expensive, but they want to procure it "for Swamiji wants it".'

Patla-da has tried to discover whether Swami Vivekananda himself made ice cream in India. He has found no suitable references and has concluded that it may not have been practical as they lacked the equipment at Belur Math which moreover had no electricity at that time.

☙

From America, Swami Vivekananda sent Swami Ramakrishnananda reports that he had been eating plenty of cold foods, as well as milk. He said that he seldom opted for yoghurt, but that whey was plentiful. When Vivekananda extolled the taste of Western cream, he used the rare Bengali word: *mathha*. He writes, 'Mathha is used in tea, in coffee, in everything. It is not the upper crust that forms on milk, but cream

The Monk as Man

of milk. Butter is also used—and ice water—abundant ice water ... and ice creams of various kinds.'

There was a time when Swamiji's legs had swelled, and, as part of his treatment at Belur, his physician advised milk. The doctor asked him not to take water or salt but only drink a little milk. Vivekananda's disciple Sharat Chandra gives us an insight into how he was able to endure such treatment. He told Swami Vivekananda. 'It is the height of summer. You drink water four to five times an hour. It will be unbearably difficult for you to follow these instructions and have your medicine as well.'

Vivekananda replied, 'What are you saying? When I decide to take the medicine, I will resolve that morning that I will not drink water, and it shall be so. For twenty-one days then water won't be allowed to go down my throat. The body is a reflection of the mind. What the mind says, it will obey. I have to do it at Niranjan's request. I cannot ignore a gurubhai's appeal.'

ᘒ

Time was running out. But Patla-da was anxious to cover two more areas: what was Swami Vivekananda's vision for the Ramakrishna Order regarding food distribution, and what traditional Bengali recipes did he prefer? Both questions are difficult to answer.

Patla-da enlightened me on the first point: 'Swami Vivekananda decided that the principal work of the Ramakrishna Order would be to provide rice for all. Who can think of such a responsibility without being a good cook as well? We see Swamiji in his role as a cook even towards the very end of his life when he tries to please his disciples by cooking for them.'

One day, Swami Vivekananda asked his disciple Sharat Chandra, who hailed from East Bengal, to cook for him. Vivekananda told him, 'You must cook for your guru.' Sharat Chandra hastened to Balaram Basu's house with fish, vegetables and other ingredients. Swami

Vivekananda had asked him to cook 'according to the East Bengal style'. Obediently, the disciple went into the kitchen and started cooking. Swami Vivekananda was also in the house and, from time to time, went into the kitchen to supervise his disciple and also encourage him. At one point, he said, 'See that the *zul* on the fish is exactly like that in the land of the "Bangals"!' It should be noted here that he used the word zul, which is the East Bengal dialect for *jhol*, meaning 'curry'.

Let us hear the rest of the story from the disciple: 'I finished cooking rice, munger dal, *koi machher jhol*, *machher tak* and *machher shuktani*. He took his bath and prepared to eat. I told him that I had not yet finished, but like a child he implored me to serve. "Please bring whatever you have cooked. I cannot wait any more. I am famished!"'

The disciple admits that he was never a good cook, but Swamiji praised his cooking lavishly. Calcuttans laugh at machher shuktani, but Vivekananda was pleased with it and said that he had never eaten anything like it. He also emphasized that none of the dishes was as hot as the machher zul. As he was having it, he felt that it was somewhat similar to the 'Bardhamani' style of cooking.

Later Swamiji told Sharat Chandra, 'One who cannot cook well cannot be a good monk.'

Some years after this event, and just a few months before he passed away, it was Swami Vivekananda who cooked for his disciple. This was during the period when he could not drink water, on his physician's orders. Previously, he had been in the habit of taking water five to six times an hour. Sharat Chandra had brought a *rui* fish to offer to the deity. He describes what happened next: 'After the fish was cut into pieces, a portion was kept aside for the deity and Swamiji took a portion, for he wanted to cook it in the English way. Everybody was concerned that he might feel thirsty if he cooked by the fire and so they asked him not to cook. But he did not listen. Swamiji used milk, vermicelli, yoghurt and other spices to cook the fish.' After the meal, he asked if the disciple liked it. The disciple replied he had never tasted anything like it before. He had never tasted vermicelli and wanted to know what it was. Swamiji said, mischievously, 'Those are English worms. I have dried them and brought them to India!' Sharat Chandra met his guru by the Ganga at Ahiritola (in north Calcutta) a few days before his demise. Swami Vivekananda was gleefully eating *chanachur* (a mixture of chickpea and nuts with salt and spices), like a young boy, from a *shal* leaf. Swamiji said to Sharat Chandra, 'Have some. It is salted and hot.'

It was around this same time that Swami Vivekananda expressed the desire to eat phuluri. The memories of his childhood were rushing through his mind. The stove was lit, the pot was placed on top and the oil poured. Then Swami Vivekananda, who won the hearts of nations, transformed himself into a phuluri-seller, the kind he had seen as a child. He sat on his wooden stool, dropped the beaten mix into the hot oil and fried them. Then he called out to his 'customers' to come and eat. He was very, very happy.

Another time, Swami Vivekananda was travelling by train. He noticed a chickpea seller in front of the first-class compartment and told his disciple, 'It would be a good idea to eat boiled chickpea. It is nutritious.' Swami Vivekananda wanted to give the chickpea seller one rupee, but his companion had already paid the man four annas. Swami Vivekananda said, 'A four-anna coin will not help him. Please give him a rupee.' Curiously, after buying the chickpeas, Swami Vivekananda did not eat them. Possibly, he only wanted to help the chickpea seller.

But the situation abroad was different: Swami Vivekananda had just delivered a series of brilliant lectures in Los Angeles. The city was abuzz with excitement. One of the organizers came to speak to Swami Vivekananda and found him munching peanuts. He was mesmerized by the simplicity of the great man.

Swami Vivekananda was an unparalleled teacher. He treated

everybody alike—his disciples and ordinary folk. This was a characteristic of his that his disciples remarked upon time and again. And, to one and all, Swami Vivekananda stressed the importance of cooking.

Swami Birajananda has narrated a story about travelling with Swamiji. They left Mayavati and went first to Champabat, then to Diuri's bungalow. Birajananda was in charge of the cooking, and unfortunately, he had added more rice to the pot than it could hold, so the half-boiled rice began to spill over. Swami Vivekananda was hungry and called out to ask if the rice was ready. Swami Birajananda was now in a quandary: should he take out a portion of the half-cooked rice and boil it separately? At this crucial juncture, Vivekananda came in to inspect the cooking. Realizing the problem, he told his favourite disciple, 'Just do this. Pour ghee into the mixture and cover the pot with an earthen plate. It will be all right and will be tasty as well.' Swami Vivekananda was an expert cook and so the result was excellent, as he had predicted. Everybody liked the preparation.

I asked Patla-da a new question, curiously, 'Did Swamiji become impatient if he had to wait long for his food unnecessarily?'

'That was only natural,' said Patla-da. 'His parents had raised him with a lot of love and affection and yet, from the age of twenty-four he led the life of a nomad wandering about from place to place. He had no idea where his next day's food would come from. So when he became ill and when a few close people were around him, it is natural to become a little sensitive. Also, he was very particular about punctuality—not for himself alone, but for everybody.'

From distant America, he instructed Swami Ramakrishnananda in 1895, 'In the name of serving prasad, please do not make people wait for hours and then give them stiff, stale rice!'

In another letter the same year, he warns his gurubhais: 'Please see to it that on Sri Ramakrishna's birthday, the whole day is not spent in feeding people.' When Swamiji thought about how best arrangements could be made for a particular situation, he was not thinking of himself. But he could be childishly simple with those who were close to him. His disciples, gurubhais and admirers knew that Swamiji could angrily refuse food if they did not comply with his wishes.

Patla-da told me about one such incident that occurred in the life of Swami Vivekananda's disciple Gupta Maharaj (Swami Sadananda), previously the assistant station master at Hatras. Swami Sadananda writes: 'Towards the end, I cooked according to his wishes. His body was slowly crumbling. One day, he got very angry and would not step out of his room. Who could dare to go near him! I prepared food, then like a bawarchi tied a towel around my waist, and went up to him and pleaded, "Maharaj, please calm down. Please relent!" But he would not be pacified. Then I said, "Please forgive me, please forgive my error." He merely said, "Get out, shala, I will not eat!" Then I became angry and retorted, "Such bad temper! If you can behave like an army man, so can I! Shala, remain hungry! What's it to me!"'

Nothing is known about what happened afterwards. But Patla-da assured me, 'I am certain that Swami Vivekananda grew calmer and finally took some food. It is impossible that others at the math will eat leaving him hungry. If they had that sort of attitude, Ramakrishna Mission would not become what it is today.'

ଓଃ

I asked, 'Patla-da, it is true that Swami Vivekananda expressed his love for all nations by cooking hundreds of dishes from all over the world, but which dish would you place at the top of the list?'

'That is a very difficult question,' he mused, 'but quite possibly the lunch that he cooked at Belur Math for Sister Nivedita and Rabindranath's niece, Sarala Ghoshal, on a Sunday.'

The date was March 1899. A few days earlier, he had cooked a surprise supper for Sister Nivedita. The menu consisted of cold mutton, bread and butter, and coffee. Swami Vivekananda sat beside her as she ate and saw her off as she took a little ferry across the Ganga to return to Calcutta.

We can read an account of the Sunday's unforgettable lunch in a letter written by Sister Nivedita to Miss Macleod: 'It was an extraordinary accomplishment. I wish you had seen the lunch, cooked as it was by our blessed Master himself.' They sat on the first floor and Sarala Ghoshal sat facing east so that she could see the Hooghly River (Ganga).

Sister Nivedita called it a 'geographical' meal because Swami Vivekananda had gathered together dishes from all across the world. He had prepared it entirely by himself. This was the menu:

YANKEE——FISH CHOWDER

NORWEGIAN——FISH BALLS——'Taught to me by Madame Agnewasan'——explained Swamiji. 'Who is Madame A., Swami?' asked Sister Nivedita. 'What does she do? I seem to have heard her name.' 'She makes fish balls, among other things,' came the answer.
ENGLISH (ORYANKEE?)——BOARDING HOUSE HASH——Swami Vivekananda assured his guests that it was properly made and contained 'nails'—— but they found only cloves and lamented the absence of nails.
KASNMIRI——MINCE PIE À LA KASHMIR——Meat with almonds and raisins.

BENGALI RASGOLLAS AND FRUIT

I was surprised to read this remarkable menu. In how many ways did the man try to comprehend the world!

Patla-da then made a significant remark: 'If one cannot appreciate the cook Vivekananda, one cannot appreciate the countless other

Vivekanandas, for instance, the Vivekananda whose ability to love was as deep as the sea. Before his death, as we have seen, Swami Vivekananda invited Sister Nivedita and cooked for her. One of the dishes was boiled seeds of jackfruit. Let readers learn more about this from contemporary accounts. It is better not to give away all the answers at once!'

'Patla-da, did Swami Vivekananda comment on the bread?'

'Yes!' said Patla-da emphatically, 'As with luchis and kachuris, so with bread. He harboured serious doubts regarding the value of these food items. He wrote: "Bread is also poison. Do not touch it. Flour changes when you add yeast to it ... If you really have to eat bread, then toast it by all means." Swami Vivekananda had a scientist's curiosity regarding everything. So, before he died, he sent a specimen of the bread baked at Belur Math to Sister Nivedita.'

'Patla-da, what did he take for lunch on that last day, Friday, 4 July 1902?'

'*Hilsa*, of course! It was July, as you know, and the Ganga was full. If it was anything else, one would have said that the man lacked sense. Nobody knew on the morning of 4 July that the last hours of his life had arrived.'

Swami Premananda reminisced about that morning, 'The year's first hilsa from the Ganga was bought today. Swamiji joked with me because I am a Bangal. Swamiji said, "Bangals worship the first hilsa of the season, so why don't you worship this hilsa?" He ate the hilsa curry with *ambal* (a kind of sour broth) and was satisfied. He said, "I am more hungry now because of the *ekadashi* (a fast observed by Hindus)."'

Patla-da glanced at his wristwatch, remembering that he still had to shop for things to take back with him to England—amtel, *amchur* and *kasundi*. Then he had to pack.

I begged him, desperately, 'Patla-da, please be my saviour! I still have a few questions. Please provide the answers. I can then be counted as an expert on Swami Vivekananda among those who are learned in the field.'

Patla-da is a kind soul. He did not raise objections. My first question was: 'You have demonstrated how his creative talent manifested itself through cooking, but what did he actually like to eat?'

'There is no easy answer to that. There are authentic Indian foods that he liked and also dishes from other countries. He liked non-vegetarian as well as vegetarian preparations. He liked hot *chachchari*, but he also loved sweets.'

Then Patla-da added, 'Those who are convinced that Swami Vivekananda did not like vegetarian food do not know anything! He did like vegetarian food, especially khichuri. Do not forget that it was because he did not want to miss the math's evening khichuri that he climbed the locked gate at Belur to reach the dining area! He also liked vegetarian curry—some call it 'hot curry'.

'Even after Swamiji became famous, he used to visit his mother and grandmother to eat *shukto* (a bitter vegetable dish) and *mochar dalna* (a banana flower dish). Sometimes he went there only to be able to eat out of his mother's plate. Once he came so late that she only had a stalk of sajne danta left on her plate. He ate that with great relish, though his mother did tell him, affectionately, that he should have come a little sooner.'

Swami Vivekananda was fond of *pnui chachchari* (a vegetable preparation with Indian spinach). Whenever he could, he used to join Jogin Ma at Bagh Bazar to taste her preparation of this chachchari with rice. Even when Jogin Ma was in Kashi (Benares), he used to visit Bagh Bazar. And when he celebrated his birthday according to the lunar calendar, he used to request for payesh.

Patla-da was a fountain of knowledge. He continued, 'One of the things that he was most fond of was *koi machh*. Do you know the joke that ran in the family of the Duttas of Simulia regarding koi? According to them, there are two kinds: one they referred to as '*Sikh koi*', the other as *'Gurkha koi'*. The former is long and thin and the latter is short and fat. When Swami Vivekananda was going abroad for the first time, he left from Bombay. He wanted to taste koi for the last time before he left, but it was difficult to get it in Bombay. So Kalipada Ghosh sent someone by train to a distant city to procure koi for Swami Vivekananda. After much search, this emissary was successful and Kalipada Ghosh had the rare honour of feeding Swami Vivekananda koi.

'Do you know that Swami Vivekananda sometimes fixed the menu for those who wanted to cook for him? Kusumkumari Debi said that he chose kalaier dal and koi machher *jhal*. One of those who had cooked for Swami Vivekananda said, "I always think of Naren whenever I cook prawns and Indian spinach." But one of his favourite combinations— hilsa and pnui shak—is terrific, or should I say, deadly! An American or German scholar could perhaps have written a thesis on it and then you would have pored over their reading, fond as you are of what foreign sahibs write!'

For Swami Vivekananda, hilsa was as necessary to Indian spinach as a lock is to a key, as a cup is to a plate, or as Shiva is to Parvati. Just as when one pulls hard on someone's ear, the whole head bends, similarly, if there was hilsa, Swami Vivekananda would automatically look for Indian spinach!

Let us hear what Manmathanath Gangopadhyay, a government official from Allahabad, has to say on this: 'Swamiji was going to Goalanda by steamer. In a boat, a few fishermen could be seen hauling a large quantity of hilsa, when Swamiji said, "I would like to eat fried hilsa." The chief fisherman understood that Swamiji wanted the entire steamer crew to eat fried hilsa as well. They said the price of a fish was an anna. Three or four would have been sufficient, but Swamiji bought a rupee worth of hilsa. So, sixteen large hilsas were bought; the fishermen offered a few free. The steamer moved on, then when it stopped, Swamiji said, "It would have been perfect if we had Indian spinach and warm rice."The village was close by. Rice was bought at a shop but there was no market, so they could not buy spinach. Then a gentleman said, "Come, I can give you spinach. I have it in my garden. But, only on one condition: I must see Swamiji first!"'

Patla-da paused for a moment, then said, 'In the final analysis, shukto with mochar dalna versus hilsa and Indian spinach, both make it to the final round. Ice cream does not go beyond the semi-final round because, after Swami Vivekananda developed diabetes, he could no longer have it.'

Patla-da wanted to know my opinion. I said, 'Hilsa and Indian spinach will win the gold medal, for Swami Vivekananda was so pleased to have them on his way to Goalanda that he offered mantra diksha to the owner of the spinach that same day! The disciple later said, "He wanted to have fish and spinach purely in order to bless me."'

Patla-da smiled. 'Yes, for that Indian spinach, he gave initiation! On the strength of this story alone, this dish should win the gold medal. But you forget what he once said after eating shukto and mochar dalna. He said, "In order to be able to eat these two things, one could be born again!" Therefore, I propose that shukto and mochar dalna combination be given the gold medal, for great men do not talk lightly about rebirth!'

The time had now come for us to take leave of each other. I have learnt so much from him. But, before leaving, he did spring one more surprise on me: 'We have not given any consideration to what was probably the most valuable and dearest item of all. It is not shukto–mocha, it is not koi, it is not spinach, it is not ice cream. This monk, Vivekananda, always carried a small bottle with him and, from time to time, sipped from it. He carried it everywhere. He said that he did not know in advance when he would need it, so he kept it with him always. "Before thousands of people, before the onslaught of civilization, before the possibility of being trampled to death by lacs and lacs of men and women, I have remained calm—only a few drops calmed me," he said.'

'What was it?' I asked eagerly, looking at Patla-da.

'Can't you guess? It was Ganga water! The water of the Ganga stored in a small bottle was always with Swamiji. It gave him the much needed strength.'

'End your piece with this,' concluded Patla-da. He put his treasure of a notebook back into his pocket and said, 'I have a few more things to write down in this notebook. If you can write well, if you can do justice to Vivekananda the cook, the next time I come to Calcutta, I will hand this over to you!'

So saying, he got into the waiting car and sped in the direction of the Calcutta airport.

CHAPTER THREE

The Monk Who Loved Tea

Tea versus coffee! It is like Rabindranath Tagore versus Haridas Pal, or William Shakespeare versus Tom, Dick, Harry. Can they be compared? Impossible! But if you can market well and raise an uproar, everything is possible in the twenty-first century. For instance, in India in recent times we have replaced our own sweetened yoghurt with imported ice cream. In this land of pleasure, how could Swami Vivekananda's own countrymen be prosaic enough to do such a thing! A commission should be set up to inquire into this.

On the subject of tea, I consulted Patla-da, himself a lifelong tea lover. He told me, 'Englishmen had predicted long before that the inferior will always drive out the superior from the market. This is Gresham's law. It is inevitable, he said. Gresham first said this about money, but the law seems to be true for every sphere of life.'

I am sure you remember that my dear friend Patla-da was once a pupil at the Howrah Vivekananda Institution. And that he was inclined, at times, to be a little overcurious and overenthusiastic about food. At school, Patla-da usually took a leading part in organizing various school programmes and frequently ate more than his share. This had led to a little bad reputation among the students.

I should have suffered the same fate, but Patla-da used to say to me, 'You are a Mukherji Brahmin. So overeating is your birthright!

But even though you are greedy, you lack the guts, so you never dare to pick up an extra packet of prasad in the school ceremonies. So your greed remains unsatisfied. I, on the other hand, am a Kshatriya and can dare to do what my heart desires. Though I admit it leads to trouble sometimes.'

Patla-da and I became close friends during our student days and have maintained it ever since. From school itself Patla-da would investigate into the life of Swami Vivekananda and concluded that he was the only man in the world who was so eager to feed the poor and the starving. Patla-da was of the opinion that Swami Vivekananda's capacity for love and his urge to feed all cannot be explained away merely by his writings on karma yoga, jnana yoga and bhakti yoga. 'Those who are selfish,' he declared, 'stuff themselves from the throat to the groin without a thought for others.'

I told him that I found our Bengali expression 'kanthha theke kunchki' (literally, from the throat to the groin) a trifle harsh. Patla-da immediately retorted that the expression had been coined by Vivekananda himself.

As you know, I was fascinated by all the things Patla-da had to say and gave him a notebook as a present to record the same. For many years, he has been faithfully collecting material on Swami Vivekananda in that notebook, particularly on the subject of eating and its extremes: gluttony and starvation.

If Patla-da had known then that a Bengali would win the Nobel Prize for economics in 1998 for his work on starvation and malnourishment in India since the 1950s, he would have sent his notebook to Amartya Sen. Both Amartya Sen and Patla-da live abroad. In Patla-da's case, this has given him access to some exclusive facts on Vivekananda from sources in the United Kingdom, Europe and America, as well as our Indian subcontinent. Whenever he comes to Calcutta for a visit, he shares his latest findings with me.

Of late, it has come to his attention that monks of the Ramakrishna Mission offer tea liberally to their guests. Patla-da attaches much importance to tea and has urged me to give it serious attention—'tea and our attachment to it'. It is a fine proposal. Prominent Bengalis of the nineteenth and twentieth centuries were fascinated by tea. Even those who, by virtue of their scientific bent of mind, were compelled to ask the question, 'What is the difference between drinking tea and drinking poison?' drank generous tea in generous quantities as they discussed the matter!

Tea was a source of inspiration for such great luminaries as Rabindranath Tagore and Swami Vivekananda, but their tastes were unique and reflected their individual personalities. *Mahakavi* Tagore exhibited his love for all nations through his fondness for Chinese tea, Japanese tea and Indian tea. And we are supremely grateful to Swami Vivekananda for saving tea from the stigma of being an addictive beverage. For the monks of the Ramakrishna Order seeking liberation, tea is not a forbidden drink. Though the poet and dramatist Girish Chandra Ghosh, who was a great admirer of Ramakrishna, had, without concealing his weakness for alcohol, declared that there were indeed those who got drunk on tea. Swami Vivekananda's philosopher brother Mahendranath too admitted jokingly that he belonged to that group.

Swami Saradananda, the writer of *Sri Sri Ramakrishna Lilaprasanga* (The Divine Play of Sri Ramakrishna), was naturally very fond of tea. It is not possible to write so lucidly on such a difficult subject without a partiality for tea!

Vivekananda's brother Mahendranath once asked Saradananda, 'Who taught you to be a tea addict?'

'Your brother, of course!' pat came the reply. 'Swami Vivekananda introduced the practice of drinking tea, which was common in your family, into the monastery at Baranagore. So we all turned into tea addicts! Your family deals with narcotics, do you understand?'

Mahendranath was born in 1869. We realize from his memoirs that tea has become a part of Bengali life only recently. He writes: 'We heard the term *'cha'* in our childhood but never knew what it was—solid or liquid! One of our aunts who had just given birth was given tea for medicinal purposes. A black kettle was brought; some chopped leaves and hot water was put into it, then boiled together; then the liquid was poured into a bowl. Milk and sugar was added and she drank the concoction.' Mahendranath goes on to say that in those days tea did not grow in India at all; it came from China.

Patla-da commented, 'The last statement is not accurate, for there is evidence that Prince Dwarakanath Tagore and some other Bengali businessmen were associated with the Assam Company. This world-renowned tea company was established in 1820 and tea worth three million English pounds was sent to Mincing Lane in London to be sold at an auction in 1864. Swami Vivekananda was only one year old then.

What Mahendranath says may be partly true, however. Tea was food for the gods, reserved only for the English folk, not ordinary Indians. Each season, the entire crop would be sent directly to wholesale dealers in Mincing Lane.

Patla-da now sweetened his tale of tea a little more: 'Mahendranath observed that his elder brother when still young had become a tea addict. He wrote, "Bar-da [elder brother] once bought a kettle for five annas from an Anglo-Indian auction house. The cover was sooty. But, O my God, as I started to polish it, I soon realized that the inside was made of pure silver."'

Tea continued to play a significant role in Narendranath's life even after the death of his father, when the family suffered serious financial setbacks.

Once, Narendranath came with his friend Kali (later Swami Abhedananda) to stay at the house at Ramtanu Basu Lane. The poverty-stricken family had nothing to offer to the guest. It was very cold.

During the night, the hunger and the cold made Kali miserable. Seeing his plight Narendranath produced a kettle from somewhere. Then he made tea for his guest thereby averting a disaster. It is worth noting here that there was neither LPG nor electricity in Calcutta in those days, so it was not easy to make tea at that hour of the night.

Another detail I learnt from Patla-da: Swami Saradananda once explained the reason behind the widespread drinking of tea at the Ramakrishna Mission. He said, 'Do you know why we drink tea even during the fast on Shivaratri? Then listen: we drank tea even when we were mourning for Sri Ramakrishna on the day of his demise (16 August 1886). Nobody could eat anything in grief. Who would light the stove and cook at such a time? But after a while, tea was prepared in a kettle and we all gulped it down. If we could have had tea on that day of intense grief, why can't we have it on an ordinary Shivaratri?'

Patla-da continued: 'One of Swami Vivekananda's gurubhais returned from Bodh Gaya so enamoured of tea that he experimented with it during *tarpan* (the custom of offering water to the deities in honour of the dead). Swami Vivekananda and Swami Shivananda sat side by side in Baranagore and Shivananda chanted in Sanskrit *anena chayena* (by the tea). Inevitably, the question was raised whether the word 'cha' was of masculine or feminine gender. If it were feminine, the monk should have said *anaya chayaya*!'

At Baranagore, whether they had rice to eat or not, the monks drank gallons of tea. They always had some tea leaves with them, and along with that a few round cups of porcelain. Cups did not have handles in those days.

One gurubhai went to Assam and discovered new merits in tea. He reported: 'There are people who mix tea with rice, just as we mix curry.'

Another gurubhai undertook an adventurous journey to Tibet. He found that Tibetans drank tea in the following manner: 'They put a lump of tea in the water, then add dried, powdered meat, then barley. When it boils, they add butter.' He noticed that Tibetans loved tea and always kept a samovar of warm tea by their side. He further commented that a rich Tibetan would always drink tea.

The tale of tea does not end here. Let us take a look at the year 1896. Swami Vivekananda meets his brother Mahendranath in London. Mahendranath has come to England to study law. Fascinated with the ritual of tea drinking among the English, Mahendranath provides many detailed descriptions of the same. He writes that Swami Vivekananda used to often partake of afternoon tea at four o'clock at the invitation of some prominent Englishman or other.

Mahendranath, Goodwin, Fox and Saradananda once took tea together at 4.30 in the afternoon. He gives a lengthy description of this very British tradition as seen through the eyes of an incredulous Indian: 'An old housekeeper came in with the teapot, a small jug of milk, thin pieces of buttered bread resembling pasteboard, sugar lumps and hot water in a large jug. They offer warm water to those who drink weak tea. The English generally drink weak tea, unlike the Bengalis. Their sailors take strong tea, which is why strong tea is referred to as sailors' tea. Mr Goodwin took up the responsibility of pouring the tea for all of us. Everybody took two slices of bread and tea. The English do not warm their milk. I took some warm milk, but it was so salty that I found the tea difficult to drink. They feed their cows too much of salt. Because they do not warm the milk, the cream that forms on the surface of the milk in Bengal does not happen in England. That is why there is no word for it in English! The sugar they use is beet sugar. It measures one square inch, and three such make a cube. It is called "lump sugar". One has to use a delicate pair of tongs made of German silver or some other white metal to pick up the "lump sugar". One can have as many as one likes. But you cannot use your fingers.'

One afternoon in London, Swami Vivekananda returned to the

apartment at four o'clock and, instead of pouring milk into his tea, put lemon in it. He put two large slices of lemon in a bowl reserved for Japanese tea, then poured the tea, and added lumps of sugar to it. As he slowly sipped the tea, he said, 'I no longer like tea, and one must not add milk to it for it is bad for the stomach. In America, people prefer tea with lemon. That is good!'

On another occasion, Swami Vivekananda said, 'Americans are excessive in everything. They drink tea with lemon and even put ice in it! In the summer, they like iced tea. They will drink only a little, but pour themselves a lot. Their practices are really arbitrary!'

We can sense Mahendranath's wide-eyed fascination in his description of Miss Müller engaged in making tea: 'Miss Müller poured hot water into a Japanese bowl and took out a box-shaped tea strainer with a rattle attached to it. She opened the box and put green tea, or Japanese tea, into it. Then she closed it by pressing the sides together. It was made of silver. Having done this, she dropped the box into the hot water and proceeded to shake it from time to time. A little while later, the water in the bowl became slightly reddish. She added milk and sugar and then drank it.'

For those who cannot conceive of tea without sugar, our chronicler Mahendranath offers us some interesting insights into the prevailing lifestyle in London in the 1890s: 'India's sugar, white or black, is powdered. One does not get *michhri* in London. English sugar is reddish; it is called brown sugar. White sugar is also available, but not much. There is yet another kind of sugar: it is thick at the top and thin at the bottom, conical in fact. It is called loaf sugar. This particular variety is used a great deal. It is generally stored in lumps or broken into smaller pieces for fear that it will absorb too much water.'

Patla-da inquired, 'Were you acquainted with the renowned scholar Shibakali Bhattacharya, the author of *Chiranjib Banousadhi*?'

'Did I know him?' I replied. 'Of course! He had great affection for me. He had gathered all kinds of material regarding ancient Indian customs and informed me about them. If he had only given the material to the right person, it would have caused a sensation throughout the world by now. According to Shibakali, there are five common words for tea in Sanskrit. This proves that our nation could not have become intoxicated by drinking Chinese tea alone! I have learnt these names by heart in case any entrepreneur should ask for my advice before bringing out a new brand of tea. They are: *shleshwari*, *girivit*, *shyamaparni*, *atandri* and *kamalarasa*. He had also discovered one more word for tea—*fant.*'

Hearing this, Patla-da got very excited. 'Fant! Then the name of the beverage—'fanta'—has Eastern origins!'

Shibakali defined fant as follows: 'If you soak something in hot water, keep it covered for some time, and strain it while still hot, the warm liquid that you get is fant. This is the way the people in the mountains have always enjoyed tea. It had no relation to either milk or sugar.'

'Then how did we get into the habit of mixing milk and sugar with our tea? Did we learn it from the English?'

Patla-da answered, 'As a matter of fact, the English are exceedingly proud of their tea. They act as if Brooke Bond and Lipton saved India by teaching the Indians how to drink tea. True, the oldest tea shop in London dates from 1659, but our Indian tradition of tea drinking goes back much further.'

After a pause he added, 'Those of us who are from Howrah can feel proud as well. The English first planted tea in the gardens of Shibpur in Howrah. Mr Kydd planted tea there thirty years after the Battle of Plassey (1757).'

'But Patla-da,' I protested, 'Kydd Sahib himself said that Howrah was not fit for growing tea.'

Patla-da: 'How time passes! Now tea is grown even in Kharagpur (West Bengal), mainly through the efforts of the Indian Institute of Technology there. I have tasted it. It is not bad.'

I contributed another detail to the conversation: 'Shibakali used to say that tea leaves should not be soaked in hot water for more than three to five minutes. If you remove them by this time, your tea will not absorb too much tannin. But if you boil the leaves or soak them for too long, you will get double the amount of tannin in your fant.'

Then I directed our attention to another Sanskrit word for tea: atandri. It derives from the root 'tandra', meaning sleep. Thus, atandri means 'lack of sleep'—which can lead one to suppose that this particular variety of tea could keep one awake!

However Patla-da corrected my theory: 'That applies to coffee. Those who have trouble sleeping are afraid to drink coffee, especially at night. Your theory does not apply to atandri tea. In this case, the word merely signifies that if you feel sleepy at the wrong time, it can be countered by drinking this tea. The tea itself will not harm you.'

So that is the significance of atandri tea, but what of shyamaparni tea? 'Parna' means leaf, and 'shyama' probably refers to the colour of the leaf, a dark green.

Patla-da clarified on this, 'Shyama is not exactly green and yet it is not black either. Shyama is a very confusing term. If you consult the dictionary, you will see that shyama may also mean fair or bright.'

Next we came to fant. Patla-da liked this word enormously. He commented, in his inimitable way, 'Not only writers, but readers may also benefit if a thousand such Sanskrit words from ancient times could be soaked in warm water, like dried tea leaves, and kept ready for our use!'

We had wandered far from our main subject and Patla-da was eager to return to Swami Vivekananda. 'A great man, he devoted much of his time thinking about the trials and tribulations of ordinary people. He himself was undeniably a tea addict, and realized that this beverage could bring genuine delight to his countrymen. One must remember that, in those days, the pundits were opposed to tea. They were of the opinion that addiction to tea was harmful for one's health. Vivekananda, a true rebel, trod on the opposite path! He banned narcotics, but introduced tea into the monastery. Read the Vedas and the Upanishads, he said, and drink tea—no harm in it! But the Bally municipality authorities misbehaved with the monks precisely because of this custom. Their then chairman increased the taxes on the math on the grounds that it was Narendranath Dutta's private garden house with tea being frequently served there.'

'Really?' I asked in amazement.

'Yes, really,' he affirmed. 'But Swami Vivekananda was not someone to tolerate injustice lightly. He sued the Bally municipality in the Chinsurah Zilla District Court. In the lawsuit, witnesses were cross-examined and they did not deny that they had taken tea at Belur Math. Fortunately, a progressive-minded British magistrate had been assigned the case. He understood the problem. On the court's orders, he himself came riding to the math on a horse to investigate the matter. The result? The charges were dismissed.'

'Did the magistrate himself drink tea at the math?'

'That I cannot say. Perhaps you can find that out from searching the records kept at the math. Bear this in mind, however, that in those days, although there were plenty of shops selling kachuris and jalebis, there was not a single tea shop. There was neither the 'double half', nor the clay pots. Swami Vivekananda was so far-sighted! He prophesied that there would come a time when there would be shops in every neighbourhood selling chops and cutlets. And of course, tea would come immediately after the snacks. More need not be said on the matter. In literature and art, this is called self-restraint—implying the meaning rather than saying it.'

Patla-da went on, 'Not only did Swamiji defend the practice of tea drinking in court, he also introduced the subject into his writings from time to time. His observations prove that he had studied it in some detail. In *Paribrajak* (Traveller), for example, he writes: "Tea is not hugely popular in any country other than England and Russia ... In Russia, people consume vast quantities of tea. Theirs is an extremely cold climate and China is close by. Chinese tea is excellent, and most of it goes to Russia. The Russian way of drinking tea is similar to that of the Chinese: they do not add milk to it. They believe that if you add milk to tea or coffee, the drink becomes as harmful as poison. The real tea-drinking races—the Chinese, the Japanese, the Russians, the people of the Middle East—drink tea without milk. Only in Russia they add a slice of lemon and a lump of sugar to the tea."

'Oh, then there are a few lines which will break your heart,' Patla-da warned me. 'Swami Vivekananda wrote, "The poor keep a lump of sugar in their mouths and then drink the tea. When one person has finished, he gives the sugar to the next person, who repeats the process."'

Patla-da now raised another point: 'There is no dearth of tea drinkers who drink it right. Some of them may be eminent people, but how many could prepare their own tea? Rabindranath Tagore, to name one, was a passionate tea drinker, but I have yet to come across any account of him going into the kitchen to make tea! There is no doubt that Swami Vivekananda could and did make tea on many occasions. One who could cook huge pots of khichuri or palanna would naturally have no trouble making tea! There are innumerable references to this—he even made tea in the middle of the night. But a teacher of men does not only learn himself, he also encourages others.'

I reflected, 'Sharadindu Bandopadhyay did the same thing in Poona. He prepared shyamaparni tea and offered me a cup. Afterwards, he invited me to prepare the tea. I could not honestly claim that I had never made tea before because I had often prepared it for guests of our headmaster, Sudhanshushekhar Bhattacharya, or Handu-da, who was deeply enamoured of Swami Vivekananda. But on that occasion in

Poona, it was not possible to get full marks. For one, I did not know how to handle a heater. Alas, had LPG been available, I might have scored a hundred per cent!'

Patla-da marvelled, 'The eminent writer Sharadindu asked an obscure writer like yourself to make tea! This only proves how affectionate and kind he was. But Swami Vivekananda was like a missionary in this respect. He even convinced the great freedom fighter Bal Gangadhar Tilak to make tea at Belur Math. Tilak came to Belur and prepared Mughlai tea for everybody! He had brought nutmeg, mace, cardamom, cloves and saffron with him. He boiled these things together, added the tea leaves, milk and sugar, and made tea.'

'That is quite shocking—Tilak, the chaiwallah of Belur! Tell me, Patla-da, what is this Mughlai tea? Did the Mughal Emperor Akbar drink tea? I do not know of any reference to tea in *Ain-i-Akbari*. I thought that tea, coffee, cocoa and chilli peppers were introduced in this country in the time of Akbar's grandson, Shah Jahan. Before that, our taste buds had been woefully deprived. It was not until the seventeenth century that Mr Oddington had tea with the baniyas of Surat and convinced them of its merit. At that time, sugar was not added, but there were spices and a few drops of lemon juice.'

Patla-da agreed, 'There may be some stray references to tea in the annals of those times, but the twentieth century is truly the era of tea! That is when Bengalis became obsessed with this beverage. They refused to listen to Acharya Prafulla Chandra Roy who warned them against it. Tea was served everywhere—in clay cups, in porcelain cups, in silverware, in paper cups, in plastic containers. I have even heard that tea lovers sometimes experimented with drinking tea out of bel shells.'

After a significant pause, Patla-da continued, 'A lot of experts hold tea responsible for the regular indigestion that Bengalis suffer from. Nobody in the world would dream of drinking tea on an empty stomach, except a Bengali! Still, I believe tea has helped us, as a nation.

At least, our tea drinkers outnumber those who consume alcohol. One may even go so far as to claim that the spread of alcoholism has been arrested in this country because of tea.'

'The twentieth century is over,' I reminded him. 'This is the twenty-first century and the reign of tea in Calcutta. Long may it live!'

Patla-da's reply was lukewarm. 'I am returning to Calcutta after a long time, but I must say that the future of tea does not look too bright, my friend. The venerable old tea shops of our city look more drab than ever before and I can no longer connect tea with our memories of youth. Coffee has made a sparkling entry.'

I empathized with my friend. 'Earlier coffee lovers used to frequent only two coffee houses—Albert Hall [now Calcutta Coffee House] or the one at Chitta Ranjan Avenue. But how many people went there for coffee? Most Bengalis went for a warm cup of tea. True Bengalis never allowed coffee into their homes, despite the best efforts of the Coffee Board. But, now, I can see that times are bad for tea. Coffee is getting widespread. One finds it everywhere, on every street and in every shop. There are cafés mushrooming all across Calcutta, and are visited by the young and the old alike who are prepared to pay double or even triple the price of tea. The true Bengali tea lover has been routed out by coffee.'

Patla-da was indignant: 'Bengalis have tea in their blood and nobody can do anything about it! Bengalis will never forget that coffee smells like burnt shal leaf, while Darjeeling tea tastes like champagne. The two are completely different! We are living with our eyes shut. Sweetened yoghurt has been replaced by ice cream at weddings. Previously, this was unimaginable! Now yoghurt has no prestige any more. Plastic cups have supplanted clay cups. The list goes on. You cannot understand the pain of rejection and being supplanted by other foods. The coffee lobbyists have been trying to foist their product onto us for the past three hundred years. They started with France. At first, King Louise

XIV, a true connoisseur of food, was not partial to the flavour of coffee. Then it was promoted with such rigour that the French began to declare that it represented their nation. The writer Pascal says, "What tea is to the English, beer is to the Germans, chocolate is to the Spaniards, opium is to the Turks, coffee is to the French!" He was a coffee missionary indeed! It is said that coffee was first served at a certain festival in Paris. Seeing its success, Pascal opened a coffee shop. Failing to attract customers however, he sent coffee vendors around the city. Later, doctors got so enamoured of coffee that they began to recommend it to their patients.'

My friend felt disappointed that nobody was trying to promote tea in Calcutta. This is obvious when you compare the number of tea shops in the city with the rapidly growing number of coffee shops. He concluded, 'If we want tea to survive, we have to emulate the French, as Swami Vivekananda did. There is a tea salon called Marriage Frères near Metro Saint Paul where one can select from three hundred different kinds of tea from twenty nations. There are also two hundred different varieties of teapots, and the tea is served by beautiful French waitresses. In our city, we have no shortage of anything—tea, teapots, shops or beautiful women. But, sadly, people lack the imagination or the enterprise. We are so close to Darjeeling, yet we have turned this city of Vivekananda into a Waterloo for tea!'

I said, 'At one time, you could get ten different kinds of tea at Bandel railway station. The experts knew which vendor sold which.'

'Calcutta has many woes. Earthenware pots are not being used to promote tea. Instead, they are being used to decorate the Durga Puja pandals!' replied Patla-da.

'Then what can we do, my friend?'

'I hope that my visits to Calcutta end before tea loses out to coffee. The only way to prevent this is to fight a duel with coffee! We have to take to the streets! We have to sit on strike in front of coffee shops, if necessary. We must tell everybody that the brightest sons and daughters of our soil never promoted coffee. They seldom stepped into coffee houses. Swami Vivekananda never drank coffee in Paris after sunset for fear that he would not be able to sleep.'

I busied myself noting down Patla-da's points. He added a final spirited challenge: 'Our Bengaliness lies in those old faded teacups; we will not surrender them. We demand tea! Coffee can go to hell! Long live Swami Vivekananda's tea!'

Patla-da rose from his seat. After all, he is an NRI. So his next move before leaving the city was to take photographs of the disappearing tea shops of Calcutta.

GENEALOGICAL TABLE 1

Duttas of Dariatona

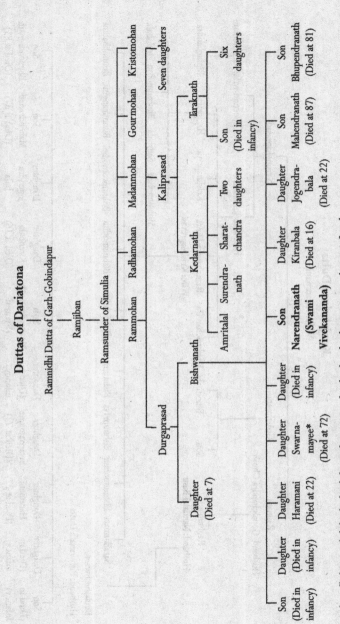

A genealogical chart of the Dutta family of Dariatona.

*Also called Swarnabala by the family, but in documents related to her the above-mentioned name is found

GENEALOGICAL TABLE 2

Kunjabehari Dutta

A genealogical chart of the Kunjabehari Dutta family.

A letter dated 17 September 1898 from a desperate Swami Vivekananda to the Maharaja of Khetri seeking financial help.

Swami Vivekananda's mother, Bhubaneshwari Dasi. This photograph was taken a few years after Swamiji's demise.

Swami Vivekananda was born in this house (3, Gourmohan Mukherjee Street, Calcutta), in 1863. Once a splendid place, this photograph shows its ruins. It was taken in 1966 by the *Times of India* photographer, Mona Chowdhury, which caught the attention of Prime Minister Indira Gandhi who wanted the house restored as a place of pilgrimage. This work was completed in 2000.

Swami Vivekananda's brother,
Mahendranath Dutta (1868–1956),
known affectionately as Mahim.

Swami Vivekananda's elder sister
Swarnamayee.

Youngest brother
Dr Bhupendranath Dutta (1880–1961),
took part in the freedom movement
and was forced to flee India after
a stint in jail.

Swami Vivekananda's
benefactor and admirer
H.H. Maharaja Ajit Singh
of Khetri.

Beloved friend and gurubhai Swami Brahmananda.
Known as Raja Maharaj (1863–1922), he became the first
president of the Ramakrishna Math and Mission.

Swami Saradananda (1865–1927), who was very
close to Swami Vivekananda. Affectionately called 'Junior Sahib',
while Swamiji was referred to as 'Senior Sahib', Saradananda is
the author of *Sri Ramakrishna Leela Prasanga*.

Researchers maintain that this is the first of the 106 available photos of Swami Vivekananda.1836, Cossipore garden house, Calcutta.

This historic group photograph was taken on 16 August 1886 following Sri Ramakrishna's *mahasamadhi*. Dr Mahendralal Sarkar came to Cossipore garden house at ten in the morning, pronounced Sri Ramakrishna dead and took out ten rupees for a photograph by Bengal Photographers Studio. Narendranath is standing in the front row, behind Sri Ramakrishna's cot.

A studio portrait of Sri Ramakrishna
Paramahansa, taken on 10 December 1881.

Sri Ramakrishna's consort, Sarada Debi,
now known as Sri Ma.

A portrait of Swami Vivekananda's friend and admirer
Josephine MacLeod by Marie Robiquet.

Sara Bull (Mrs Ole Bull). Swami Vivekananda called her 'dhira mata',
the calm and quiet mother. When Swamiji was ill in America, he drew
up a will making her the beneficiary.

Sister Nivedita (Margaret Noble), Swami Vivekananda's stormy
disciple who later took part in India's struggle for freedom.
Rabindranath Tagore called her the 'mother of the people'.

Swami Vivekananda in Madras in February 1897—photograph by
T.G. Appavan Mudaliar from Madras.

Swamiji's portrait photographed by Thomas Harrison, at his studio in Central Music Hall, Chicago. Seven such 'Chicago style' cabinet card photographs —known as the Harrison series—were taken in September 1893 during the World's Parliament of Religions. Coloured posters based on this photograph were printed by a lithographic company and displayed all over Chicago.

One of the seven Vivekananda photographs
that were taken at Bushnel Studio,
San Francisco, 1900.

The ailing Swamiji in Shillong.

Possibly the last photograph of Swami Vivekananda.
It was taken in Shillong.

The Ramakrishna temple at Belur Math.

CHAPTER FOUR

Swamiji's Health

We have an expression in Sanskrit—*shariram byadhimandiram*—which means 'the body is the temple of diseases'. It comes to my mind every time I seek further information about Swami Vivekananda's health. My own father died young. And that is why I am still distressed by the early deaths of male elders and their impact on middle-class households. Perhaps that is the reason why the whole question of Swamiji's health became a subject of my enquiry.

Narendranath's father, Bishwanath Dutta, died in 1884 at the age of fifty-two. According to the Calcutta Corporation death register, he died of diabetes. Swami Gambhirananda's account however differs in this respect. He says that Narendranath went to Baranagore in the afternoon of Monday, 23 February. He enjoyed himself there, sang and chatted with his friends until eleven o'clock at night and then went to take rest. His friend Hemali came to inform him at two in the morning that his father had died. Gambhirananda reports that Bishwanath had a weak heart. Almost a month before his death, he had suffered from a heart attack. On the day he died, he complained of chest pains to his wife. After dinner, an ointment was massaged onto his chest. He then smoked a hookah and started reading. Then at nine o'clock the vomiting started, and he breathed his last an hour later. Mahendranath

Dutta's memoirs reveal that Narendranath went directly to the Nimtala burning ghat from Baranagore. The municipal death register bears his signature in English.

In Swami Vivekananda's paternal line, there is no real evidence of a long life. In addition, a number of his brothers and sisters died in infancy or as children. However, from this we cannot conclude that there was a hereditary tendency towards early death in the Dutta family. Vivekananda's sister, Swarnamayee, lived to be seventy-two, Mahendranath lived to be eighty-seven and Bhupendranath, eighty-one. For all her suffering, Bhubaneshwari lived to the age of seventy-two, when she succumbed to meningitis, and her mother lived to be ninety. Bhupendranath writes that his 'mother and grandmother were very strong and hardy.'

If we had to draw up a chart, we would have to say that Vivekananda was genetically predisposed towards diabetes and heart problems, but the constitution of his family members was, on the whole, sound. In Swamiji's case, his health problems were aggravated because of the great demands that he placed on his body. We already know a vast deal about his spiritual accomplishments. Now I would like to draw your attention to how much he had to endure physically and in spite of which he managed to achieve such extraordinary things.

First, let us examine Swami Vivekananda's appearance—how tall he was, his weight, his complexion, the shape of his feet and so forth. Indians rarely offer substantive information of this kind. At best, the personality or appearance of a great figure must be gleaned from a few vague remarks. And so it is with Swami Vivekananda.

Pramathanath Basu tells us that Vivekananda was well built, and his features had the grace of a lion. That is all. The description offered by Manmathanath Gangopadhyay yields some more details. He puts Swami Vivekananda's height at 5 feet 9 inches. Then he goes on, somewhat fancifully, 'He was well built with a wide chest, his hands and feet were very soft ... he had wide bones, his wrist was wide ... The arms were long and touched his knees.'

From other Indian sources, we learn that Swami Vivekananda's feet were thin, long and narrow. His fingers were, similarly, slender, elongated and pointed. His face was round and full. His lips were thin and occasionally firm. His long nose was similar to a lion's. His hands were shapely. Swami Trigunatitananda says they 'were more beautiful than those of a woman'. The back of his head was flat and he had a high forehead.

This is perhaps the sum total of the description of Swami Vivekananda offered by his countrymen. So we need to turn to Romain Rolland and other Western writers for greater accuracy and detail. Were it not for them, we would have lost some vital information.

Josephine Macleod writes of 'the fiery missionary whose physique was like a wrestler's and whose eyes were deep black'.

Romain Rolland is more precise: 'His athletic form was the opposite of the fragile and tender, yet wiry, body of Sri Ramakrishna. He was tall (five feet eight and a half inches), square-shouldered, broad-chested, stout, rather heavily built; his arms were muscular and trained for all kinds of sports. He had an olive complexion, a full face, a vast forehead, a strong jaw, and a pair of magnificent eyes—large, dark, with heavy lids, and beautifully shaped like a lotus leaf.'

In a footnote, he adds that the line of his jaw was more similar to those of the Tartars than the Hindus.

Rolland continues, 'He had a beautiful voice (so Miss Josephine Macleod told me), like a violoncello, grave and even, whose reverberations filled both hall and hearts. Once he had enraptured his audience, he could make it sink to an intense "piano", piercing the soul of his listeners.'

The French singer Emma Calvé, who knew him, described his voice as 'an admirable baritone, having the vibrations of a Chinese gong'.

According to Rolland, Swami Vivekananda weighed about 170 pounds. It is possible that his weight fluctuated, for one American journalist has estimated it to be around 225 pounds. We know that sometimes Vivekananda himself chose to lose weight and reports indicate that he was able to gain and lose pounds easily.

The first time Swamiji was in the United States, he wrote to Mary Hale from Thousand Island Park about dieting. The letter is dated 22 June 1895: 'I am living mostly on nuts and fruit and milk, and find it nice and healthy. I hope to lose 30 to 40 lbs this summer. That will be right for my size. I am afraid I have forgotten Mrs Adams's walking lessons. I will have to renew them when she comes to New York again.'

The first time Swami Vivekananda went to America, he was examined by Dr Edgar C. Beall of the Phrenological Society of America and his statistics were published in the *Phrenological Journal of New York*. It reports: 'Swami Vivekananda is, in many respects, an excellent specimen of his race. He is 5 feet 8½ inches in height, and weighs 170 pounds. His head measures 21″ in circumference, and 14″ from ear to ear ...'

Vivekananda always joked about his own weight. After one lecture in the United States, an appreciative listener asked him if he had seen God. He answered that he was surely too fat to have seen God! He often referred to himself as 'the fat maharaj'.

It is nearly impossible to get an accurate record of the variations in someone's weight after a gap of so many years. As far as sources go, we do have scattered reminiscences of his contemporaries and disciples, as well as Swami Vivekananda's own letters, written primarily in English and Bengali, but also containing elements of Sanskrit and French. We are also fortunate to have a number of photographs, taken at various points in time, which show Swamiji's fluctuations in weight. It is probable that diabetes and renal complications were responsible for much of this fluctuation.

For example, Swami Vivekananda appears quite thin in a photograph taken at Belur Math before he went abroad in 1899. But after a few months, photos of him in California show that he had put on weight.

Swami Vivekananda's weight decreased again a few months later when he was in Paris. He lost a whopping thirty pounds. This fact was not lost on his American admirers. Josephine Macleod wrote to her friend Sara Bull that Swami Vivekananda looked like a boy now. His American friends analysed the photographs from Paris and said he was not only thinner but was also looking remarkably handsome.

Before we proceed, let us recall another of Swami Vivekananda's delightfully candid remarks about himself. After he first returned from America, he fell ill in Almora. While recuperating there, he wrote to Marie Halboister on 25 July 1897: 'I am having a good deal of riding and, exercise, as well, but I had to drink a lot of skimmed milk per prescription of the doctors, with the result that I am more at the front than back! I am always a forward man though——but do not want to be too prominent just now, and I have given up drinking milk.'

Swami Vivekananda's non-Indian biographers are of the view that he never had full control over his weight, even though he sometimes reduced his food intake drastically. According to them, during his historic lectures in Chicago in 1893, his weight was stable, but possibly it did start rising after that period. There is a photograph of his, taken at the house of George W. Hale some time after the lecture at the Parliament of Religions, in which he looks decidedly heavier.

ભ

What was Swami Vivekananda's complexion like? What an Indian might consider 'fair', a Westerner would disagree with. For the Western understanding of this term is vastly different from ours. Swami Vivekananda was not fair then. According to Romain Rolland, his skin was olive. Swami Trigunatitananda reminisces that Swami Vivekananda's complexion underwent changes—one day he would look slightly dark, another day a little brighter, but there was always a hue to the skin that could be called 'golden'.

There are conflicting opinions on this though: 'Not dark and not very fair', 'olive', 'dark', 'light', 'with a golden hue'. In the face of such differing descriptions, it is hard to establish an accurate portrait, but I believe Trigunatitananda's description of the changes in Swami Vivekananda's complexion is dependable.

There is some discrepancy also regarding the shape of Swami Vivekananda's head. Some have talked about his full, round face, while others have emphasized on his firm chin. Photographs taken from various angles have led to added confusion.

One can easily see from the photos, however, that Swami Vivekananda had a thick head of wavy hair, neither frizzy nor curly. Macleod confesses she had once 'crept behind him with a pair of scissors and cut off a lock of it.' Swami Vivekananda was quite embarrassed by this devotion. Afterwards, she kept the lock in her jewellery box and always carried it with her.

Swami Vivekananda's hair, when released from his turban, used to fall across his forehead, nearly touching his eyes. He had his beautiful hair shaved off as soon as he returned to India. When he was once more ensconced at Belur Math, he used to have it cropped short every month. One day, as the barber was casually discarding the pile of hair, Swami Vivekananda joked, 'Just see … Soon, there will be a clamour across the world for a lock of Swami Vivekananda's hair!'

Swamiji had long, tapering fingers. Mahendranath once compared them to the buds of the *champa* flower. Such fingers are indicative of an unwavering, fearless mind. Swami Vivekananda's nails were slightly reddish in colour and rounded in shape. In Sanskrit, such nails are called *nakhamani*. When Vivekananda delivered his lectures, he was in the habit of closing together the fingers of his right hand and then spreading them wide. His hands were very expressive.

Mahendranath also speaks about Swami Vivekananda's gait—it was neither fast nor slow. It was the gait of 'somebody lost in thought, who walked with deliberation, desiring victory'.

There are no conflicting opinions about Swami Vivekananda's eyes. All those who met him were arrested by his magnetic gaze. We come across expressions such as 'very large and brilliant eyes' time and again in memoirs and newspaper articles. Such adjectives as 'flowing', 'graceful', 'bright', 'radiant', 'fine', 'flashing' and 'full of light' are frequently employed. Those who were bent on defiling his character, but failed, generally concluded their attack by saying that American women were more attracted to his magnetic eyes than to his ideals.

Romain Rolland describes a certain regal quality about Swami Vivekananda's eyes: 'In intelligence, in expressiveness, in humour, in compassion, those eyes were radiant, absorbed, imbued with a spiritual light; they could penetrate effortlessly, deeply, into the consciousness, become fiery when angry. Nobody could escape the magic in them.'

Swami Nirlepananda (a grandson of Yogin-ma) said: 'Those eyes are incomparable!' Swami Saradananda wrote, 'What those eyes were— how can I say?' Still another swami commented that when Swami Vivekananda 'slept in Balaram-babu's hall, his eyelids remained almost half-open, the eyes of Shiva—truly!'

Swami Vivekananda's Shiva-like eyes have been praised widely. The fire in those eyes have, time and again, destroyed the world of maya and enchanted many a truth-seeking devotee. But we should know that those eyes remained sleepless for days on end. For him it was a rare joy to be able to fall asleep as soon as he lay down. A number of his letters reveal his chronic insomnia.

In a letter to Dr Shashi Bhushan Ghosh dated 29 May 1897, Swami Vivekananda confides, 'I never in my life could sleep as soon as I got into bed. I must toss for at least two hours. Only from Madras to Darjeeling (during the first month) I would sleep as soon as my head touched the pillow. That ready disposition to sleep is gone now entirely, and my old tossing habit and feeling hot after the evening meal have come back. I do not feel any heat after the day meal!'

It was vastly different during his student days. Then he had to fight against overwhelming sleep. He has described how he used to keep a cup of tea or coffee by his side when he sat down to study. He would tie a rope around his foot, so that should he fall asleep, he could feel the pull and wake up. It is difficult to imagine that this is the same person who later appealed to his youngest disciple, Swami Achalananda, 'If you can only put me to sleep, I will give you whatever you want.'

Achalananda reported, 'Swami Vivekananda could not sleep for long. He was in constant pain. He told me he could never sleep for more than four hours at a stretch. Of late, he has not been sleeping at all.'

As a child, was Naren able to sleep well? Fortunately, this is one area regarding which we do have some concrete information. We know that he used to lie with his face on the pillow. He did not fall asleep instantly. As soon as he closed his eyes, he could see a ball of light changing colours. It would slowly expand and at last burst, bathing his whole body in a white radiance. Watching this light, he would fall asleep. When he told Sri Ramakrishna of this phenomenon years later, Ramakrishna said that only yogis were able to see this light. I confess that I am a bit curious about what modern medical science has to say on this matter.

Insomnia was such a persistent problem for Swami Vivekananda that long afterwards he could remember the few times in his life when he did manage to sleep well. In May 1901, he narrated to Sharat Chandra Chakrabarty about his visit to the house of the great devotee Nag Mahashay in Dacca, East Bengal: 'The house is so beautiful! It is an abode of peace. There I swam in the village pond after which I fell into such deep sleep that I woke up at half past two in the afternoon.

Of the few days I had sound sleep in my life, that was one. Waking, I had a lavish meal.'

Nag Mahashay had been to see Swami Vivekananda at Belur Math in early 1899, just before his departure to the West for the second time. Vivekananda had told him then, 'One has to be healthy to be able to work. I have not been well since I came back; I was well there.'

Nag Mahashay replied, 'Thakur Sri Ramakrishna said that if one has a body, one has to pay the price. You are a box of precious stones; it needs to be taken care of. Who will take care of it? Who will understand? Only Thakur understood.'

Although Swamiji was not well, he tried to keep himself physically fit. He told a disciple in January 1899: 'I still exercise. I use the dumbbell.'

We hear of an incident that occurred in the house of Balaram Basu in north Calcutta. Swami Vivekananda was weary and wanted to sleep. After lunch, the conch shells were blown and the house filled with the melody of the conch shells and the piercing cries of the ladies. Hearing the celebration, Swami Vivekananda told a companion, 'The eclipse has just begun. I am feeling sleepy. Please massage my legs.' The eclipse started and the afternoon darkened like the evening. Vivekananda slept briefly and woke up about twenty minutes before the eclipse got over. He commented, 'It is said that what one does during an eclipse, one gets in abundance thereafter. Since Mahamaya has made it impossible for me to sleep, I thought that if I could sleep now, I should be able to sleep well always. But that did not happen. I could sleep for only fifteen minutes.'

Another time, in the same house, Swami Vivekananda had difficulty sleeping. At 4.30 a.m., he declared that he was famished. The faithful Sarojini immediately prepared luchis, *halua* and other fried dishes. Swamiji smiled and told Tulsi Maharaj (Swami Nirmalananda), 'See what a devoted disciple I have got!'

Vivekananda's circle of disciples and admirers anxiously tried to create an atmosphere that would be conducive to his sleep, especially when he was not feeling well. On 2 June 1897, Swamiji wrote to Marie Halboister from Almora that he was unwell and hoped to recover soon. He went on, 'I am living in a beautiful garden house belonging to a merchant of Almora—a garden abutting several hill of mountains and forests. The night before last, a leopard came here and took away a goat from the flock kept in this garden. It was a frightful din the servants made and the barking of big Tibetan watchdogs. The dogs are kept chained at a distance all night since I am here, so they may not disturb my sleep with their barks. The leopard then found his opportunity and got a decent meal, perhaps, after weeks.'

Sadly, sleep was such a trouble! The previous year, on 6 February, 1896 the tired Vivekananda had written to his *dhira mata* (Sara Bull) from New York complaining that he was unable to sleep at all. He said: 'My health has nearly broken down. I have not slept even one night soundly in New York since I came ... I wish I could go to the bottom of the sea and have a good, long sleep.'

On 10 February, just four days later, he wrote to Mary Hale: 'I have not slept for a single night soundly this winter.'

I began by talking about the beauty of Swami Vivekananda's eyes and have ended up describing the lack of sleep that showed in these very eyes. Vivekananda suffered from chronic insomnia. He was treated for it, but to no avail.

In 1902, Sharat Chandra described Swami Vivekananda's routine at Belur Math: 'Swamiji does not sleep. He gets up at three in the morning.'

Some idea of Swami Vivekananda's health is gradually starting to emerge, but it is not clear yet. Some further inquiry is needed.

സ

We know that Swami Vivekananda suffered from diabetes like his father and that during his lifetime, suitable drugs were not available. As a result, Swami Vivekananda tried different modes of treatment, ranging from allopathic, homoeopathic to ayurvedic. He also took advice from all kinds of quasi-medical experts from various countries. He allowed them to treat him and, in a way, conduct experiments on his body.

By June 1901, he was tired of these treatments though. He said that he tolerated them merely out of regard for his gurubhais, regardless of whether they yielded results or not. When one disciple ventured to say that he considered ayurveda the most effective, Swamiji retorted, 'According to me, it is better to die in the hands of a physician who knows science than to be cured by quacks who guess in the dark, cite ancient books, and may heal a few.'

We do not have many letters written by Swami Vivekananda to his doctors. In a letter from Almora to Dr Shashi Bhushan Ghosh on 29 May 1897, he feels triumphant about his current good health and compares it with his childhood: 'I have scarcely felt so well since I was a boy and used to have *kusti* (wrestling) exercises. I really began to feel that it was a pleasure to have a body. Every movement made me conscious of strength——every, movement pulse of the muscles was pleasurable. That exhilarating feeling has subsided somewhat, yet I feel very strong.'

At the end of the letter, Vivekananda refers again to his new-found strength: 'You ought to see me Doctor, when I sit meditating in front the beautiful snowpeaks and repeat from the Upanishads: *na tasya rogo na jara na mrityu; praptasya yogagnimayam sarirmu*——He has neither disease, nor decay, nor death; for, verily he has obtained a body full of the fire of Yoga.'

Let us go back a little to the early accounts of Narendranath. From them we get to know that he was a healthy child. Once he had an accident and, as a result, bore a scar above his eye all his life. A second misfortune occurred when a schoolteacher hit him so violently that blood oozed out of his ear and soaked his garment. Fortunately, this injury did not have serious repercussions. Sports and physical exercises kept Narendranath busy while he was growing up.

Later in life, when he was suffering from ill health, Swami Vivekananda recalled his robust health as a child. We have to remember that unhygienic conditions were a common feature in the Calcutta of those times, and, as a result, diseases such as cholera and typhoid were pretty widespread. Swami Vivekananda's mother, Bhubaneshwari Dasi, told her youngest son, Bhupendranath, that without proper plumbing in the city, every summer families would lose a member or two to cholera.

With such a high death rate, disposal of the bodies became a major concern. As a youth, Narendranath's favourite duty was to help burn the dead. His brother Mahendranath reveals that 'Naren burnt thirty to thirty-five dead bodies ... that was his chore every evening. Father used to get annoyed. Had he not been very healthy, this would not have been possible.'

ℭℬ

We have already seen that after his father's death, Narendranath began to suffer from severe bouts of headache and frequently took camphor for its cooling effect. One wonders if these headaches signified high blood pressure.

In later life, when he was staying in Mayavati, Swami Vivekananda told his disciple Swami Birajananda, 'Learn from my experiences. Don't be so hard on your body and ruin your health. I have harmed mine. I have tortured it severely, and what has been the result? My body has become ruined during the best years of my life! And I am still paying for it.'

On 25 February 1897, after his return from the United States,

Swami Vivekananda wrote from Calcutta to Sara Bull, 'I am almost dead ... I am so, so tired. I do not know whether I would live even six months more or not, unless I have some rest.'

It is obvious that around this time he was diagnosed with diabetes. From the memoirs of Krishnalal Maharaj, another of his disciples, we learn that it was in Colombo that the first signs of this disease were detected in Swamiji. This was long before the discovery of insulin. Physicians recommended that he eat regularly and try to avoid stress.

ᚼ

Here is a list of the various diseases, medical conditions and other ailments that Swami Vivekananda suffered from during the course of his life:

1. Severe headaches (migraines)
2. Tonsillitis
3. Diphtheria and influenza/cough
4. Asthma
5. Typhoid
6. Malaria
7. Other kinds of persistent fevers
8. Liver disease
9. Indigestion and other stomach ailments/gastroenteritis
10. Accumulation of water in the stomach
11. Dysentery and diarrhoea
12. Dyspepsia and abdominal pain
13. Gallstones
14. Lumbago (lower back pain)
15. Neck ache
16. Bright's disease (acute nephritis)
17. Kidney ailments

18. Dropsy
19. Albuminuria
20. Bloodshot eyes
21. Loss of vision in the right eye
22. Insomnia
23. Premature greying of hair and beard
24. Neurasthenia
25. Body heating up after dinner
26. Inability to tolerate heat
27. Excessive fatigue
28. Sea sickness
29. Sunstroke
30. Diabetes
31. Heart problems

In his letters and memoirs, we get both passing references and detailed descriptions of these health complications. It is wonderful that he should have accomplished so much in spite of this long list of ailments. Swami Vivekananda's body was, indeed, a mystery and those who fuss over minor physical discomforts should draw inspiration from his example.

CB

Swami Vivekananda had tremendous mental courage. He realized that the work he had begun would never be completed if he wasted time fussing about his health. But his gurubhais did worry about him constantly.

'Why are you alarmed? Can a grain of sand be destroyed so soon? The evening lamp has just been lighted, a whole night of singing is still left. I am not so irritable any more, and the fever is just because of the liver—I can see that clearly. I shall also bring it under my control—what is there to fear?' These are the spirited words Swami Vivekananda wrote to his gurubhai Swami Brahmananda from Almora on 20 May 1897.

Two months later, on 24 July 1897, he wrote to Swami Akhandananda: 'I have started with new enthusiasm. One has to die, but why should it be through laziness? It is better to wear out than to rust out. And even if I die, my bones will work wonders! So what is there to worry?'

What plagued Swami Vivekananda all his life were various stomach ailments. When Sri Ramakrishna passed away and Narendranath became a sannyasi, his lifestyle changed dramatically and from that point on he began to suffer from abdominal problems. He was alternating between two lifestyles—that of luxury and poverty—and this sharp contrast continued throughout his life. He himself was aware of this. The second time he left the shores of India, accompanied by Sister Nivedita, he told her that he was a bundle of extremes. He could eat a great deal and also starve himself. He could be a chain smoker but, again, refrain from smoking altogether. He could control his senses, but also indulge in them, otherwise, he said, what was the point of control?

Swami Vivekananda once wrote to Nivedita from New York about these apparent contradictions in his nature. He told her that his peculiar constitution could produce the greatest music but also wail alone in the dark.

It would not be very just to hold the austere lifestyle at Baranagore monastery entirely responsible for Swami Vivekananda's ailments. While he was still a student, he suffered from chronic malaria. Swami Gambhirananda says in his book *Yuganayak Vivekananda* that malarial fever prevented Narendranath from regularly attending classes in his first year of college. Due to his poor attendance record, he had problems being allowed for his FA examination.

Around the same period, Thakur Sri Ramakrishna told Narendranath, 'All parts of your body bear auspicious signs. Only when you sleep, you release your breath with great force. Yogis say that such people do not live long.'

In the summer of 1887, Narendranath fell gravely ill due to lack of food and overstrain. His temperature ran high and his fever showed no signs of abatement. He lay on a cot in a large room inside the Baranagar monastery. One Dr Chandra prescribed him medicines. Balaram-babu also informed Narendranath's mother and she came with one of her sons. At intervals he would be in his senses and would remain silent. At other times the fever made him delirious. When he saw his mother, he shouted, 'Why did you allow a woman to come in? I was the one who made the rule and it is for me that the rule is being broken!' He was suffering terribly and his illness worsened during the night. His pulse had become very weak. Baburam Maharaj (Swami Premananda) could not contain himself any longer and started weeping. At this, Narendranath said indistinctly, but with great firmness, 'Do not cry. I am not dying now. There is a lot of work that remains to be done. I can see them in front of my eyes. I have no time to die.'

During this period in Baranagore, Narendranath also suffered from gallstones, then called the 'gravel-stone disease', and was forced to stay with his mother and grandmother for some time. Dr Rajendralal Dutta, the eminent homoeopath, came to visit him. It sounds incredible but this doctor would always carry a gift for his patients when he visited their homes. For Narendranath he had got a huge marmelo. Eventually, his treatment alleviated Narendranath's pain.

But Vivekananda's woes were not over yet. Next he fell ill of acute diarrhoea and found himself unable to digest any food. Swami Saradananda obtained a bottle of 'Fellow's Syrup' from his father's shop and carried it to Narendranath's grandmother's house. Baikuntha Sanyal brought a pot of *magur* fish, which is supposed to be good for diarrhoea. What could be the reason for the attack? According to Mahendranath Dutta, it was probably the fact that 'he was used to eating meat, but as a monk he lived on alms; that and the uncertainty of food ruined his health.'

Balaram Basu persuaded Narendranath to stay with him for a couple of days in order to recuperate, but Narendranath did not like the mild diet that he was being given to treat his diarrhoea. So he privately asked the housemaid, Bhabini, to prepare a pumpkin curry and a few rotis for him. Surprisingly, Bhabini's food cured him of diarrhoea for some time.

In the summer of May and June 1887, Narendranath suffered from typhoid and problems in his urinary tract. The deterioration in his health was compounded by two more ailments: tonsillitis and gastroenteritis.

Tonsillitis was hereditary in the Dutta family. Narendranath was treated by a famous homoeopath, Dr Salzer, who examined him at the house of Atul Chandra Ghosh, brother of Girish Chandra Ghosh. Dr Salzer assured him that medicine was not needed; it was enough to gurgle with cold water and apply cold compresses to the throat area. After diagnosis, the doctor spent three or four hours discussing the scriptures with Narendranath.

While travelling, Vivekananda's tonsillitis recurred and he was placed under the care of Dr Hem Chandra Sen, a renowned physician in Delhi.

Narendranath's abdominal pains too were a source of great anxiety for all at Baranagore. It was recommended that he take small quantities of opium to minimize the pain. This agitated Atul Chandra Ghosh very much. He said, 'What are they doing? Teaching him to take opium! They will ruin this man of keen intellect!'

ଉଷ

Fever and stomach infections figure prominently in the next phase of Swami Vivekananda's life. Premadadas Mitra, who lived in Benares, received a letter from one of Vivekananda's gurubhais at Baranagore in early 1889 informing him that Swami Vivekananda had fallen ill while walking to Kamarpukur, the birthplace of Sri Ramakrishna: 'On the way to the village, the Master ran a temperature and threw up as one does if one has cholera. The fever recurred after three or four days. Now he is so weak that he cannot walk a step ... I am also unfit for travel.'

On 21 March 1889, Swami Vivekananda informed Premadadas, 'I am very ill at present; there is fever now and then, but there is no disorder of the spleen or other organs. I am under homoeopathic treatment.'

A further letter to Premadadas, dated 7 August 1889, reveals: 'It is more than a week since I received your letter, but having had another attack of fever, I could not send a reply all this time, for which please excuse me. For an interval of a month and a half I kept well, but I have suffered again for the last ten days; now I am doing well.'

In December, he wrote from Baidyanath, 'I am not keeping well, probably due to excessive iron in the water.'

A month later, Swami Vivekananda was in Ghazipur. From there, he wrote: 'Of the few places I have recently visited, this is the healthiest. The waters of Baidyanath led to indigestion ... The few days I passed at Benares, I suffered from fever day and night—the place has malaria in the air.'

By February 1890, another ailment had developed. On 11 February, Swami Vivekananda wrote from Ghazipur: 'I am suffering from back pain which started in Allahabad. I had recovered from it sometime back, but it has recurred. So I will have to stay here a while longer ...'

In April, still in Ghazipur, he wrote to Swami Abhedananda: 'I cannot get rid of this back pain. Cadaverous!'

Swami Vivekananda returned to Baranagore in May 1890. On 10 May, he wrote to Premadadas: 'I could not write to you because of various distractions and a relapse of the fever.'

When Premadadas Mitra learnt about Swami Vivekananda's family's financial constraints, he offered to help. Vivekananda wrote back: 'You have sent me a twenty-rupee note. You are very kind. But it is unfortunate that the pride of my mother and brothers has proved to be an impediment. I cannot accept the money on their behalf, and, therefore, your prime wish cannot be fulfilled. But your second wish will be fulfilled as I will be gratified to use the money for my tour to Benares.'

When Swami Vivekananda went to Benares for the last time, in February 1902, he met Premadadas's son, Kalidas. Swamiji was then very ill. He wore a sweater and a pair of woollen socks. Leaning against the cushions, he breathed with difficulty.

Vivekananda told Kalidas, 'I am in bad health. I suffer.' When Kalidas Mitra asked what disease he was suffering from, Swami Vivekananda answered, 'I am unable to name the disease. In Paris and in the United States, I have been to so many physicians. Even they could not cure me.'

This was the same Vivekananda who had once joked about his health. He had said, 'All my illnesses stem from the stomach. Do people suffering from stomach ailments grow so listless and turn renunciates?' Yet, he continued to battle his fever and dyspepsia and travel across the length and breadth of the country.

Somehow he could not bring his stomach problems under control. Because of this condition, H.H. the Maharaja of Khetri had purchased a first class ticket for Vivekananda's voyage to the West. On board the steamer, Swamiji wrote a letter to the Maharaja telling him that earlier he had to go to the toilet at least twenty-five times a day, but on the ship he was much better.

It is perhaps worth noting here that Sri Ramakrishna also suffered from stomach ailments.

From time to time, Swami Vivekananda used to ponder over the impact of dyspepsia on the national health. He once said, 'Bengalis are too sentimental. That is why they suffer from such acute indigestion.'

Another time, he asked his disciple Sharat Chandra Chakrabarty, who was from East Bengal, 'Is it true that people in the villages of East Bengal do not even know what indigestion is?'

Sharat Chandra replied, 'Yes, sir. There is no such disease in East Bengal. I first heard of it after I came here. We take rice and fish for our two meals every day.'

Swami Vivekananda said, 'Yes, eat as much as you like. Dyspeptic monks who live on vegetables have flooded the country. That is a sign of *tamas*: laziness, indolence, ignorance and sleep.'

Swamiji's letters reveal that even after returning to India from the United States, his stomach problems persisted. He wrote to Swami Brahmananda from Almora on 20 May 1898: 'My health is much better, but the gas and acidity is still there and the insomnia has recurred. It will be of great help if you can send a good ayurvedic medicine for indigestion.'

❦

Let us examine the various medical problems that Swami Vivekananda faced during his stint as a wandering monk in India. We have seen how, in the summer of 1889, he vomited on the way to Kamarpukur. Then he was assailed by fever after he came back to Baranagore. Next, in Shimultala in Bihar, he got diarrhoea due to excessive heat.

In 1890, Swami Vivekananda went to Ghazipur in the middle of the Ganga Valley in north India to meet the saint Pavhari Baba who, according to him, 'was one of the greatest masters he [had] loved and served'. Pavhari Baba lived inside a long underground cave by the side of the Ganga and survived on a diet of neem leaves and chilli peppers.

While he was in Ghazipur, Swami Vivekananda had suffered from lumbago (pain in the lower back region). He had also succumbed to a stomach virus. Perhaps food that he could gather by begging did not agree with him. There were some lemon trees near the house where he was staying and he subsisted on lemons for some time.

Later, on the way to Badrinarayan, Vivekananda had a high fever and one of his companions, Swami Akhandananda, came down with severe cough. The party also consisted of Saradananda and Kripananda, plus a porter. All of them stayed in an inn called 'Salarkar' while the sick recovered.

When they eventually arrived in Hrishikesh, Swamiji had a relapse of malarial fever. Unfortunately, there were no physicians in the vicinity and he became delirious. Swami Gambhirananda, who was present, later wrote: 'Swamiji alternately sweated and turned cold; his pulse had become very feeble ... Those present were afraid he would die. Then a monk we barely knew fed him some honey and some powdered peepal leaves. Immediately there was an impact. Swamiji opened his eyes and muttered something indistinctly.'

Meerut was the next destination. Here Swami Vivekananda went to visit Swami Akhandananda, who was staying with Dr Trailokyanath Ghosh. Vivekananda had become quite emaciated by this time and Akhandananda was concerned to see the thin, weak body of his gurubhai. Swami Vivekananda had turned 'a shadow of his former self'. The spectre of the severe illness in Hrishikesh still seemed to hover over him.

Dr Trailokyanath was able to give him proper treatment in Meerut. Afraid that his fever might recur, Swami Vivekananda obediently took whatever was prescribed to him.

Some say that Vivekananda's stay in Meerut lasted for only a few weeks; others claim that he was there for around three months. According to Swami Akhandananda's memoirs, it was four to five months and Swamiji did not leave for Delhi till January 1891. It was here that he was treated for tonsillitis by Dr Hem Chandra Sen.

In the town of Alwar, Rajasthan, Swami Vivekananda met yet another doctor. This was Dr Gurucharan Laskar. Laskar had made arrangements for Swamiji's stay. While he was there, a disciple inquired, 'Does one benefit from massaging oil?' Swami Vivekananda replied, 'Yes, of course! If a *chatak* (58 g) of oil is massaged well into the body, it is as good as eating a *poa* (233 g) of ghee.'

Swami Vivekananda then met his gurubhai Swami Akhandananda in the village of Mandabi again. The latter noted that Swamiji's health had greatly improved by then. It was almost as if he had acquired a new body. 'His beauty and grace delighted everyone!'

Vivekananda was against the indiscriminate use of pills and drugs. One of his admirers, the forest officer Haripada Mitra, was used to regular intake of all kinds of medicines. Swamiji told him that he should take drugs only if the situation was bad enough that he could not get out of bed. At least 90 per cent of his nervous ailments were imaginary, Swamiji declared, and he advised his disciple to enjoy life more.

Unfortunately, Swami Vivekananda's own nervous ailments were very real. In March 1900, during his visit to San Francisco, his health took a turn for the worse. Writing to Brahmananda, he said: 'I really require rest. My disease is called neurasthenia—a disease of the nerves. Once afflicted, it continues for some years. Only after a complete rest of three or four years is it cured. This country is the home of that disease, but I hope I survive it. Don't you worry about me.' Another letter in Bengali says, 'Alas, sickness, sorrow and pain have been my companion for the last two years. Tell Sharat that I am not going to work so hard any more. But he who does not work enough to earn his food will have to starve to death.'

I have now managed to present a picture of Swami Vivekananda's health before his first voyage to the US. From a letter written to Maharaja Ajit Singh in June 1983, we even come to know of an unexpected improvement in his health on the ship. Now we shall explore further Swamiji's physical condition in the West.

Fortunately, in the first phase of his stay in an unfamiliar territory, there was no major illness. A few excerpts from his letters of that period support this theory. Swami Vivekananda wrote to Miss Mary Hale from Detroit on 30 March 1894: 'I am all right—in sound body and mind.'

He also enjoyed good health during the Christmas of 1895, as he wrote to Mrs Ole Bull on New Year: 'I enjoyed my visit to the Leggetts exceedingly. It has braced me up for further work. I am well both physically and mentally.'

Financial help was not always easy to procure, but tremendous strength of mind and incredible hard work brought Swami Vivekananda success in a foreign land. Perhaps Swamiji hastened to complete his work, for he feared that his health would soon fail him. He once told Hari Maharaj (Swami Turiyananda) that he had achieved all that he desired within the first twenty-nine years of his life.

Yet, it may perhaps be said that Swami Vivekananda's triumph in Chicago was not his last or his greatest work. Perhaps more significant was the establishment of the Ramakrishna Mission, the impact of which has proved to be more enduring than his brilliant successes in America and Europe.

The first signs of ill health in the United States did not manifest themselves until early 1896, when Swamiji was staying in New York. Thus the beginning of 1896 marks the start of the last phase of Swamiji's short life. This phase has two chapters, as we shall see: the first extends from 1896 to 1899, when he returned to the West for the second time; the second covers the period from 1899 to 1902.

ॐ

On 6 December 1895, Swami Vivekananda arrived in New York once more after crossing the Atlantic from Europe. His voyage had not been pleasant. On 8 December, he wrote to Sara Bull: 'I arrived last Friday after ten days of a very tedious voyage. It was awfully rough and for the first time in my life I was badly seasick.'

It was then the middle of the winter season in New York and Swami Vivekananda often had to cross the Brooklyn Bridge by cable car. Not surprisingly, he caught a bad cold. In the letter to Sara Bull on 6 February, he wrote: 'My health has nearly broken down. I have not slept even one night soundly in New York.'

Vivekananda's American disciple, Swami Kripananda, was worried that Swamiji might fall severely ill. He saw how hard he worked and paid for the rent, advertisements and printing without a care for himself.

Swami Kripananda's fears were not unfounded. From January 1896, Vivekananda's health began to deteriorate. He was only thirty-three years old. He confided in his American friend, Miss S. Ellen Waldo, 'Ellen, it is the strangest thing. I cannot remember how I look. I look and look at myself in the glass, but the moment I turn away, I forget completely what I look like.'

In April 1896 Swami Vivekananda returned to London. This time, he took precautions against seasickness and was able to write to the Hale sisters from Reading on 20 April, 'The voyage has been pleasant and no sickness this time. I gave my treatment to avoid it.'

It was in London that Swami Vivekananda met his brother Mahendranath. Some reliable sources have surmised that he suffered a mild heart attack during this period. We have already had glimpses of the difficult circumstances in which Vivekananda found himself in London. By August, he was determined to travel to Switzerland, partly for health and partly to escape the London scene.

He wrote from Switzerland to J. J. Goodwin on 8 August 1896: 'I am now taking rest ... [and] I am much refreshed now. I look out of the window and see the huge glaciers just before me and feel that I am in the Himalayas. I am quite calm. My nerves have regained their accustomed strength; and little vexations, like those you write of, do not touch me at all.'

Sadly, this period of calm did not last long. On 23 August, Swami Vivekananda wrote to Mr Sturdy from Lucerne, 'I am suffering from a very bad cold indeed.' Swamiji was anxious about his brother as well. He goes on, 'I hope by this time Mohin's money from the Raja has arrived to your care. If so, I do not want the money I gave him back. You may give him the whole of it.'

Swami Vivekananda returned to Britain and wrote to Mary Hale on 17 September: 'Today I reached London, after my two months of climbing and walking and glacier seeing in Switzerland. One good it has done to me—a few pounds of unnecessary adipose tissue have returned back to the gaseous state. Well, there is no safety even in that, for the solid body of this birth has taken a fancy to outstrip the mind towards infinite expansion. If it goes on this way, I would have soon to lose all personal identity even the flesh—at least to all the rest of the world ... I have come over here among my friends, shall work for a few weeks, and then go back to India in the winter.'

He had suddenly decided to return home. He told Josephine Macleod on 3 December 1896: 'Three lectures next week, and my work in London is finished for the season. Of course, everybody here thinks it foolish to give up just now the "boom" is on, but the Dear Lord says, "Start for Old India." I obey.'

Swami Vivekananda's sojourn in the West ended on 16 December 1896 when he left London for Ceylon. On 3 January, on board his ship, he wrote to Mary Hale: 'The ship is rolling as hard as she can ... From Suez begins Asia. Once more Asia. What am I? Asiatic, European, or American? I feel a curious medley of personalities in me.'

03

Swami Vivekananda's steamer reached Colombo on 15 January 1897 and he was given an elaborate welcome. He described the festivities in a letter to Mary Hale on 30 January: 'From Colombo in Ceylon, where I landed, to Ramnad, the nearly southernmost point of the Indian continent where I am just now as the guest of the Raja of Ramnad, my journey has been a huge procession—crowds of people, illuminations, addresses, etc., etc. A monument forty feet high is being built on the spot where I landed. The Raja of Ramnad has presented his address to "His most Holiness" in a huge casket of solid gold beautifully worked. Madras and Calcutta are on the tiptoe of expectation as if the whole nation is rising to honour me.'

But the long journey and the extended celebrations wearied Swami Vivekananda and he began to feel unwell. His diabetes became apparent, though whether it was first detected in Colombo, Madras or Calcutta is unclear. Doctors in Madras advised him to drink the juice of tender young coconuts instead of water, so his friends and admirers presented him with lots of coconuts for his onward journey by steamer. Nonetheless, he was in pretty poor health by the time he reached Calcutta on 19 February.

Shortly afterwards, on 25 February, he wrote to Sara Bull from the Alambazar monastery: 'I have not a moment to die as they say, what with processions and tomtomings and various other methods of reception all over the country; I am almost dead ... I am so, so tired. I do not know whether I would live even six months more or not, unless I get some rest.'

Swami Vivekananda left for Darjeeling on 8 March 1897, on the advice of his doctor. The heat in Calcutta was proving to be too much for him. However, he did visit the city to spend time with H.H. Maharaja Ajit Singh who was in Calcutta between 21 and 26 March. After his departure, Vivekananda returned to Darjeeling immediately.

By 28 April 1897, we find Swami Vivekananda writing to Mary Hale:

'My hair is turning grey in bundles, and my face is getting wrinkled up all over; that losing of flesh has given me twenty years of age more. And now I am losing flesh rapidly, because I am made to live upon meat and meat alone—no bread, no rice, no potatoes, not even a lump of sugar in my coffee! ... I am going to train a big beard; now it is turning grey. It gives a venerable appearance ... O thou white hair, how much thou canst conceal, all glory unto thee, Hallelujah!'

Vivekananda's speaks about his sorry state of health further in a letter to Sara Bull from the Alambazar math on 5 May 1897: 'I had to go to Darjeeling for a month to recover my health and I am glad to tell you that I am much better, and would you believe it, without taking any medicine, only by the exercise of mental healing! I am going again to another hill station [Almora] tomorrow.'

He wrote encouragingly to Swami Brahmananda from Almora on 20 May: 'The feverishness is all gone. I am trying to go to still a cooler place. Heat or the fatigue of walking, I find, at once produces trouble of the liver ... nowadays my temper also is not very irritable, and feverishness is all due to the liver—I see this clearly. Well, I shall make that also come under control—what fear?'

At Swami Vivekananda's request, Dr Shashi Bhushan Ghosh sent a letter and two bottles of medicine from Calcutta to Almora. After acknowledging receipt Vivekananda urged him, 'Please do not listen to Yogen. He is a hypochondriac himself and wants to make everybody so. I ate one-sixteenth of a barfi in Lucknow, and Yogen says that was what made me ill in Almora!'

Swami Vivekananda confirmed that his health had indeed improved in a letter to Swami Shuddhananda, written in Sanskrit, where he states that open air, controlled food habits and plenty of exercise has made his body strong and pleasing to the eye.

Swami Vivekananda's thoughts from Almora now once again turned to the West but, as he wrote to Marie Halboister on 2 June 1897,

'My physicians would not allow me to venture into work so soon. For going to Europe means work, isn't it? No work, no bread. Here the yellow cloth is sufficient, and I would have food enough ... don't you like to have a good rest, say for some years and no work? Sleep, eat and exercise; exercise, eat and sleep—this is what I am going to do some months yet.'

In a letter written the following day to an American devotee, Vivekananda said that he was suffering from indigestion and trying to cure himself through sheer willpower (according to the tenets of Christian science). It had worked for him in Darjeeling. If his health did not improve in India, he would go to America.

The symptoms of diabetes were probably not so acute around this time. Swami Vivekananda wrote from Almora to Swami Brahmananda on 20 June 1897: 'I am all right now, with plenty of muscular strength and no thirst. The liver, too, acts well. I am not certain as to what effects Shashi's medicine had. So I have stopped using it. I am having plenty of mangoes. I am getting exceptionally adept in riding, and do not feel the least pain or exhaustion even after a run of twenty or thirty miles at a stretch. Milk I have altogether stopped having for fear of corpulence.'

It may surprise the reader to hear that Swami Vivekananda was absorbed in physical activities during this period. That his body was infested with various diseases does not appear to have perturbed him.

Swami Vivekananda wrote some stirring thoughts on this subject in a letter to Mary Hale from Almora on 9 July 1897: 'Ay fools, neglecting the living god and His infinite reflection with which the world is full, and running after imaginary shadows! Him Worship, the only visible, and break all other idols.'

The next day, he wrote to Swami Brahmananda: 'The kind of work that is going on at Berhampore [the Ramakrishna Mission's first work for the famine-stricken] is exceedingly nice ... Philosophy, yoga, and penance—the worship rooms ... your sunned rice or vegetable offerings—all these contribute the religion of one man or one country, doing good to others is the one good, universal religion.'

Swami Vivekananda's all-encompassing vision for the Ramakrishna Mission fully occupied his mind and life. He wrote to Swami Shuddhananda on 11 July: 'I am sorry to learn that you are getting only babus from Calcutta as visitors. They will not be able to do anything. What we want are brave young men who will work, not fools.'

Swami Vivekananda gives special attention to the organizational aspect of the Ramakrishna Mission in this important letter. He said that at least three *mahantas* (heads) should be elected in the math. One would look after the administration, another, the spiritual affairs and the third, matters of the intellect.

Vivekananda concluded this letter by saying: 'I expect more from my children [his disciples] than from my brethren [his gurubhais]. I want each one of my children to be a hundred times greater than I could be. Everyone of you must be a giant ...'

From Almora, to Swami Akhandananda, he goes on to say: 'Go on working at top speed. Never fear! I, too, am determined to work. I have started with new enthusiasm. One has to die, but why should it be through laziness? It is better to wear out than to rust out. And even if I die, my bones will work wonders! So what is there to worry? Money and all will come of themselves, we want men, not money. It is man that makes everything, what can money do?'

In spite of his brave words, Swami Vivekananda was far from well at this time. He was suffering from asthma and a severe cold. The bright sun hurt his eyes—another symptom of diabetes. He also had a relapse of tonsillitis and fever. However, Vivekananda was more concerned about the welfare of his gurubhai, Swami Ramakrishnananda, than about his own health.

We have some additional information about Swami Vivekananda's health during this period. On the way from Almora to Kathgodam, he was obliged to stay in Bhimtal for a day where he fell ill. He reached Bareilly in the foothills of the Himalayas on 9 August 1897, but his fever continued unabated for two more days. Nevertheless, he delivered lectures there. He also confided to Swami Achyutananda of the Arya Samaj that he would not live for more than five or six years.

Swami Vivekananda reached Ambala on 12 August, and was suffering from severe abdominal pains. He delivered a ninety-minute lecture, but did not take any food.

On the way to Dharamsala in the Kangra Valley, Swami Vivekananda fell ill yet again, this time in Amritsar. He was forced to take a two-wheeled horse-drawn carriage to Murree. But he was unwilling to rest. He passed his time singing devotional songs for the local people.

At last, on 20 September 1897, Swami Vivekananda sent some good news from Kashmir to Swami Ramakrishnananda: 'As my health is much better, I have decided to tour again as before.'

In the same letter, he revealed that he was currently plagued by financial worries: 'None of my countrymen has yet offered me even a pice towards my travelling expenses ... you can easily understand how difficult it is to move about in a group. I feel ashamed to ask for money only from my English disciples. And so have decided to go out on my own again with only a blanket.'

Swami Vivekananda had the constant urge to wander on his own, but he was far from well. He wrote to Swami Brahmananda on 11 October: 'I feel I have been working as if under an irresistible impulse for the last ten days, beginning from Kashmir. It may be either a physical or mental disease. Now I have come to the conclusion that I am unfit for further work. All that I could have done, I was led to do, and I was forced to give all that I could, both bodily and mentally, by the Divine Mother. Her will be done! I now understand that I have been very harsh to all of you—but what has happened is now past. What is the good of repentance? I do not believe in it. This is all Karma. Whatever of Mother's was to be accomplished through me, she made me do, and has now flung me aside breaking my body and mind. Now I retire from all this work.

'In a day or two, I shall give up everything and wander out alone. I shall spend the rest of my life quietly in some place or other. Forgive me if you all will or do what you like. I have never shied away from the battlefield—shall I now? Either one wins or one loses. But I believe that cowards die only to be born again as worms. They will not be saved, even if they pray for ages. Am I going to be born again as a worm? ...

'To me, this worldly life is but a play. It will always remain so. So, I do not care about insults or petty losses; I am a man of action. I see that people give advice upon advice—this one says this, that one says that; again, that one threatens and this one frightens.

'To me, this life is not so sweet that one has to be concerned with fears of all kinds ... I understand only this: that I fought tooth and nail and whoever says to me, "Do not worry, be fearless. O brave one, here I am by your side!" I am all for that person. To me, such people are like heroes, like gods, like saviours. To such a person, I offer a million salutations. They are the ones who are saving humanity. It is their presence that purifies the world. And those who always wail, "Oh, do not go forward, there is *this* danger, there is *that* danger"—those dyspeptics!—they tremble with fear. But through the grace of the Divine Mother, my mind is so strong that even dyspepsia cannot make a coward of me. What can I tell the cowards? Nothing whatsoever!'

Swami Vivekananda returned time and again to the subject of death. In a letter written from Lahore to Srimati Indumati Mitra, he said: 'It will ease my anxiety if a math is established in Calcutta. Then I can hope that the work for which I have struggled all my life enduring all sorts of privation and suffering will not die out when I cease to live in this mortal body.'

And yet, on the same day—15 November 1897—Swami

Vivekananda has this to say to Swami Brahmananda from Lahore: 'My health is good, only I have to get up at night once or twice. I am having sound sleep, sleep is not spoiled even after exhausting lectures, and I am doing exercise every day. I have been living on rice for the last three months and there is no trouble at all. Now come on, work with redoubled energy!'

By 24 November however, Swami Vivekananda was asking Swami Premananda from Dehra Dun to send him some very old ghee to rub on his neck as he had been suffering for a while from ache at the back of the neck. 'You are sure to get it from Habu or Sharat [a lawyer],' he wrote.

At the end of the year, Swami Vivekananda came down with a bad cold in Delhi.

CS

Swami Vivekananda seemed to be slowly spending his last bit of energy in working tirelessly. He wrote to Sister Nivedita in August of the following year asking her not to overwork: 'Do not work yourself out. It is of no use; always remember—"Duty is the midday sun whose fierce rays are burning the very vitals of humanity." It is necessary for a time, as a discipline; beyond that, it is a dark dream. Things go on all right whether we lend them our helping hands or not. We in delusion only suffer.'

On 17 July 1898, we find Swami Vivekananda writing to Swami Brahmananda from Srinagar, encouraging him to go there: 'If you can spend a winter here, you are sure to recoup your health. If the house is a good one and if you have enough fuel and warm clothing, life in a land of snow is nothing but enjoyable. Also, for stomach trouble, a cold climate is an unfailing remedy ... I am fine and do not usually have to get up during the night, even though I take rice, potato and sugar twice a day and, in fact, eat whatever I can lay my hands on! Medicine is useless—it has no action on the system of a Knower of Brahman! Everything will be digested— dont be afraid of.'

Exactly two months later, he wrote from Srinagar to Haripada Mitra: 'Recently my health was very bad and so I have been delayed. Otherwise, I had intended to leave for Punjab this week ... The doctor had advised me to go to the plains at the present time.' He then asked Haripada Mitra to send him fifty rupees, if it was not inconvenient for him. 'It will be a great help to me, for I have incurred much extra expense of late owing to my illness and I feel a little ashamed to depend always on my foreign devotees.'

The same day he wrote to Maharaja Ajit Singh: 'Your Highness, I have been very ill here for two weeks. Now getting better. I am in want of funds. Though my American friends are doing everything they can to help me, I feel shame to beg from them all the time, especially as illness makes one incur contingent expenses. I have no shame to beg of one person in the world and that is yourself.'

When Swami Vivekananda returned to Calcutta, he went in search of a good doctor. He was suffering from diabetes, insomnia and heart problems. From Swami Brahmananda's diary we get to know that he arranged for the eminent doctor R.L. Dutta to treat Swami Vivekananda. This doctor advised rest and Vivekananda often stayed at the house of the late Balaram Basu during this period of treatment.

Swami Vivekananda's gurubhais paid a great deal for the services of such a distinguished doctor. His fees was forty rupees and the medicine itself cost ten rupees. I urge the reader to discover for himself what fifty rupees in 1898 is worth today! Somehow, the money was obtained, but even after that Vivekananda's gurubhais did not rest. They consulted an ayurvedic doctor.

Nothing cured Swami Vivekananda, however, and on 19 December 1898 he left for a health resort in Deoghar with Brahmachari

Harendranath. They stayed at the house of Priyanath Mukhopadhyay, but here Vivekananda suffered greatly from asthma and so was compelled to return to Calcutta on 22 January.

Swami Gambhirananda writes in his *YuganayakVivekananda* that when Vivekananda was in the throes of an asthmatic attack, his face went red, he writhed in agony, and it appeared as if he would die any moment. Swamiji would lean against a cushion and wait for death to come.

In spite of this physical hardship, Swami Vivekananda began to think of travelling to Europe once again. He wrote to his American disciple, Sister Christine, on 26 January 1899: 'The fact is, I was once more in the vale of death. The diabetes has disappeared, but in its place has arrived what some doctors call asthma, others dyspepsia. It is a cause of great worry, for it seems my breath is going to stop any moment. I am fittest in Calcutta, so am here for some rest and quiet. If I get well by March, I will go to Europe.'

On 2 February 1899, he reaffirmed his intention in a letter to Josephine Macleod: 'The change at Vaidyanath did me no good. I nearly died there, was suffocating for eight days and nights! I was brought back to Calcutta more dead than alive, and here am struggling to get back to life again. Dr Sarkar is treating me now. I am not so despondent now as I was. I am reconciled to my fate. This year seems to be very hard for us ... I hope to rally again by March, and by April I start for Europe. Again Mother knows best.'

April arrived and we find him writing: 'Two years of physical anguish have taken away twenty years of my life. Well, but the soul changeth not, does it? It is the same *atman*, intent upon a single idea.'

Around this time, Sister Nivedita got a sharp rebuke from Swami Vivekananda for having his horoscope examined again. According to this new horoscope, he should have no fear of death for nine more years because Jupiter was his ruling planet. But he would continue to remain ill. Swami Vivekananda dismissed this as superstition.

On 20 June 1899, Swami Vivekananda, accompanied by Sister Nivedita, boarded the *S.S. Golconda*, in Calcutta bound for Europe. Among those who came to see them off was Shachindranath Basu. He observed that Vivekananda did not look well. However, Nivedita later wrote that Swami Vivekananda kept quite well during the voyage as he had controlled his smoking habit.

Just over one month later, on 31 July, the steamer arrived at the Tilbury dock in London. A devout admirer who was present there reported that Swami Vivekananda looked very thin and bore the appearance of a boy. Swamiji wrote to Brahmananda on 10 August to say that he had suffered from gastroenteritis after reaching London.

A respected doctor whom Swami Vivekananda consulted in London asked him to follow a vegetarian diet and avoid lentils. According to him, an excess of uric acid was the cause of all his physical problems. Meat and lentils led to an increase in the amount of the acid and were, therefore, best avoided. The doctor further informed him that he had albumin, not sugar, in his blood. His pulse was strong, but his heart weak. Swami Vivekananda decided to follow the doctor's advice and live on boiled rice and ghee for some time.

He stayed for only a short time in London and reached New York on 26 August 1899. Seeing Swami Vivekananda's complicated health issues, his American disciples were not averse to calling on the assistance of quasi-medical experts along with eminent doctors. In September, for example, Vivekananda wrote to Mary Hale from Ridgely Manor to report that even she could not cure him with her firm faith in Christian science: 'I am losing much faith in your healing powers. … I was growing grey fast, but somehow it got checked. I am sorry, only a few grey hairs now; I like it and am going to cultivate a long white goaty.'

In the same letter, he asks if she knows anything of osteopathy. 'Here is one in New York working wonders really. I am going to have my bones searched by him in a week.'

In the second week of November that year, Swami Vivekananda made the trip from Ridgely Manor to the house of Dr Egbert Guernsey in New York. Dr Guernsey advised him to place himself under the care of an osteopath by the name of Dr Helmet. Vivekananda did so. He also suffered from severe cold while staying at Dr Guernsey's house.

In December 1899, he was persuaded to try magnetic treatment. Writing to Sara Bull on 22 December, he says: 'As for me, I had a slight relapse of late, for which the healer has rubbed several inches of my skin off.'

The next day, he wrote with greater enthusiasm to Sister Nivedita: 'Yes, I am really getting well under the manipulations of the magnetic healing! . . . There was never anything serious with my organs—it was nerves and dyspepsia. Now I walk miles every day, at any time—before or after meals. I am perfectly well—and am going to remain so, I am sure.'

It was Josephine Macleod who arranged for him to be treated by Mrs Milton, a healer who rubbed magnets on the body. Vivekananda wrote to Sara Bull from Los Angeles on 27 December to report that Joe has 'unearthed a magnetic healing woman' and he was improving, although he was not sure if it was because of the treatment, or the high quantity of ozone in the California air, or the end of the present spell of bad karma. He told Mrs Bull that he could now walk three miles even after a heavy dinner and felt very reassured by this.

By 4 March 1900—three months later—his tone was less enthusiastic. He wrote to Mrs Bull from San Francisco: 'My health is about the same; don't find much difference; it is improving, perhaps, but very imperceptibly. I can use my voice, however, as I did twice in Oakland, and get good sleep too after two hours of speaking.'

Three days later, on 7 March, Swami Vivekananda was very unwell. He wrote: 'I have not yet found any real benefit from the magnetic healer, except a few red patches on my chest from scratching!'

Vivekananda had by this time already started Debising ways to collect the necessary funds for his trip back to India. 'I have some hopes yet in England. It is necessary for me to reach New York in May.'

On 12 March, he wrote to Swami Brahmananda from San Francisco: 'Tell Sharat that I am not going to work so hard any more. Alas, sickness, sorrow and pain have been my companions for the last two years. But, he who does not work to earn his food, will have to starve to death ... I crave rest.' He goes on to tell his gurubhai that he was suffering from neurasthenia and asks him not to worry.

What exactly happened to Swami Vivekananda under Mrs Milton's care? She was a woman who could neither read nor write, nor could she express herself well in English. After an initial improvement, Swamiji's health deteriorated and he himself said that he was yet to find any real benefit from her treatments.

At least they seemed to have cured him of his insomnia, if only temporarily. He told Sister Nivedita on 28 March 1900: 'I work every day, morning and evening, eat at any hour—and go to bed at 12 p.m. in the night—but such deep sleep! I never had such power of sleeping before!'

He wrote to Josephine Macleod in much the same vein on 30 March: 'I am working hard—making some money—and am getting better in health. Work morning and evening, go to bed at 12 p.m. after a heavy supper—and trudge all over the town! And get better too! So Mrs Milton is there, give her my love, will you?'

On 18 April, as evident from a letter to Miss Macleod from Alameda, California, a sadder mood seemed to have overtaken him: 'I am well, very well mentally. I feel the rest of the soul more than that of the body. The battles are lost and won. I have bundled my things and waiting for the great deliverer.'

Two days later, he summarized the whole experience to her: 'I am going on, sometimes well and at other times ill. I cannot say, on my conscience, that I have been the least benefited by Mrs Milton. She has been good to me, I am thankful. My love to her. Hope she will benefit others.' He later went on to say, 'Even the magnetic healer could do nothing for me. Well, things will go on anyhow. I do not care ...'

By the end of April, Swami Vivekananda was gripped by fever and neurasthenia. He wrote to Sister Nivedita on 2 May 1900: 'I have been very ill—one more relapse brought about by months of hard work. Well, it has shown me that I have no kidney or heart disease whatsoever, only overworked nerves. I am, therefore, today going in the country for some days till I completely recover, which I am sure will be in a few days.'

In the letters of this period, there is mention of a Dr Milburn H. Logan. This particular doctor was very affectionate and kind to Vivekananda. He lived at 770, Oak Street and for some time, Swami Vivekananda was bedridden there. Dr Logan advised Swami Vivekananda not to travel before he was fully well; he was bent on making him strong and curing his stomach and nerve problems.

Another doctor who attended Swami Vivekananda was Dr William Forster of 1510, Market Street.

Throughout his trials, Swamiji always retained his sense of humour. Writing to Mary Hale from New York on 23 June, he told her that he could not digest her letter 'as the dyspepsia was rather bad the last few days.'

❈

In August that year, Swami Vivekananda crossed the English Channel to Paris. On 14 August, he made yet another allusion to his impending death when he wrote to John P. Fox: 'I like boldness and adventure and my race stands in need of that spirit very much. Only ... my health is failing and I do not expect to live long. Mohin must see his way to take care of mother and family. I may pass away any moment.'

He made arrangements to stay with an acquaintance in Paris and informed Hari Maharaj (Swami Turiyananda) on 1 September: 'Yesterday, I went to see the house of the gentleman with whom I shall stay. He is a poor scholar, has his room filled with books and lives in a flat on the fifth floor. And as there are no lifts in this country, as in America, one has to climb up and down. But it is no longer trying to me.'

During an afternoon lunch, the legendary singer Emma Calvé told her friend Josephine Macleod that she intended to visit Egypt. When Miss Macleod expressed an eagerness to accompany her, Madame Calvé invited Swami Vivekananda to join the party as her guest. Vivekananda agreed. Calvé had once, out of despair, sought to take her own life, when she met Vivekananda in the United States and became imbued with a new lease of life. Since then she felt a deep gratitude for him and called him 'Baba'.

The party also included the French poet Monsieur Jules Bois, and the scholar-theologian Père Hyacinthe Loyson together with his wife who were going as far as Constantinople.

Swami Vivekananda wrote to Sister Christine on 14 October: 'I shall travel with Madame Calvé, Miss Macleod and M. Jules Bois. I shall be the guest of Madame Calvé, the famous singer. We shall go to Constantinople, the Near East, Greece and Egypt. On our way back, we shall visit Venice.'

On 24 October 1900 they boarded the famous train, the Orient Express, in Paris. This tour, Swamiji's last in the West, came to an end on 26 November when he boarded the Italian ship *S.S. Rubatino* from Port Taufiq in Egypt. The ship was bound for Bombay.

During the tour, Swamiji did not fall ill. He was cheerful and lively throughout. He was not only experiencing new countries, seeing places of significant historical interest and writing the first drafts of his collection of Bengali essays, *Paribrajak* (Traveller) for *Udbodhan* (the Bengali magazine of the Ramakrishna Mission started by Swami Vivekananda in January 1899), but also entertaining and enlightening his friends. All these different facets of his personality come alive in the memoirs of Madame Calvé and Josephine Macleod. *Paribrajak* also offers us delightful glimpses of the tour.

Here is the itinerary as we know it: On 24 October, the Orient Express left Paris and travelled through the east of France to Strasbourg. Crossing into Germany, most of the next day was spent en route to Stüttgart and Münich. The next day, the train reached Vienna where the party alighted and explored the old city. Swami Vivekananda wrote: 'Three days in Vienna were sufficient to tire me. Seeing Europe, after Paris, is like tasting the dessert after an elaborate meal—the same fashion and eating habits, the same odd black suit, and the same queer hat.'

They continued on their journey, passing through the Balkans. Here Swami Vivekananda had reason enough to be happy though. The chilli peppers of the Balkans were sufficient even to make the south Indians ashamed, he said. Finally, on 30 October, Swami Vivekananda and his companions reached Constantinople.

How long did they stay there? Some say two to three days. Miss Macleod, in her memoirs, suggests nine days. Researcher Marie Louise Burke accepts this latter version.

One day in Constantinople, they decided to cross over to Scutari and visit Père Hyacinthe. Swami Vivekananda describes a unique encounter: 'On the way we saw the seat of a Sufi fakir. These fakirs cure diseases, which they do in the following manner: First they read some lines from their scriptures, swaying their body to and fro; then they begin to dance and gradually fall into a trance, after which they heal the disease by treading on the patient's body.'

Swami Gambhirananda reports that one day Swami Vivekananda spotted some fried chickpeas. He immediately purchased some and munched them happily as a child, while his friends tasted Turkish delicacies.

On 10 November, they journeyed from Constantinople to Athens. They stayed in Greece for three days and then, either on 13 or 14 November, crossed the Mediterranean to Egypt on board the Russian steamer *Czar*.

The focus now turned to Cairo. Here, Swami Vivekananda talked extensively about the Egyptian civilization. Mme Calvé writes: 'Swamiji was always absorbingly interesting, even under ordinary circumstances. He had magic in his voice that would enthral his listeners. Repeatedly, we would miss our train, sitting calmly in the waiting room, captivated by his discourse and quite oblivious of the lapse of time.'

She describes one memorable occasion where they lost their way in the streets of Cairo and found themselves in a squalid locality 'where half-clad women lolled from windows and sprawled on doorsteps'. Vivekananda's companions tried to usher him out of the area, but he 'detached himself gently from our group and approached the women on the bench.' Drawing close to them, he began to weep. The women were abashed and one of them said to him, in Spanish, 'Humbre de Dios, humbre de Dios (Man of God)!'

Some incidents, such as this, were not known in India until relatively recently. Only many years after Swami Vivekananda's death did Mme Calvé write her memoirs: 'What happened in Cairo that made Swami Vivekananda suddenly so restless to return to India?'

I personally heard from the publisher Ranjit Saha, now no more, that according to Swamiji's family, he fell ill there and had to be taken to a hospital. His illness precipitated his decision. Ranjit Saha has published Sister Nivedita's letters in English and also Bhupendranath Dutta's biography of his brother. Therefore he had access to a great deal of confidential information.

There is no concrete evidence, however, to support this theory. We only know that as soon as Vivekananda received word that Captain Sevier was on the point of death, he decided to return to India.

Nevertheless, the principal authorities on Swami Vivekananda are not entirely happy with this explanation. According to Swami Gambhirananda, the reasons go deeper. He writes that Vivekananda visited the Cairo museum, the sphinx and the pyramids. 'The lost, lifeless monuments brought about a weariness in him, and he wanted to return to his homeland.'

Miss Macleod and Mme Calvé have provided additional information in their memoirs. Also, the copious notes that Mme Verdiere took of her conversations with both Calvé and Vivekananda furnishes fresh material. We learn that one day Calvé had gone to sing somewhere. When she returned, she heard that Swami Vivekananda was in a melancholic mood and wanted to return to India. She asked him why he wanted to break the journey midway. Swami Vivekananda said he longed to go back to his gurubhais. He was given assurance of monetary help. The ticket would be bought by Mme Calvé, if necessary. But why did he want to leave them, she persisted. Swami Vivekananda's eyes filled with tears. He said he wanted 'to return to his country to die, to be with his gurubhais'. Calvé said they would not allow him to die for they needed him. Then came the explosion: Swami Vivekananda declared to Mme. Calvé that he would die on 4 July.

A ticket was purchased on the first available boat and on 26 November 1900, Vivekananda boarded the *S. S. Rubatino* alone to return to Bombay. Three days after his departure, Sara Bull received a letter from her friend Miss Macleod informing her that Swami Vivekananda had not been keeping well. In Cairo, he had suffered 'another heart attack'. It is evident from her words that this was a second heart attack. In that case, the heart attack that claimed Swamiji's life on the evening of 4 July 1902 must have been his third.

Some researchers however, including Marie Louise Burke, are sceptical about the possibility of a heart attack in Cairo because Swami Vivekananda did not appear to be ill at all during this tour.

CHAPTER FIVE

Thirty-nine Years, Five Months and Twenty-four Days

And now that beginning of the end. With trembling hearts and faltering steps we approach the day when Swami Vivekananda shed his mortal frame—4 July 1902. Traditionally, the death anniversary of a great man is not observed at the Ramakrishna Mission.

'We celebrate birth; death is an act of discarding old clothes for new ones!' A venerable old monk of the Ramakrishna Mission had this insightful remark to make on the subject. Over the last hundred years therefore, those who have been working tirelessly to spread the message of Swami Vivekananda have not attached any particular importance to the day of his death.

Still 4 July does have a special significance in the minds and hearts of countless men and women of India. We wonder what greater impact Swami Vivekananda could have had on India and the world had his life not been cut short in 1902. What other gifts could we have received from him?

The great messengers of God have often died young, whether it be Christ or Adi Shankaracharya. But Lord Buddha lived to be eighty. Josephine Macleod once lovingly reminded the learned Swami Vivekananda that 'the Buddha did not do his great work until between forty and eighty.'

In this chapter, I shall explore if there are really valid reasons behind this sheer disregard for death, particularly that of an eminent personality. And I shall keep in mind that the person who is the focus of this inquiry once advised regarding his own master: 'Ponder, collect the materials, and write a biography of Sri Ramakrishna with all its supernatural aspects firmly tucked away.' Implying that even if there are mystical aspects to a great man's life, there's no need to be absorbed by them. He came of his own and stayed for a short while with us of his own free will, but even if this is true, he must tread the path shown by other great men in the past.

Shankari Prasad Basu, who is an authority on Swami Vivekananda, has encouraged me to pursue this line of inquiry. In his works, he has described with great poignancy the events that took place on 4 July 1902. Some foreign devotees of Swamiji's have also conducted extensive research on the subject and these contribute valuable information on Swamiji's final hours.

But still one feels tempted to write. One recalls Tagore's words: 'Who are you that sit and read my poem after a hundred years?' And I wonder——who are you that read the accounts of the last day of Swami Vivekananda's life after a hundred years? If there are still some who are eager to read of such things, should one not write? Should one not rise to the challenge? Let it be my account that is read!

I would like to emphasize on the struggle of this great man we now adore and elevate to those who are reading about him across a gap of a hundred years or more. He achieved unlimited success and fame but had to battle for basic survival every day. Why did Swamiji say that life is a constant attempt to express oneself in adversity? And why do Indians relegate less importance to the dates of death than those of birth? The reasons will be clear by the end of the chapter. But before that let me offer a brief overview of my inquiry.

There are several issues to be addressed here: What are the factors that led to the early death of this great man? Why are great souls always persecuted by the world? How do they manage to achieve their goals through sheer hard work in spite of such acute adversity? In this context, one recalls the famous statement by a German philosopher: 'If you have respected a great man, do not mourn his death, but work towards fulfilling his dreams.'

Since Narendranath was a healthy young lad when he first began treading the perilous path of asceticism, I am curious to learn how his health got ruined subsequently. Why did he not regain it? He did not live long in the past. Why, then, did he have to suffer from medical conditions that were treatable during his time? These questions have been asked by other writers before me. It is not that I have any new information; I am merely presenting a common thread, as it were, drawn from a variety of sources.

ଔ

After Sri Ramakrishna's death, Narendranath was assailed by a variety of illnesses. His constitution found it difficult to adjust to the harsh poverty of life at Baranagore and, later, to the erratic life of an itinerant monk. We shall examine these in some detail, and also take a look at the various hereditary diseases which victimized members of the Dutta family.

We learn from brother Bhupendranath that 'Bishwanath contracted diabetes at a young age.' Narendranath and his two brothers inherited the disease. Nevertheless, both Mahendranath and Bhupendranath lived to be fairly old men. I have personally got to know from the late Ranjit Saha, who was close to Vivekananda's brothers, that Bhupendranath avoided sweets. Both these younger brothers also suffered from hypertension. Narendranath may also have been prey to the disease for, even at a young age, he suffered severe headaches.

Bishwanath Dutta died at the relatively young age of fifty-two. It is reported that, during his final days, it was his heart that failed to function properly. Many years later, on 5 July 1902, when his family received the news of Swami Vivekananda's demise, his grief-stricken mother 'wanted to know the cause behind the sudden death of her eldest son'. Bhupendranath's reply was, 'The same as with father.' Bishwanath Dutta had had a heart attack around nine o'clock in the evening. He was smoking a hookah, then suddenly he vomited and died immediately after.

In spite of these various hereditary illnesses, it would not be wrong to say that most of Swami Vivekananda's sufferings were brought about by his life as a wandering monk. Most of all, he was handicapped by stomach ailments. When he travelled by train, it became almost impossible for him to travel in the third class because of his need to use the train toilet frequently. During my school days, I had heard that if anybody offered to buy a train ticket for Swami Vivekananda, he would request a second-class ticket.

One may suggest, however, that Swami Vivekananda's stomach problems inadvertently benefited India. When he went to the United States for the first time, he travelled with a first-class ticket. If Khetri's maharaja had not bought him a first-class ticket, he would not have met Jamshedji Tata, the father of Indian industry and the founder of the Tata empire!

Tata was on his way to Japan to arrange for the import of matches. Vivekananda inspired the rich businessman to cultivate industry in India. He also told him that it was necessary to foster greater scientific and technical education among the youth. Later, Jamshedji went on to found Tata Steel and the Indian Institute of Sciences. The interchange of ideas between the two has recently come to light from the publication of the letters that they exchanged.

Thanks to American researchers, we have a great deal of information about Swami Vivekananda's mental and spiritual state while he was in that country. We also have precise details regarding his illnesses and eating habits. We come to know that he was a heavy smoker, that he was exceedingly fond of ice cream, that he was capable of an immense quantity of hard work, and that he acquiesced to different forms of medical treatment—both modern allopathic methods and non-standard approaches.

Towards the end of his life, a disciple in Dacca asked him, 'Why has your health deteriorated in spite of the fact that you are so young? Why did you not take care of it earlier?' Swami Vivekananda's reply was that he had no sense that he had a body when he was in America.

ख

Where do we get the first indication of a major illness? The answer is in Mahendranath's memoirs: in 1896 when Swami Vivekananda visited London from America. Did he have a heart attack in London at the time? The answer is, without doubt, in the affirmative. According to Mahendranath, after lunch one day, Swami Vivekananda was relaxing with John P. Fox and Mahendranath. 'Suddenly, I saw his face,' Mahendranath writes. 'It had contorted with pain. He sighed after some time and told John P. Fox that he was suffering from a heart attack. "My father died of this disease. I just suffered a pain in my chest. This runs in the family."' Swami Vivekananda was just thirty-three at the time.

The question now is: How did Swami Vivekananda's heart deal with this first attack?

Two years later, in 1898, it seems all was not well during his arduous pilgrimage to Amarnath (a holy cave high in the mountains of Kashmir). A doctor who examined Swamiji said that he might have suffered a cardiac attack after climbing the mountains and that the physical strain of this undertaking had caused a definite enlargement of his heart. When Vivekananda returned to Belur Math after this expedition, he had a red spot in his right eye—a blood clot according to a doctor. The damage proved to be permanent and he began to lose sight in that eye.

Sharat Chandra, the writer of *Swami-Shishya Sambad*, met Swami Vivekananda around this time and later remarked that Vivekananda retained his sense of humour despite this setback. Swamiji would merrily compare himself to the one-eyed Indian sage of ancient times, Shukracharya. Perhaps, had he lived longer, he would have gone completely blind.

CB

Let us return to our story. Swami Vivekananda returned from the West for the second time by the *S. S. Rubatino*, reaching Bombay on 6 or 7 December 1900. Thus ended his travels abroad.

In Bombay, Vivekananda had to wait at the railway station for a considerable length of time to catch a train to Calcutta. There he happened to see his friend Manmathanath Bhattacharya, who however failed to recognize him, perhaps because of his Western attire. Later, they both laughed over it.

Swami Vivekananda travelled alone by the Bombay–Howrah Express alone. Arriving in Howrah unannounced, he made his way to Belur Math, climbed over a small, locked gate still wearing his Western clothes, entered the compound, made his way to the dining area and ate khichuri—his favourite dish—with his gurubhais. The date was 9 December 1900. Swamiji was in good humour and announced that as soon as he heard the dinner gong he hurried, for fear that if he was late, he would get nothing to eat! His gurubhais could detect no signs of serious illness in him then.

But one can find hints of his rapidly deteriorating health scattered throughout his letters of the previous six months. In June, he had joked about his indigestion and dyspepsia. Around the same time, he wrote to Sister Christine from New York—'All the past fear of kidney troubles has passed away. "Worry" is the only disease I have, and I am conquering it fast.' By 14 August 1900, Swami Vivekananda was writing to John P. Fox that he was in very bad health and also alluded to his imminent death: 'Only as my health is failing and I do not expect to live long, Mahin must see his way clear to take care of mother and family. I may pass away at any moment.'

He wrote to Swami Turiyananda from Paris in August 1900: 'I have completed my work, that's all. I am indebted to Guru Maharaj. I have paid off my debts and have worked very hard for it! What can I say? I have given up my claims over everything in deed. I will only do the bossing, that's all!'

After his return to India in December 1900, Swami Vivekananda wrote to the Maharaja of Khetri that he was not well: 'As for me, my heart has become very weak. Change, I do not think, will do me any good ... I feel that my work in this life is done. Through good and evil, pain and pleasure, my life-boat has been dragged on—the one great lesson I was taught is—that life is misery, nothing but misery.'

It would not be long before the final curtain would fall, scarcely eighteen months after. Although Vivekananda was severely ill, he could never remain inactive. It was his nature to remain busy at all times and his ill health did not deter him.

The last week of December 1900 found him in Mayavati in the Himalayas. On the way there, he stayed for a day at Kathgodam, where he had a mild fever. In Mayavati, he confided to his disciple Swami Birajananda that he had himself imposed severe hardships on his body, which cost him the best years of his life.

In January 1901, he was once more at Belur Math. He wrote to Sara Bull in the last week of January: 'The moment I touch Bengal, especially the math, the asthmatic fits return! The moment I leave, I recover. I am going to take my mother on pilgrimage next week. It may take months to make the complete round of pilgrimages. This is the one great wish of a Hindu widow. I have brought only misery to my people all my life. I am trying at least to fulfil this one wish of hers.'

Prior to this Swamiji writes on 6 January, 1901 to Dhiramata Mrs. Bull: 'The first day's touch of Calcutta brought the asthma back; and every night I used to get a fit during the two weeks I was there.'

Towards the end of March, Swami Vivekananda and his party set out for Dacca. From there, he took his mother to Chatragram, Kamrup, Kamakhya and Shillong. He paid little heed to his health, though he was constantly troubled by asthma throughout the trip. In Dacca, one courtesan begged him to cure her asthma. Swamiji expressed his helplessness and explained to her kindly that he was himself a victim of the same disease. Would he be suffering so if he had the power to cure himself, he asked her.

In Dacca, Swami Vivekananda's diabetes worsened considerably. In Guwahati, his asthma attacks took a serious turn and deteriorated further in Shillong. When he was in the throes of an attack, he would place pillows on his chest and lean forward to counter the pain. The level of albumin in his blood rose dangerously too and his body swelled.

Back at Belur Math, he wrote to Josephine Macleod on 14 June 1901: 'As for me, I was thrown *hors de combat* in Assam. The climate of the Math is just reviving me a bit. At Shillong—the hill sanatorium of Assam—I had fever, asthma, an increase of albumin, and my body swelled to almost twice its normal size. These symptoms subsided, however, as soon as I reached the Math.'

The chief commissioner of Shillong, Sir Henry Cotton, had asked the local civil surgeon to care for Swami Vivekananda during his stay and used to himself inquire after Swamiji's health twice a day.

One is relieved to hear that these illnesses subsided as soon as he returned to Belur Math and, in the letters of this period, he mildly criticized the benefits of hill resorts as being overrated.

Swami Vivekananda's relief from his health problems, however, was only temporary. On 5 July 1901 he wrote to Mary Hale: 'My health has been and is very bad. I recover for a few days; then comes the inevitable collapse.'

The downward trend continued and, in a further letter to her dated 27 August, he states frankly, 'I would that my health were what you expected—at least to write you a long letter. It is getting worse, in fact, every day, and so many complications and botherations without that. I have ceased to notice it at all.'

At the end of January 1902, however, Swami Vivekananda was on the move once again. He went to Bodh Gaya with the Japanese artist Mr Okakura, and the following month he went by train to Benares. Clearly, he did not wish to stop travelling. His mind was willing, even though the body was not! Those who are curious to know about the extent of his travels in January and February 1902 can refer to several other records of Swamiji's life. For I would now like to move directly to the events that led up to that fateful Friday—4 July 1902.

03

Swami Vivekananda came back to Belur from Benares on 7 or 8 March 1902. Let scholars argue over the precise date. I prefer to concentrate on the state of his health around that time.

Fortunately, he himself regularly wrote about his health during this period in his letters to Sister Christine. The letters have recently been brought out in the ninth volume of the *Complete Works of Swami Vivekananda* in English, published with painstaking care by the Advaita Ashrama.

These letters express a sharp swing from hope to despair. Sometimes

Vivekananda writes that he is sleeping very well and his health is not troubling him; at other times, he complains of ill health.

An example of the former is the letter that Swamiji wrote to Sister Christine on 2 September 1901 from Belur Math: 'Of course, Bengal brings the asthma attack now and then, but it is getting tame, and the terrible things—Bright's disease and diabetes—have disappeared altogether.'

It is an established fact that diabetes often leads to the kidney ailment Bright's disease, also referred to as acute nephritis. As far as his asthma was concerned, Swami Vivekananda was convinced that it would not have been a problem had he been living in a dry climate. The frequent attacks took a toll on his body—he lost weight although afterwards, he said reassuringly, it did not take him long to regain it.

Next day in a continuation of the same letter to Sister Christine, Swami Vivekananda reveals: 'My whole body is covered by big patches of prickly heat. Thank goodness, there are no ladies about! If I had to cover myself in this state of things, I surely would go crazy.' He admits he is getting irritable frequently. 'I am half-crazy by nature; then my overtaxed nerves make me outrageous now and then. As a result, I don't find anybody who would patiently bear with me! I am trying my best to make myself gentle as a lamb. I hope I shall succeed in some birth.'

The summer of 1901 was extremely long. Even as late as October, Swami Vivekananda was complaining about the heat to Sister Christine: 'Our heat, too, has been fierce and is continuing unusually long this year. I am blacker than a Negro now.'

Considering all his symptoms together, Dr Subrata Sen confided in me: 'This is tricky, because the darkening can occur due to renal failure as well.'

In many countries, it is now customary to review the health of great heroes and heroines of the past in a scientific manner, taking into account their various symptoms. In India, we are lagging far behind in this.

By 12 November 1901, Swami Vivekananda was writing to Sister Nivedita about his prolonged ill health: 'Since the Durga Puja I have been very ill ... We had a grand puja here, lasting nearly four days; but alas, I was down with fever all the time.'

The same day, he wrote to Sister Christine: 'I am expected to leave Calcutta and Bengal in a few days, as this country becomes very malarious this month, after the rains.'

At the end of the year, Swami Vivekananda had two pieces of bad news to convey to Sister Christine. On 25 November, he wrote: 'My right eye is failing me badly. I can see very little with that one. It will be hard for me for some time either to read or write and as it is getting worse every day, my people are urging me to go to Calcutta and consult a doctor. I will go soon, as soon as I recover from a bad cold I have.' It seems the condition was aggravated by his diabetes. Two days later, he laments, 'I am just under another spell of catarrh and asthma.'

Then, on 12 December, he tells her that his albuminuria has returned with renewed force: 'You know, the last three years I have been getting albuminuria now and then ... The kidneys are structurally all right. Only they throw out albumin now and then. This is worse than throwing out sugar in diabetes. Albumin poisons the blood, attacks the heart and does all sorts of mischief. Catching cold always increases it. This time it has caused a small blood vessel in the right eye to burst, so that I scarcely see with that eye. Then the circulation has become very rapid. The doctors have put me to bed; and I am forbidden to eat meat, to walk or even to stand up, to read and write.'

The ayurvedic doctors who attended to him gave him powders made of finely ground metals. Swami Vivekananda comments on this wryly: 'Our old school physicians pour in tons of iron and other metals—

including gold, silver, pearls, etc.——down our throats. I should be a man of iron by this time!'

The sickness did not lessen. When he reached Benares, three attendants by turns fanned his overheated body, but sleep continued to elude him. On 4 March 1902, he wrote to Sister Nivedita, trying to underplay his condition: 'It is night now, and I can hardly sit up or write ... My condition is not at all serious, but it may become [so] any time; and I don't know what is meant by a low fever that almost never leaves me and the difficulty of breathing.' His legs had also swelled up and he could not walk.

In June 1902 Swami Vivekananda went to Bara Jagulia. He travelled first by train; then a bullock cart carried him the remaining distance. On 14 June, buoyed by hope, he wrote to Sister Christine that he was 'much stronger than before; and when seven miles of jolting in a bullock cart and railway travel of thirty-four miles did not bring back the dropsy to the feet, I am sure it is not going to return.'

The following day, he explained to her the source of his optimism: 'Anxiety is one thing I must avoid to recover ... I am slowly recovering.'

Swami Vivekananda was sometimes hopeful, sometimes despairing. If he allowed his body to rest and, especially, to sleep, the effects of his diabetes and albuminuria were far less pronounced.

Generally, he did not want his disciples to worry about him. On 21 June, he wrote to Sister Christine: 'You have not the least cause to be anxious. I am getting on anyhow and am quite strong. As to diet, I find I have to restrict myself and not follow the prescription of my doctor to eat anything I like. The pills continue, however. Will you ask the boys if they can get some *amalaki* fruits in the place now? We cannot get them in the plains now. They are rather sour and puckery eaten raw; but make marmalade of whole (ones)——delicious. Then they are the best things for fermentation I ever get.'

Swami Vivekananda concludes this 21 June letter in a lighter vein by reporting that he is 'laying on adipose tissues fast—especially about the abdominal regions'.

🕉

Vivekananda's gurubhais always tried to ensure that there were enough doctors of various kinds all around Swami Vivekananda who would attend to his diabetes, his albuminuria, or his asthma and prescribe their own treatments. The main ayurvedic doctor was Kabiraj Mahananda Sengupta, the one who had asked Swami Vivekananda to abstain from taking water or salt for twenty-one days. Vivekananda resolved to obey him, thereby stretching his enduring capacity to its limit. By way of liquid, he was permitted to have milk only. He used to rinse his mouth with water, but refused to swallow it.

This treatment did achieve good results. Swami Vivekananda wrote to Josephine Macleod on 21 April 1902 to announce: 'I am getting on splendidly, they say, but yet very weak and no water to drink. Anyhow the chemical analysis shows a great improvement. The swelling, about the feet and the complaints have all disappeared.'

Swamiji's gurubhais also arranged for him to be treated by a renowned allopathic doctor from Calcutta, Dr Saunders.

Vivekananda's health was undoubtedly exacerbated by his financial worries. In his letter to Sister Nivedita on 4 March 1902, from Benares Cantonment, he says: 'I have spent the little money I brought from Europe in feeding my mother and paying her debts. What little remains I cannot touch, as that is the expense for the pending lawsuit.'

Around the same time, Swami Ramakrishnananda came up from Madras and offered all his savings—400 rupees—to Swami Vivekananda. It overwhelmed Swamiji—where could you find such love! Vivekananda accepted the gift but gave it to the math with special instructions regarding what to do with the money in his 4 March letter to Sister Nivedita: 'Well, if I pass away, see that that Rs 400 is paid back—every rupee to him.'

For the entire year before his death, Swami Vivekananda could not sleep. Moreover, his body had become hypersensitive to human touch. He told his disciple, 'Why ask after my health? It gets worse every day. I was born in Bengal and, therefore, have never been free from diseases. Bengal is not good for your health. And if you work too hard, the pressure ruins your health.'

It was Swami Vivekananda's goal in life to be continuously engaged in work, even in death. According to him, man is not born to waste his life in idle pursuits.

As the days passed, his dropsy got more acute. Moreover, insomnia made him impatient and irritable. He brutally scolded his near and dear ones, even making them weep on occasions.

On some memorable days, when he was involved in discussions with the monks, Swami Vivekananda would spend the whole night sitting in a chair. Once, in the garden of Nilambar Mukherjee, the discussion continued until two o'clock in the morning. Just two hours later, Swamiji asked Akhandananda to wake everyone up for meditation. Sleeping was not the purpose of the math, he said. Inactivity of any kind was anathema for Swamiji.

Sleep eluded him during this period, but he never conceded defeat. Even on the day of his death, he had rebuked the monks for their morning naps. He told them, 'Was the math built for you to sleep?'

Swamiji was rarely annoyed, but he frequently scolded others. He would not allow mistakes. As death approached and the burden of work intensified, the number and intensity of his rebukes increased. Much of the brunt was borne by Rakhal Maharaj (Swami Brahmananda) from whom Swamiji demanded nothing but perfection.

Swami Vivekananda's long-standing desire had been to establish an exceptional math. To achieve this, the practices, routines and cultivation of the *shastras* (scriptures) there had to be flawless. He demanded the same perfection from himself too. He never felt it to be a matter of shame to clean the heavily soiled cooking pots himself. Or if the latrines smelled, he would set to clean them with buckets of water, covering his mouth with a towel. This surprised and embarrassed his disciples. 'Swamiji, not you!' they would exclaim. To this, Vivekananda would retort, 'Is that all you can come up with?'

The Bally municipality imposed heavy taxes on Belur Math by awarding it the status of an amusement park. To seek justice, Swamiji had to appear in court even.

We learn from the memoirs of Hari Maharaj (Swami Turiyananda) that once Swami Vivekananda became extremely annoyed about something and left the math. But his anger would subside quickly as well. The root for it usually lay in the fact that he had tremendous expectations from the monks. He once proclaimed that he would consider his life fulfilled if they sacrificed their lives for the greater good of humanity.

Swami Brahmananda, the first president of the math, confessed that it was extremely difficult to live with Swamiji. Knowing him from books and knowing him personally were two different things. Many a time, after feeling the lash of his tongue, Brahmananda had considered quitting the math. Once, a particularly merciless scolding from Vivekananda brought tears to his eyes. Seeing how badly he had wounded his gurubhai, Swamiji was immediately repentant. He explained that his scoldings were an expression of his love and so were often misunderstood.

ରଃ

Towards the end of his life, Swami Vivekananda complained of a continuous burning sensation in his body and a degree of mental confusion. He said that he should be mercifully killed, just like a useless racing horse. His loss would not be felt, because his job was done.

Swami Brahmananda had planted five *shaddock* (citrus) plants in the math gardens for Vivekananda. Doctors had advised Swamiji to drink the juice of the fruit. One day, he said to Brahmananda: 'I must get desperate now. Either I will cure myself through meditation and prayer and immerse myself fully into work, or I shall leave this broken cage altogether.'

Swami Gambhirananda tells us that there were days when Swami Vivekananda's health did not permit him to leave his room on the first floor. When he felt well enough to venture out, he would take a stroll. Sometimes on these walks he would have on only a loincloth with the torso bare; at other times, he would be draped in a saffron robe or wrap himself in a dark cloak. Often he would be seen wearing chappals and carrying a hookah and a stick with him. He was completely absorbed in his own world.

Several biographers have described how Swami Vivekananda forged a special bond with the animal world around this time. His letters are sprinkled with references to his delightful relationship with them. Swami Akhandananda believed that this new-found interest was a result of his disappointment with human beings. But more likely, this was the result of the memories of his childhood pastimes exercising a strong influence on him.

As a boy, Narendranath was very fond of animals. He kept pigeons, monkeys and goats as pets and used to feed them. His peacock died, however, because the people of the locality pelted it with stones. The monkey got very troublesome and Naren had to get rid of it. The goat remained for a while under the puja room that was attached to the house. All these we learn from Mahendranath's memoirs.

Swami Vivekananda wrote to Sister Christine at the end of June 1901: 'Do you know how I am taking rest? I have got a few goats and sheep and cows and dogs and cranes! And I am taking care of them the whole day! I am not trying to be happy; what for? Why should one not be unhappy as well—both being nonsense?—but just to kill time.'

In his letter to her on 2 September, he speaks of his expanding circle: 'I have a lot of cows, goats, a few sheep, dogs, geese, ducks, one tame gazelle, and very soon I am going to have some milk buffaloes.'

On 7 September, he wrote to Sister Nivedita: 'Well, about the rains—they have come down now in right earnest, and it is a deluge, pouring, pouring, pouring night and day … The rain-water stands at places some feet high. My huge stork is full of glee, and so are the ducks and geese. My tame antelope fled from the Math and gave us some days of anxiety in finding him out. One of my ducks unfortunately died yesterday. She had been gasping for breath more than a week … One of the geese had her plumes falling off. Knowing no other method, I left her some minutes in a tub of water mixed with mild carbolic, so that it might either kill or heal; and she is all right now.'

Swami Vivekananda cared for his ducks with mixed success. On 12 November 1901, he wrote to Sister Christine: 'I tried to keep them alive on cow's milk, but the poor things died in the night! Two of my ducks have hatched their eggs. As this is their first time and the male ones do not help a bit, I am trying my best to keep up their strength by good feeding them well. We cannot keep chickens here—they are forbidden. We have fenced in a lot of our grounds to protect the vegetables from our cows and goats and sheep.'

This latter move was at the urging of Swami Brahmananda who was in charge of the gardens. It seems that Swamiji personally paid for the upkeep of his animals, sometimes paying up to 100 rupees for their food.

Vivekananda took great delight in his new animal friends: swans, ducks, pigeons, dogs, cranes, cats, cows, deer, lambs and goats. He often talked to them. He named the she-goat Hansi and her kid, Matru. The duck was called Yashomati and the swan, Bombete. Swamiji would often visit his little friends paying little heed to his doctor's instructions. He was specially concerned about a timid swan. It preferred staying alone and seemed sad and miserable.

Swamiji used to go up to the she-goat Hansi and ask for her permission to draw some milk for his tea. Whether or not she gave, depended on her.

Vivekananda had placed a string of bells around Matru's neck and it would follow him around the math. He played with it like a child but it died all of a sudden and Swamii was deeply saddened at the loss. He felt convinced that he knew Matru from a previous birth. 'How strange!' he exclaimed. 'Whoever I love, dies early.'

Swami Vivekananda named one of his dogs Bagha. Shankari Prasad has carefully collected a host of anecdotes relating to this remarkable animal. The other two dogs were called Tiger and Mary.

Bagha was not an ordinary dog. He used to escort eminent guests at the math. Shankari Prasad tells us, 'Once he was exiled to the other side of the river. But Bagha did not like the arrangement. He loved the monastery and could not live without Swami Vivekananda. So he got into a boat in the evening. The boatman and the passengers tried to get rid of him, but could not. He bared his teeth and growled at them and scared them ... Swami Vivekananda was going to take his bath at four in the morning, and suddenly something touched his feet and he saw it was Bagha ... He patted him and reassured him, and told everybody that Bagha could not be exiled any more, whatever he did.'

When Swami Vivekananda went to Benares in 1902, he had lost the use of one eye, but this tragic state of things did not make him forget to request Swami Brahmananda to look after his goat while he was away. On 27 May 1902, Vivekananda wrote to Sister Christine about some new additions to his circle of friends: 'I have just now two kids and three lambs added to the family. There was one more kid, but he got himself drowned in the yellow fish tank.'

Swami Akhandananda said that Swami Vivekananda's animals died soon after he passed away. Swami Subodhananda gave some of them to Akhandananda, but none of them lived long except Bagha. When this unusual dog died, his body was offered to the Ganga. The body was washed away, but the waves brought it back in the evening. A brahmachari buried Bagha, with the permission of the monks, in the grounds of the math, at the place where he was found.

೦೪

Sometimes, Swami Vivekananda would saunter out alone along the lonely paths of Belur. Or, he would enter the kitchen and cook for his brother monks. Or, sometimes he would leaf through books or look at paintings.

His disciple Sharat Chandra once saw him on the other side of the river, by Ahiritola ghat. Vivekananda was munching chanachur from a shal leaf in his hand. He was eating gleefully, like a boy. He beckoned the disciple, 'Have some. It is salted and hot!'

From several other accounts, it is evident that the various medical treatments he was undergoing did have a demoralizing effect on him. On doctors he said, 'What do they know? After reading only a few books, they think they know a lot and act as if they know everything, understand everything.'

A week before his demise, Swami Vivekananda met Asim Bose of north Calcutta. Asim inquired after his health, and Swamiji sadly replied that the doctors and the kabiraj had done all they could, but unfortunately, he had the 'disease of death'.

೦೪

The day Swami Vivekakanda passed behind the curtain of eternity has been described by biographers as a day of liberation. Sister Nivedita gives a detailed account of the events that preceded his departure and her recollections are a rich source of information on Sri Ramakrishna and Swami Vivekananda.

It is important here to go over several key points before we look at the day itself:

Swami Vivekananda was feeling relieved during this period after putting an end to the family feud around his family house.

On Wednesday, 2 July, the day of *ekadashi* (the eleventh day of the new moon, traditionally a day of fasting), Swami Vivekananda cooked for Sister Nivedita. Enthusiastic experiments were being conducted at the math on the ways to bake bread and, before he died, Swami Vivekananda also sent some brown bread to Nivedita's house in Bagh Bazar.

On 7 April, Kabiraj Mahananda finally allowed the patient to resume eating fish, oil and salt. From late June, ayurveda did not remain the sole mode of treatment. Dr Mahendranath Majumdar of Baranagore was consulted.

In April, Swami Vivekananda told Josephine Macleod: 'I have nothing in the world. I haven't a penny for myself. I have given away everything that has ever been given to me.'

Also in April, Swamiji told Miss Macleod, 'I shall never see forty.' He was thirty-nine at the time.

ೞ

Friday, 4 July 1902. This last day of Swamiji's life has been poignantly depicted in quite a few books. Sister Nivedita was the first to undertake the task and a number of devout disciples of Sri Ramakrishna followed. A summary of their accounts has been presented here for industrious readers.

EARLY IN THE MORNING

Swami Vivekananda emerges from his room very early and goes to the puja room for prayers. No sign of bad health.

AROUND BREAKFAST

Swami Vivekananda laughs and jokes with everyone. He drinks tea, coffee and milk, as usual. The first hilsa fish of the year has been brought. Swamiji talks and jokes with Swami Premananda. He cuts jokes with a disciple who hails from East Bengal and tells him to worship the hilsa with due rites, since it is known that people from East Bengal worship the first hilsa of the year.

MORNING WALK

Swami Vivekananda walks with Swami Premananda. During the course of their conversation, Swamiji tells him, 'Why should you imitate me? Thakur forbade that. Do not be as erratic as I have been.'

8.30 A.M.

Swami Vivekananda tells Swami Premananda: 'Close the doors and prepare the puja room for me.' He enters the room alone for meditation.

11.00 A.M.

Swami Vivekananda's meditation is over. He sings, in Bengali:

> *Is Kali, my Mother, really dark?*
> *The naked One, though black She seems,*
> *Lights the lotus of my heart ...*

11.30 A.M.

Lunch. Swami Vivekananda eats with great relish the hilsa curry with rice, fries and ambal (a preparation with fish). He eats with everybody present. He says, 'The observance of ekadashi has whetted my appetite. With difficulty I resisted the temptation to eat up the utensils!'

12.30 P.M.

Swami Vivekananda rests for fifteen or twenty minutes. Then he tells Swami Premananda, 'Come! A monk must not sleep during the day ... I could not sleep today. I have got a headache now that I meditated.'

1.00—4.00 P.M.

Swami Vivekananda instructs the brahmacharis and monks in the library for three hours, ninety minutes earlier than the designated time. The subject is Sanskrit grammar, possibly, Panini's *Laghukaumudi*. Swami Vivekananda is a little tired afterwards.

4.00 P.M.

Swami Vivekananda drinks a cup of warm milk and goes out for a walk with Swami Premananda to Belur Bazaar. They cover a distance of nearly two miles. Of late, he has not been walking such long distances.

5.00 P.M.

Swami Vivekananda returns to the math. He sits under the mango tree in the courtyard and declares, 'I have not felt so well for many days.' He smokes, then goes to the bathroom and returns, declaring that he is feeling very well. There in that spot, he speaks to Swami Ramakrishnananda's father, Ishwar Chandra Bhattacharya, for some time.

6.30 P.M.

A few monks drink tea. Swami Vivekananda asks if he may also have a cup.

7.00 P.M.

As the bell rings for worship in the evening, Swami Vivekananda goes to his room. Brahmachari Brajendra, who is from East Bengal, is with him. Swamiji asks for his mala beads and then requests Brajendra to go outside the room and meditate. Swamiji sits in meditation, facing east towards Dakshineshwar, on the other side of the Ganga.

7.45 P.M.

Swami Vivekananda calls out to Brajendra, 'I feel warm. Please open the windows.' He lies down on a bed that has been made up on the floor. His mala beads are in his hand. Then he says to the disciple, 'You do not have to fan me. Please could you massage my legs?'

9.00 P.M.

Swami Vivekananda is lying on his back. Then he turns on his right side. His right hand trembles for a while. Perspiration appears on his forehead. Then he begins crying like a small child.

9.02—9.10 P.M.

Swami Vivekananda breathes deeply. His head starts shaking and then it falls on the side of the pillow; his eyes dilate. A celestial light beams on his face and a smile appears.

9.30 P.M.

Everybody comes in running. Initially, they think he has fallen into a trance. Swami Bodhananda tries to check his pulse and then stands up. He begins weeping. Someone says, 'Go fast. Fetch Dr Mahendra Majumdar.' Dr Majumdar lives in Baranagore, on the other side of the Ganga. Swamis Premananda and Nishchayananda begin to chant aloud the name 'Ramakrishna' to try to bring Swami Vivekananda out of samadhi.

10.30 P.M.

Dr Majumdar, Swami Brahmananda and Swami Saradananda arrive at Belur Math. The two swamis had been in Calcutta during the evening. Dr Majumdar examines Swami Vivekananda and finds that his heart had stopped functioning. He tries to induce artificial respiration but fails.

12.00 MIDNIGHT

Dr Majumdar declares that Swami Vivekananda is dead. He cites heart attack as the cause of death.

CB

Swami Vivekananda left this world when he was thirty-nine years, five months and twenty-four days old. He kept his word. He had said that he would not see forty.

Just a few months earlier, on 28 March, he had told Sister Nivedita, 'I have given all that I had to give. Now I must go.'

Then, just two days before he passed away, he said, 'The spiritual power that has been set in motion in Belur will continue for fifteen hundred years. It will take the shape of a huge university. Do not think I imagine it; I see it.'

On 1 July, while walking across the grounds of the math, he had pointed to a spot by the Ganga and said, 'When I cast off my body, I would like to be cremated there.'

CB

The next morning: 5 July. Swami Vivekananda's eyes were as red as the *jaba kusum* (hibiscus flower) and there were signs of blood flowing from his nostrils and mouth. Dr Bipin Bihari Ghosh said it was apoplexy. Dr Mahendra Majumdar gave sudden heart failure as the cause. Other physicians thought the signs were consistent with the rupture of a blood vessel in the brain.

Sister Nivedita arrived at seven in the morning and stayed by the body, fanning it, until one in the afternoon. Bhubaneshwari received the news in the morning. Bhupendranath came with his cousin to Belur and, after some time, Bhubaneshwari arrived with her eldest grandson, Brajamohan Ghosh. The monks persuaded Bhubaneshwari to go back home.

Girish Chandra Ghosh came when fire was being applied to the pyre. Swami Niranjanananda said to him, 'Naren is gone.'

'No, not gone,' replied Girish. 'He has only discarded his body.'

An imprint of Swami Vivekananda's feet was taken on a white handkerchief.

Bhupendranath says that Sister Nivedita asked Girish Chandra Ghosh why they asked his mother to go home. The monks explained it to her.

The obsequies were over by six in the evening. During the cremation itself, Sister Nivedita had a most significant experience which she later described in a letter to Josephine Macleod: 'At two o'clock we stood there, and as I told you in the letter that seems to have been lost, I said to Swami Saradananda, seeing a certain cloth covering the bed-top—"Is this going to be burnt? It is the last thing I ever saw him wear." Swami Saradananda offered it to me there, but I would not take it. Only I said, "If I could only cut a corner off the border for [Josephine]!" But I had neither knife nor scissors, and the seemliness of the act would have been doubtful—so I did nothing. At six o'clock—or was it five?—my first letter told you; I think it was six—as if I were twitched by the sleeve, I looked down, and there, safe out of all that burning and blackness, there blew to my feet the very two or three inches I had desired out of the border of the cloth. I took it as a Letter from Him to you, from beyond the grave.'

Here ends the summary of the events. A few lingering questions remain:

- Why was the local municipality late in granting permission to hold the cremation within the precincts of the math?
- Many researchers have seen Sri Ramakrishna's death certificate. But has anyone seen Vivekananda's death certificate?
- Swami Vivekananda was famous across the world. His obsequies were over by the evening of 5 July. Why was the news of his passing away not published the next day?
- Two high court judges were asked to preside over the condolence meeting. They not only refused, but treated the offer with withering scorn. One of them went so far as to say that if Bengal had a Hindu king, Swami Vivekananda would have been hanged before then.
- Why was it so difficult for the math to raise funds to erect a small temple over the site where Swami Vivekananda was cremated? The work was not begun until January 1907 and was completed many years later, on 2 January 1924.

I can only conclude that even though Swami Vivekananda captured the hearts of men and women all over the world, his own people took time to accept him. Over the last hundred years, the Ramakrishna Mission has kept his vision alive. Were it not for them, perhaps we would have not known Swami Vivekananda today.

For accounts of Vivekananda's death and the day of his cremation, we must depend on Sister Nivedita's letters and the memoirs of Bhupendranath. Mahendranath had not yet returned to Calcutta.

Recently, however, another invaluable memoir has come to my attention. It has been written by Chandrashekhar Chattopadhyay. It was originally published in 1948, in Bengali, in the August–September issue of *Bishwabani*—forty-six years after the passing away of Swami Vivekananda. I will include here a substantial excerpt from this brilliant narrative:

'Swamiji's disciple Kanai Maharaj (Swami Nirbhayananda) came to our house in Ahiritola to convey the news of his death. I was worshipping in a temple nearby. I returned home before nine in the morning, however, to find my mother sobbing with grief. When I inquired, she said, "You have been ruined. The math's Swamiji is no more. He is dead. You never arranged for me to meet him even once!"

I said, "All the monks are referred to as 'Swamiji'. Who are you referring to? You must have made a mistake!"

She answered, "No, no. Kanai came early this morning to tell us that the senior swami passed away last night at nine o'clock. Kanai has asked you to go to the math."

I consoled my weeping mother and told her, "One must not mourn the death of a monk."

Just then, my friend Nibaran Chandra (a disciple of Sarada Debi) arrived. I decided not to go to the office that day (Saturday, 5 July). I went to Belur Math with Nibaran and my younger brother Dulalshashi to see Swamiji for the last time. We went to the Ahiritola ghat, crossed the Ganga by boat and went along Salikha–Ghusuri road on foot to reach Belur at ten in the morning.

It was drizzling. I saw that our respected Rakhal Maharaj (Swami Brahmananda) and a few other monks were decorating a cot with beautiful flowers on the ground floor verandah on the Western side of the math building. When Rakhal Maharaj saw us, he burst into tears. He could not speak, so he pointed to the steps and indicated that we should go upstairs.

We went into Swamiji's room and saw that his body had been laid on a beautiful carpet. He was besmeared with ashes, his head crowned with flowers and his body covered with a new saffron robe. His mala beads were looped around the fingers of his right hand. His eyes were half-closed, like the eyes of Lord Shiva. Incense burners had been placed on either side of his head and its sweet fragrance filled the room.

Sister Nivedita sat on Swamiji's left, tears streaming down her face. She was fanning Swamiji with a palm-leaf. His head was to the west and his feet to the east, towards the Ganga. At his feet, Brahmachari Nandalal sat in grief-stricken silence. The three of us bowed down and touched his feet in obeisance and then sat down. His body was as cold as ice.

I then touched the mala beads around the fingers of his right hand and chanted my mantra. Meanwhile, many devotees, disciples and distinguished people from Calcutta and other places were pouring in to see Swamiji for the last time. One after another, they bowed and touched his feet and left. Sister Nivedita, Nandalal and the three of us remained.

When I finished my prayers, Sister Nivedita asked me softly, "Can you sing, my friend? Would you mind singing those songs that our Thakur used to sing?"

I told her that I could not sing. Then she requested, "On my behalf, will you please ask your friend to sing?"

My friend Nibaran Chandra sang a few songs full of pathos: *Keep your beloved Mother Shyama in your heart; Who cares for Gaya, Ganga, Prabhas, Kashi or Kanchi?; Who says Shyama is dark? If my Mother is dark, how can she light up my heart?; At the blue lotus-feet of Shyama, my mind yields like a bee; O my mind, chant the name of Kali. If you say Kali, you will not fear Kala [death]'* ...

At one o'clock in the afternoon, Sharat Maharaj (Swami Saradananda) came up the stairs and addressed Nandalal and us: "We are completely heartbroken and have no strength left. Will you be able to carry Swamiji's body downstairs?" Immediately, Nandalal and we three householder disciples got up and carefully carried Swamiji's body down the steps to the lower verandah and placed it on the cot decorated with flowers. A few pomegranates, apples, pears and grapes were placed on his chest. Then Swami Advaitananda told Nandalal: "O Nandalal!

Swamiji loved you immensely. Be the one to perform the last rites."

Rakhal Maharaj and the other swamis agreed. Nandalal then offered flower garlands, fruits and sweets and chanted prayers.

It was suggested that we should take a last photograph of Swamiji, but Rakhal Maharaj objected: "Swamiji has so many nice photographs. This sad sight will be heartbreaking for everyone later." Then Rakhal Maharaj, the other swamis and the brahmacharis offered flowers at Swamiji's feet. Finally, Haramohan Mitra, who once studied with Swamiji, followed by other householder disciples, offered flowers. The soles were dyed red and an imprint was taken. Sister Nivedita also took an imprint on a new handkerchief. I smeared sandalwood paste on a large rosebud and touched his soles with it, then kept it in my pocket as a memento.

After these rituals, Sharat Maharaj again asked the four of us to carry the cot, this time to the spot where Swamiji was to be cremated. All the swamis and devotees followed. It had rained in the morning, so the grounds were wet and slippery. And they were covered with sharp spear grass. We crossed the vast space slowly and cautiously, and placed the cot on the pyre. Swamiji's aunt from Simulia, his cousin Habu Dutta and members of Habu Dutta's family arrived then and began to lament loudly.

Sharat Maharaj told us, "Please take a bundle of *pankati* (the dried stalks of jute), each one of you. Light it, then circle the platform seven times and, finally, place the bundle below the cot under Swamiji's feet and bow and touch his feet in obeisance."

Swamiji's body was offered to the fire, which had begun to burn the logs of sandalwood. The grief-stricken devotees sat like stone statues. The body was set ablaze. Gradually the fire rose higher and higher, extending its many tongues to consume the body. The poet Girish Chandra Ghosh, Upendranath Mukhopadhyay from Basumati, the writer Jaladhar Sen, Master-mashai (M.), Akshay Kumar Sen

(Shakhchunni Master) and other devout householder disciples sat on a rock under the marmelo tree and watched the heart-rending sight.

Broken-hearted, Girish-babu began to lament, "Naren! You were supposed to live and spread the glory of Thakur by letting the world know of the story of my transformation. But all is in vain now. I am old and yet I live to see this? You are Thakur's son; you are now in Thakur's arms. How could you leave us so suddenly? How unfortunate we are!"

Hearing these words, Sister Nivedita could no longer check her grief. She got up and began to circle the blazing funeral pyre. Fearing her gown might catch fire, Maharaj-ji (Swami Brahmananda) asked Kanai Maharaj to take her away. Kanai Maharaj took her by the hand and made her sit by the Ganga and tried to console her.

The lower part of Swamiji's divine body turned to ashes in a short while, there being a favourable wind. But amazingly, the fire would not touch his chest, face or hair. His half-closed eyes were enchanting.

At this point, one of the distinguished householder disciples made a strange remark. Nobody knows who inspired him to say such a thing. It was lamentable, so I cannot publish it. Everybody was deeply upset and Swamiji's disciple, Nischayananda, said, in great agitation: "Whoever beats on Swamiji's skull, I will break his skull with a stick! I will go and get whatever amount of wood is needed." So saying, he climbed an old tree and cut some branches. Then he came back and put the logs on Swamiji's face, thereby covering it.

Rakhal Maharaj took me aside and giving me a ten-rupee note said, "Please go with Nibaran. Take Girish-babu's boat and go across the river to Baranagore. Buy some sandesh and other food for us. The monks have not had a sip of water since last night, and many of the others present have not eaten either."

Nibaran and I got up. Then Bipin Saha, who lived in Baranagore, gave me five rupees more and came with us to the other side of the river. He arranged for a shop there to prepare hot luchis, kachuris and sandesh for us and then came back with us to the math, bearing the basket on his head. When we reached the math a little before dusk, the pyre had been extinguished and the remains of Swamiji had been collected by the monks. The others were bathing and making offerings to the Ganga ...

In the evening, food was offered to the deity and, after worship, the prasad was distributed on the ground floor. Tea and water were served. Afterwards, the broken-hearted householder disciples slowly left and returned home.

To fulfil Swamiji's last wishes, Goddess Kali was worshipped at Belur Math on the next *amavasya*, after 4 July. No outsiders were invited. Only Swamiji's youngest brother Bhupendranath Dutta came ...

The puja began on the first floor in the shrine room after ten in the evening. Ramakrishnananda's father, Ishwar Chandra Chakraborty, a renowned worshipper of Kali, was the priest. The swamis and brahmacharis prayed to the goddess and then went and sat in Swamiji's room to meditate. In the math, early in the evening, food was offered to the deity as usual and Maharaj-ji told Swami Premananda, "Please give prasad to Bhupen and these two devotees; we are fasting today."

After having prasad, the three of us lay down in the large room to the west on the ground floor. During the night, Swamiji's old disciple Swami Nityananda lamented piteously. The math reverberated with the sound of his wailing.

Sharat Maharaj came to the room after three in the morning and woke us up. He asked us to go upstairs. When we went there, Marahaj-ji asked me to purify myself with water first and then pray. After a while, we assembled downstairs and then sat around the *homa* (sacrificial) fire in the courtyard, facing the verandah in the west, and prayed.

After we had completed the rituals, we all went to Swamiji's cremation site. We circled it seven times and bowed in respect. Then all of us prayed under the marmelo tree and returned to the shrine room. We bowed again in obeisance and came down to take the prasad.'

CB

Once again, I return to my original question: In India, traditionally, we like to celebrate the birthdays of great men. But why do we feel it unnecessary to notice the days when they leave us? Our elaborate inquiry has provided us with the answer: Death is proof of a life lived before. Those who rise to prominence, however, begin to live in our minds and hearts from the day they die.

Sister Nivedita was once asked if she could define the difference between Sri Ramakrishna and Swami Vivekananda. Her answer was: Sri Ramakrishna is the symbol of all that India has thought about for the past 5,000 years. Swami Vivekananda is the symbol of all that India will think for the next 1,500 years.

If this is true, it is not at all necessary to observe the day of Swami Vivekananda's demise.

Vivekananda wrote a very prescient letter to Josephine Macleod from Almora in April 1900, two years before his final departure. I do not believe it is possible for any one to write such a letter if he is not convinced of his imminent death. I would like to leave the reader with Swami Vivekananda's words in this letter. I have lost count of the number of times I have read these lines. But each time I read them, they appear fresh, as though I am reading them for the first time.

He writes: 'I am glad I was born, glad I suffered so, glad I did make big blunders, glad to enter peace. I leave none bound, I take no bonds. Whether this body will fall and release me or I enter into freedom in the body, the old man is gone, gone for ever, never to come back again! The guide, the guru, the leader, the teacher has passed away; the boy, the student, the servant is left behind. Behind my work was ambition, behind my love was personality, behind my purity was fear, behind my guidance the thrust of power! Now they are vanishing, and I drift. I come! Mother, I come!'

Perhaps this Vivekananda will be enshrined in people's hearts, always.

The Monk as Man